CHRISTOPHER H. K. PERSAUD

ISRAEL AGAINST ALL ODDS

ANTI-SEMITISM FROM ITS BEGINNINGS TO THE HOLOCAUST YEARS

(VOLUME I)

i

ISRAEL AGAINST ALL ODDS

Anti-Semitism From Its Beginnings to the Holocaust Years

(Volume I)

Christopher H. K. Persaud

Christian Publishing House

Cambridge, Ohio

CHRISTIAN PUBLISHING HOUSE
CONSERVATIVE CHRISTIAN BOOKS
APOLOGETIC DEFENSE OF GOD, THE
FAITH, THE BIBLE, AND CHRISTIANITY

ISRAEL AGAINST ALL ODDS Anti-Semitism From Its Beginnings to the Holocaust Years by Christopher H. K. Persaud

ISBN-13: 978-1-949586-72-5

ISBN-10: 1-949586-72-3

Table of Contents

INTRODUCTION

I endured a great measure of emotional and psychological agitation as I contemplated whether to write *ISRAEL – AGAINST ALL ODDS* (Volumes I & II). As firm as I may be in my convictions about the nation of Israel and its place in the annals of history, and the identity and purpose of people of Jewish ancestry, including observations from a standpoint of Biblical or theological rumination, I acknowledge there exists much controversy relative to the foregoing topics in the minds of many people around the world. As a matter of fact, to many observers, the issues are sensitive and/or profound enough as to elicit expressions of approval or disapproval that sometimes translate into physical confrontation and bloodshed.

The foregoing reflections notwithstanding, I remain deeply committed to disseminating to those who would read this book what I unaffectedly feel is the truth about a unique race of people that has persisted over a course of thousands of years of intimidation, persecution, and ostracism, and has survived numerous attempts by its adversaries to annihilate it. Against all odds, the people of Israel, and Jews everywhere remain steadfast, undeterred and hopeful of the future.

A primary goal of the deliberations contained in *ISRAEL – Against All Odds* (Volumes I & II) is to put into proper perspective the historical account of the Jewish people and the unremitting hardships they endured, many a time at the hands of hateful enemies who sought to chastise, subjugate and/or eradicate them from the face of the earth.

In *ISRAEL – Against All Odds (Volume I)*, I address the following topics.

(a) Anti-Semitism – A Global Hatred in Many Forms

(b) A Brief History of Anti-Semitism

(c) The Shameful Sin of Christian Anti-Semitism

(d) Zionism – The Reestablishment, Development & Protection of the Nation of Israel

(e) The Holocaust

Anti-Semitism – A Global Hatred in Many Forms—Jew-hatred, or anti-Semitism, originated since the time of the Old Testament prophets. Anti-Semitism is a global phenomenon of hate and dislike and is the single most profound reason for the persecution and murder of people of Jewish ancestry around the world. Anti-Semitism has experienced a global rise in recent decades and continues to grow unabated. There are various forms of anti-Semitism. The mindset is an evil that continues to increase in today's world instead of diminishing. Some guises of anti-Semitism are political anti-Semitism, religious anti-Semitism, economic anti-Semitism, racial anti-Semitism, and social anti-Semitism.

Brief History of Anti-Semitism—Throughout history, Jews suffered expulsions from places in which they settled, in some instances for many hundreds, even thousands of years, and never gained readmission to such lands. Jews were first exiled or expelled from their homeland during the time of the Assyrian kingdom (734-724 B.C.) and the Babylonian kingdom (586 B.C.). Pagan Rome practiced the strategy of removing Jews from its capital cities, considering them rebellious and undesirable. There were major expulsions of Jews from England in 1290, France in 1306 and 1394, and Spain and Portugal during the years 1492 to 1497.

Governmental authorities prohibited Jews from living in Russia from the 15th century until 1772. There were Jewish expulsions from Moscow (Russia) in 1891, Lithuania in 1495 and Germany and northern Italy during the 14th to 16th centuries. During World War I, Russians expelled over 600,000 Jews from Poland, Lithuania, and the Baltic countries to the deep interiors of Russia. European Holocaust (see below) survivors migrated to the allied controlled region of Europe after the Second World War. A Jewish exodus from Arab and Muslim countries took place between 1947 and 1972, whereby a Middle Eastern and North African Jewish population of 900,000 in 1948 dwindled to about 8,000 by the end of the period.

Other Jewish expulsions included those from Egypt in 1947, 1948, 1956 and 1957, after much abuse of Jews by Egyptians. More than 75,000 Algerian Jews migrated to France and Israel in 1962. During the 1960s to the 1980s, thousands of Polish Jews left Poland because of the Polish political crisis. State-sponsored persecution in the Soviet Union prompted hundreds of thousands of Soviet Jews to flee the region during the 1970s to the 1990s.

The Shameful Sin of Christian Anti-Semitism—Over the centuries after the founding of the Christian faith, many leaders of the worldview were guilty of misrepresenting Christ's Gospel to the detriment of people of Jewish heritage. Christian leaders accused Jews of various heinous crimes and made them suffer horrendously. People who professed to be Christian leaders leveled unconscionable, outlandish charges of "Christ killer," "blood libel," and "host desecration" crimes against Jews and prodded others to hound, persecute and kill Jews for alleged practices they viewed as unpardonable trespasses.

Replacement Theology or *Supersessionism* teaches that the nation of Israel is no longer Almighty God's flagship or chosen people. The ill-advised doctrine advocates the premise that God's promises made in the Old Testament to Jews as forerunners of his glorious plan for the redemption of all humankind were transferred to the so-called universal Christian Church after Jews (actually, a minority of them) rejected Christ and helped occasioned his trial, conviction, scourging, and crucifixion. Indeed, adherents to the replacement theology teaching blame and condemn all Jews, past, present, and future, exclusively for Christ's suffering and death on the cross. The doctrine of replacement theology has been vehicular in fostering the dreadful sin of anti-Semitism over many centuries.

Zionism – The Reestablishment, Development & Protection of the Nation of Israel—Zionism is an unfairly demonized concept, as it really relates to the centuries-old undertaking by Jews to reassemble in their traditional homeland of Israel after being scattered by their enemies into foreign lands throughout history. Introduced by the Hungarian political activist Theodor Herzl (1860-1904) in the late 18th century, Zionism is a form of positive nationalism. Israel welcomes people of all ethnicities, races, and religions and does not discriminate against anyone simply because he or she is non-Jewish. Of course, as it is with any democracy, there is the expectation that everyone upholds and honors the laws of the land.

The Holocaust—Tantamount to the refutation of the claims of "occupation" by Israel's adversaries, especially by Middle Eastern Arabs and Muslims, including the Palestinians—the name is really a misnomer for a people transplanted into a region they do not, and never owned—is the necessity to establish the understanding that the West Bank and Judea and Samaria regions are part of Israel and belong to the Jews, not the so-called Palestinians. Israel, in which about six and one half million Jews reside, measures less than one percent of the entire Middle Eastern region occupied by Arabs. The latter number over 370 million. Arabs and Muslims are not satisfied with coveting over ninety-nine percent of the region that they overran over the centuries—they want it all!

Anti-Semitic sentiments reached a high point in the mid-twentieth century during the Second World War when the Nazis slaughtered six million Jews in Europe under the inspectorate of one of history's vilest madmen, Adolf Hitler. The Holocaust is history's most shocking and extreme genocidal undertaking to date.

Notwithstanding the unmitigated butchery of millions of Jews and an additional five million non-Jewish people by the Nazis and their collaborators during the Holocaust, there is an unfeeling, misguided minority of people who deny the Holocaust ever took place. Many of these disseminators of untruth claim the Jews invented the Holocaust story to gain the sympathy of the world at large and to help them justify a so-called Zionist cause.

The forgoing encapsulations about the lives of Jews throughout history represent just a prevue of the innumerable, unbelievably dreadful experiences Jews have suffered at the hands of their hateful enemies. In *Israel – Against All Odds (Volume I)*, I endeavor to present various analyses on the aspects of the history of the Jews and the nation of Israel, and on other incidents as well. Above all else, I purpose to show, despite all that transpired over the centuries, Israel, and Jews everywhere, stand tall, and though Jews are relatively few from a standpoint of global population statistics, they tower over those who continue to loathe and want to destroy them.

The Jews, after centuries of hateful, unmitigated assaults on their physical, religious and cultural wellbeing by every adversary imaginable, after incredible loss of life and possessions, after unbelievable instances of harassment and expulsions, firstly, from their traditional homeland and then from foreign places of abode in which they settled, in some cases, for thousands of years, remain a group of people undeterred, unmovable, and totally committed to survival, success and prosperity—against all odds!

The entire world, including the Jews' multitudinous adversaries, like their predecessors, stand in awe!

Israel – Against All Odds (Volume II) represents a continuation of *Israel – Against All Odds (Volume I)* and examines an additional number of essential issues as they relate to the nation of Israel and people of Jewish ancestry. The second volume contains in-depth discussions about the following:

(a) The United Nations & Israel – A History of Discrimination

(b) The Israeli-Palestinian Conflict

(c) The Boycott, Divestment & Sanctions (BDS) Movement

(d) The Iranian Nuclear Deal

(e) The Shocking Truth about the Iranian-American Hostage Exchange

(f) "Shalom" Will Come

Notes:

1. Throughout this book, the terms "Israel" and "Jews" are used interchangeably. This is how the terms are used in the Holy Bible, especially the Old Testament. This is how the world at large views the nomenclature, including those who may be categorized as anti-Semites in today's myriad societies. Unbridled detestation, many a time, does not acknowledge semantical boundaries.

   The connection between Israel and Jews, regardless of where the latter's transitory journeys took them over past centuries, represents an unbreakable bond or association that extends into perpetuity. Consequently, any surmised disassociation between the Jew and Israel becomes blurred into irrelevance.

2. Not all references in this book are intended to refer to allude to anti-Semites or terrorists. There are many Palestinians who do not subscribe to the hateful, anti-Jewish and ant-Christian agenda of Hamas, the Palestinian terrorist regime. As a matter of fact, many Palestinians themselves suffer under the inspectorate of the malevolent government.

Chapter One

ANTI-SEMITISM – A GLOBAL HATRED IN MANY FORMS

Some people like the Jews and some do not. But no thoughtful man can deny the fact that they are, beyond any question, the most formidable and the most remarkable race which has appeared in the world.

Sir Winston Churchill – Former Prime Minister of the United Kingdom (1951-1955)

ANTI-SEMITISM AROUND THE WORLD - ANTI-DEFAMATION LEAGUE (ADL) POLLS

The statistics imparted below bare the disquieting reality of the rise of global anti-Semitism. The information appeared in an *American Free Press* article that referenced a survey conducted in May 2014 by the *Anti-Defamation League* (ADL).[1]

The ADL Global 100: An Index of Anti-Semitism evaluators presented 11 statements to people and asked whether each was "probably true" or "probably false." A tally of six or more "probably true" answers resulted in a respondent being rated as having anti-Semitic attitudes. The statements included such declarations as (a) Jews have too much power in international financial markets (b) Jews have too much control over the global media (c) Jews have too much control over the US government and (d) Jews have too much control over global affairs.

The undertaking encompassed questioning 53,100 adults in 102 countries and territories in an unprecedented endeavor to conduct a comprehensive data-based survey about the level and intensity of anti-Jewish sentiment around the world. The ADL conducted the survey in the following regions.

(a) Western Europe

(b) Eastern Europe

(c) Middle East & North Africa (MENA)

(d) Sub-Saharan Africa

(e) The Americas

The ADL Global 100 Index on Anti-Semitism findings were as follows:

1. One in four adults worldwide embraces anti-Semitic feelings.

2. The highest concentration of people harboring anti-Semitic attitudes exists in the Middle East and North Africa (MENA). Almost three-quarters (74 percent) of the people polled exhibited anti-Semitic sentiments.

3. In the West Bank and Gaza in the Middle East, anti-Semitic feelings permeate society, with about 93 percent of the people viewing Jews with animosity. (See 9 & 10 below for listings of various countries and the levels of anti-Semitic sentiments therein)

4. More than one quarter on the people surveyed i.e. 26 percent, hold anti-Semitic views, which translates into a staggering sum of about 1.09 billion adults.

5. Only 54 percent of the survey's respondents ever heard about the Holocaust. Two out of three people questioned either never heard of the Holocaust or did not think historical accounts of the atrocity were accurate.

6. Greece is easily the most anti-Semitic nation in Europe, with 69 percent of its adult inhabitants satisfying the criteria for classification as "anti-Semites." Poland comes next with 45 percent, followed by Bulgaria with 44 percent. France has a score of 37 percent.

7. Eastern Europe is presumably more anti-Semitic than Western Europe, with a score of 34 percent versus 24 percent.

8. Christians in Catholic and Eastern Orthodox nations are more likely to contemplate anti-Semitic leanings than those in Protestant countries. Protestant nations such as the United States, the United Kingdom, and Sweden exhibit anti-Semitic tendencies of nine percent, eight percent and four percent respectively.

9. The following countries/territories exhibit the highest level of anti-Semitic attitudes:

> West Bank and Gaza – 93%
>
> Iraq – 92%
>
> Yemen – 88%

Algeria – 87%

Libya – 87%

Tunisia – 86%

Kuwait – 82%

Bahrain – 81%

Jordan – 81%

Morocco – 80%

10. Countries with the lowest level of anti-Semitic sentiments are:

Laos – 0.2%

Philippines – 3%

Sweden – 4%

Netherlands – 5%

Vietnam – 6%

United Kingdom – 8%

United States – 9%

Denmark – 9%

Tanzania – 12%

Thailand – 13%

The foregoing findings, although they are responses to questions about the influence and power of Jews and not necessarily about their religious, racial or ideological characteristics, signal a cause for serious concern. Continued and uninhibited hatred directed at people of Jewish ancestry around the world can only engender widespread animosity and tragic consequences as diverse religious and philosophical players take to participation on an international stage.

Anti-Semitism in America - Anti-Defamation League (ADL) Polls

Further to the 2014 Anti-Defamation League (ADL) Global 100 project, the results of two newer polls conducted in the United States in October 2016 and January and February 2017 revealed the views of American toward Jews and other religious minorities.[2, 3]

In keeping with the theme of this book, the immediate subsection deals with the way Americans feel about Jews, and not about other religious minorities.

Results of the surveys revealed that although anti-Semitic attitudes in the USA grew to 14 percent, most Americans are respectful of Jews. The ADL, for the first time in one of its polls, determined that the majority of Americans i.e., 52 percent, fear for the safety of Jews, whom they feel face violent attacks by anti-Semites. Very significantly, 84 percent of the ADL survey respondents thought it was important for the US government to address the issue of combating anti-Semitism in the country. Seventy (70) percent of Americans shared such a concern in 2014.

The ADL has been conducting polls on anti-Semitic sentiments in the US since 1964. Surveys disclose a pronounced decline in anti-Jewish feelings over the past 50 years. ADL's most recent *Survey of Anti-Semitic Attitudes in the US* carried out in 2016, divulged that approximately 34 million American adults, or 10 percent of the population, harbor anti-Semitic convictions. The recent ADL Global 100 survey included the attitudes of American Muslims toward Jews for the first time. Thirty-four (34) percent of American Muslims consider themselves anti-Semitic.

Other findings of the 2016 and 2017 ADL surveys were as follows:

1. Thirty-one (31) percent of Americans believe that Jews are "more loyal to Israel than to America," a finding consistent with the results of similar polls dating back to 1964.

2. Thirty (30) percent of Americans accept the anti-Semitic postulation that Jews "killed Jesus Christ."

3. Twenty-five (25) percent of Americans think "Jews still talk too much about what happened to them in the Holocaust," a revelation consistent with the findings of previous surveys.

The relatively sobering statistics about anti-Semitism in the USA notwithstanding, Jew hatred from a global perspective is at an all-time high. Jews face persecution more than any other religious group, except maybe Christians.

A GLOBAL RISE IN ANTI-SEMITISM

In recent times, the precept and practice of radical Islam emboldened anti-Semites in the Middle East and other parts of the world as hatred of Jews (and Christians) assumed alarming proportions. The emergence of ISIS or the Islamic State of Iraq and Syria, an inhumanly savage and merciless fringe organization bent on instituting a worldwide caliphate whereby a Muslim ruler or rulers would exercise unencumbered domination over all peoples, contributes in no small way to the rising tide of anti-Semitism, especially in Muslim autocracies around the world. In addition, the continuing conflict between Israel and the terrorist group Hamas, the latter the official government of Palestine, seems to serve as a catalyst toward anti-Jewish sentiment as people readily accede to the revisionist contention that Israeli-controlled territories such as the Gaza Strip, East Jerusalem and the West Bank, which comprised the ancient regions of Judea and Samaria, belong to the Palestinians and not to the Jews.

Disturbingly to the sane and commonsensical intellect, the global increase in anti-Semitism apparently also proceeds from the misguided resentment of Jews because of their excellence in various fields of endeavor relating to business, finance, science, and medicine. There is the perception that Jews exercise disproportionate ascendancy in the disciplines wherever they study, live and work, which, notwithstanding their stymied, sparse presence in most instances, is just about anywhere in the world. The nation of Israel, for instance, is at the forefront of hi-tech, biomedical and environmentally friendly innovations. The Jewish nation invests more of its Gross Domestic Product (GDP) in research and development than any other country in the world.[4]

Anti-Semites seek to fault a people who dedicate themselves to hard work and resiliency in the accomplishment of their goals, and who further the interests of the myriad communities in which they reside. The hatemongers, from an incomprehensibly irrational standpoint, allow jealousy and prejudice to garble what should be admiration and thankfulness.

The term "anti-Semitism" is really a misnomer. The word is a derivative of the Greek words *"anti,"* which means "against" and *"Semite,"* which refers to a descendant of Shem, the eldest son of Noah of the Holy Bible. The term "Semitic" refers to a group of Afro-Asiatic languages originating in the Middle East and includes Aramaic, Arabic, Amharic, Tigrinya, Hebrew, and Maltese, among others. A "Semite," from a standpoint of linguistic familiarity, is an individual who speaks a Semitic language. Over time, the meaning of the term evolved to refer to cultures and ethnic groups that spoke Semitic languages.

Wilhelm Marr (1819-1904), a German agitator and politician, initially in favor of liberating Jews as an oppressed group, became embittered after the failure of the 1848-1849 German Revolution to democratize Germany, and over his own dwindling political aspirations. Marr somehow felt led to venting his frustration upon the Jews. His organization, *The League of Anti-Semites*, introduced the word "anti-Semite" into the political lexicon, and the group, in embracing the term's connotations, consequently became the first popular political movement fully predicated on anti-Jewish sentiment.[5] The widespread use of the term "anti-Semitism" today to characterize anti-Jewish sentiments notwithstanding, a more accurate description of the mentality would be "Jew Hatred or Anti-Jewishness."

A simple and forthright reason for a delineation between "anti-Semitism" and the other terms is that Arabs, who make up more than 99 percent of the population of Middle Eastern countries,[6] are also a Semitic people, and Arabs and Jews, as even a novice analyst knows, are markedly dissimilar from religious, social, ideological, economic, racial and cultural perspectives.

Many Middle Eastern Arab nations spare no effort in voicing their hostility toward Jews and, more particularly, the nation of Israel. Iranian leaders, for instance, repeatedly express their obsession with destroying Israel and annihilating its Jewish inhabitants. The majority of the world's nations, including some in the Middle East, are distrustful of Iran and categorize this Arab, or more specifically, Persian nation, as the globe's chief exporter of terrorist activities. Given the foregoing observation, it is unfathomable that six of the world's leading democratic nations, i.e. the USA, with its then-President Barack Obama leading the charge; the United Kingdom, France, Russia, China, Germany and the European Union would enter into a nuclear deal in 2015 with Iran, and allow the release of billions of dollars to the Middle Eastern nation for use in developing and/or enhancing its nuclear program in return for Iran's theocratic leaders' promise to direct their efforts and utilize funds toward only industrial improvement.

The P5+1 and the European Union enacted the JCPOA agreement with Iran despite the latter's record as an egregious party to international negotiations. The author directs the reader to *Israel – Against All Odds (Volume II)* Chapter Two - *The Israeli-Palestinian Conflict* and Chapter Four - *The Iranian Nuclear Deal* for more on the aforementioned subjects.

THE DIFFERENT FORMS OF ANTI-SEMITISM

Louis Harap (1904-1989), the noted Jewish scholar and philosopher, identified six categories of anti-Semitic behavior pervading modern society.[7] The very thought there would be six defined areas of attitude and conduct attributed to a single ethnic group or race, and that such classifications would encompass unbridled animosity, is disquieting. The targeted group—in this case, the Jews, must either be (a) intrinsically evil and/or out of touch with reality, or (b) unjustly despised and ostracized.

Harap concluded anti-Semites expressed their hatred for Jews in the following spheres of thinking and comportment.

1. Religious

2. Racial

3. Economic

4. Ideological

5. Social

6. Cultural

The author expands somewhat on each of the forms of anti-Semitism in the following paragraphs.

Religious Anti-Semitism

Religious anti-Semitism may be said to have begun in Biblical times. Abraham, the patriarch of the world's three major monotheistic religions (Judaism, Christianity, and Islam), relocated from his homeland (presumably the City of Ur in ancient South Mesopotamia) to the land of Canaan around 1,000 years B.C. and birthed a new nation—the nation of Israel. Mesopotamia is a historical region in Western Asia situated within the Tigris-Euphrates river system, in modern days roughly corresponding to most of Iraq, Kuwait, parts of Northern Saudi Arabia, the eastern parts of Syria, Southeastern Turkey, and regions along the Turkish-Syrian and Iran-Iraq borders. It was accepted protocol during that time for newcomers to a region to adopt indigenous religions and worship the idols of the kingdoms of the host territory. The Jews' refusal to worship gods unfamiliar to them led to resentment by the people already resident in the location.

Early Christian church fathers, as far back as around 400 A.D., after the worldview became the official religion of the Roman Empire, sought to establish Christianity as the predominant religion. As Christianity and Judaism both proceeded from the Old Testament, Christians strove to authenticate their belief system by claiming it supplanted Judaism. The Jews did not recognize Jesus as the Messiah, which essentially amounted to a denial of the Christian faith. Roman and Christian leaders perceived the

Jews' rejection of Christianity as subversion and a threat to the new religious hierarchy. Anti-Semitic sentiments unsurprisingly ensued.

Matthew 27:24-25 King James Version (KJV)

24 When Pilate saw that he could prevail nothing, but that rather a tumult was made, he took water, and washed his hands before the multitude, saying, I am innocent of the blood of this just person: see ye to it.

25 Then answered all the people, and said, His blood be on us, and on our children.

The forgoing scriptural passage has been used by misguided Christians over the centuries to assign blame for Christ's death to the Jewish crowd in Jerusalem at the time of Christ's trial and condemnation, and to Jews everywhere, for all time. Jews, in the eyes of many Christians, including many church leaders since the second century A.D., became "Christ killers" and "murderers of God." Additionally, as far back as the early Middle Ages, Christians accused Jews of the "blood libel" crime, whereby they claimed Jews killed Christian children and used their blood for ritual purposes. These false and unsubstantiated claims gave rise to intense anti-Semitic feelings over the years and often resulted in the persecution and murder of Jews. Lamentably, the "Christ killer" and "blood libel" accusations persist among many Christians to this day. (See Chapter Three - *The Shameful Sin of Christian Anti-Semitism* for detailed discussions on the foregoing topics)

Racial Anti-Semitism

Racial anti-Semitism grew out of the development of technological progress and scientific knowledge in the latter part of the nineteenth century. Increased inquiry in the fields of human biology, genetics, and psychology spurred some behavioral scholars and politicians to nurture an ill-conceived, racist perspective of Jews. Racist thinkers also used evolutionary theory, the scientific veracity of the premise or its absence thereof notwithstanding, to advocate a pseudo-scientific philosophy called "social Darwinism."

Social Darwinism taught that human beings did not comprise a single species but were spread among several different races. The subspecies, through biological instinct, fought one another in order to survive and/or progress, with the victors, or races with superior qualities, prevailing in a continuous struggle via warfare and aggression. Social Darwinism, whether evolutionary theory and its adjuvant premise of "survival of the fittest" is scientifically defensible, is a failed postulation. There is no biological or scientific substantiation of the idea even though racially motivated hatemongers vigorously attempted to validate it for over half a century. Social Darwinists essentially rehashed the age-old iniquity of racial anti-Semitism, only under a different guise i.e. the suggestion that Jews were an inferior race and could not change for the better because of innate ethnic and cultural qualities inherited from the beginning of time through an evolutionary path.

Social Darwinists, like other revisionists obsessed with a hierarchy of racial ascendancy, alluded to the involvement of the controversial practice of eugenics, albeit from an unconventional perspective of the pseudoscience, in their twisted agenda to relegate people of Jewish ancestry to a status of racial inferiority.

While positive eugenics refers to improving the qualities of the human species or a population, especially through encouraging reproduction by individuals presumed to possess desirable inheritable traits, negative eugenics refers to the strategy of discouraging procreation through reproduction by individuals having genetic defects or undesirable inheritable traits. Social Darwinists proposed the ludicrous allegation that Jews deliberately circumvented eugenic praxis (positive and negative) by intermingling with non-Jews in central Europe and consequently weakening them biologically. The Jews, they said, "polluted" so-called pure Aryan blood through intermarriage and sexual relations with non-Jews. Social Darwinists argued Jews did this deliberately to sap the will and ability of Germans, Frenchmen, and Hungarians to resist a biologically determined "Jewish drive" for world domination.[8]

The forgoing accusation by social Darwinists was both aberrant and preposterous. Firstly, Jews would have had to acknowledge they were an inferior race, which in the absence of scientific corroboration of such a claim, borders upon the asinine. Secondly, Jews would have had to admit that Germans, Frenchmen, Hungarians and others who were non-Jewish, were members of a physically and intellectually nonpareil Aryan super race. In truth, Adolf Hitler used the term "Aryan" incorrectly to refer to a pure-blooded master race, the members of which had pale skin, blond hair, and blue eyes. Etymologists trace the word "Aryans" to a people who spoke an Indo-European language, and who invaded northern India in the 2nd millennium B.C. and displaced the Dravidians and other aboriginal inhabitants.

The German dictator Adolf Hitler (1889-1945) and Austrian politicians Georg von Schonerer (1842-1921) and Karl Luger (1844-1910) were infamous racists who capitalized on the growing culture of traditional and racial anti-Semitism in the late nineteenth century. Hitler, for his part, was the world's most infamous practitioner of the pseudoscience of eugenics. The Nazis murdered tens of thousands of people who were disabled and sterilized hundreds of thousands they deemed inferior and medically deficient. The eugenics movement, which began in America during the early part of the 20th century, was widely criminalized and condemned after World War II and the Holocaust.

Economic Anti-Semitism

The association of the Jewish psyche with the greed for money is one of the most persistent and toxic anti-Semitic canards. Purveyors of the economic anti-Semitism theory claim Jews control global finances. Russian anti-Semites promoted the foregoing contention in the disingenuous *Protocols of the Elders of Zion* or *The Protocols of the Meetings of the Learned Elders of Zion* (1903). The American industrialist Henry Ford later funded the publication of over 500,000 copies of the fraudulent text for distribution throughout the USA in the 1920s. The Nazis used the anti-Semitic text to ignite hatred against the Jews. German educators taught the anti-Jewish accusations contained in the *Protocols* as established fact and sought to indoctrinate German schoolchildren after Adolf Hitler assumed power in 1933.[9]

The Protocols of the Elders of Zion was a specious and inauthentic endeavor at averring a Jewish scheme for world domination. The fallacious allegations, first published in Russia in August-September 1903, were translated into multiple languages and disseminated internationally in the early years of the 20th century. Some of the publishers of the propagandist literature declared the *Protocols* were actually the minutes of a late 19th-century meeting during which Jewish leaders discussed their plan for global supremacy through undermining the morals of non-Jewish peoples and through regulating and manipulating the press and the world's economies. *The Times of London* thoroughly discredited The Protocols of the Elders of Zion in 1921, but such exposure did not deter anti-Semites around the world from utilizing the fabricated story to encourage contempt for and animosity toward people of Jewish ancestry.

The Secret Relationship between Blacks and Jews (Volume One) was another contemptible attempt at denigrating Jews and relegating them to a status of notoriety as racists and economic exploiters. Produced in 1991 by the Nation of Islam, an African American political and religious movement known for insolently baring its prejudices and indiscretions, the book claims Jews dominated the Atlantic slave trade. A second book, *The*

Secret Relationship between Blacks and Jews (Volume Two), with the subtitle *How the Jews Gained Control of the Black American Economy,* appeared in 2010. Writers of the book blamed Jews for promoting a myth of black racial inferiority and made a range of conspiratorial accusations about Jewish involvement in the slave trade, and in the cotton, textiles and banking industries.

Scholars widely criticized the writers of the books for advancing anti-Semitism and for neglecting to present an objective analysis of the role of Jews in the slave trade. Henry Louis Gates, Jr, head of the department of Afro-American studies at Harvard University, referred to The Secret Relationship between Blacks and Jews (Volume One) as "the Bible of new anti-Semitism" and added that "the book massively misinterprets the historical record, largely through a process of cunningly selective quotations of often reputable sources."[10]

Historian Wim Klooster, Professor of History at Clark University, Massachusetts, USA, offered the following statement about *The Secret Relationship between Blacks and Jews.*

> *In no period did Jews play a leading role as financiers, ship owners, or factors in the Transatlantic or Caribbean slave trade. They possessed far fewer slaves than non-Jews in every British territory in North America and the Caribbean. Even when Jews in a handful of places owned slaves in proportions slightly above their representation among a town's families, such cases do not come close to corroborating the assertions of The Secret Relationship.*[11]

Jews, as far back as the Middle Ages, when they endured political, economic and social discrimination, could not own land. Conversely, Christians, because of religious constriction, could not loan money for profit. Jews consequently became moneylenders. Their involvement in the questionable trade of usury—the practice of lending money and charging interest at a high rate—gave rise to a new stereotype i.e. Jews as an acquisitive, covetous people. The foregoing notwithstanding, indigenous rulers tolerated the Jews as long as the latter served their schemes to construct buildings and fund military endeavors. When the demand for their services as moneylenders was no longer required, Jews met with denigration and expulsion from society e.g. from England in 1290, from France in 1394, and from Spain in 1492.

Cultural Anti-Semitism

Cultural anti-Semitism may be defined as antipathy toward people of Jewish ancestry based on their comprising a detached minority culture that ostensibly threatens to contaminate a main culture and/or even replace the latter with Jewish thinking and customs.

The Jewish Diaspora, or the dispersion of Israelites and Judahites from their ancestral homeland (the Land of Israel), effectively began in 733 B.C. and ended around 73 A.D. and led to the relocation of Jews all over Africa, Asia, and Europe, among other parts of the world. Accordingly, it was inevitable that the Jewish culture would infiltrate the customs of foreign countries. Sadly, many host nations refused to recognize Jewish practices and treated Jewish immigrants with disdain. Also, the traditional disinclination by Jews to abandon their religious and cultural beliefs and to assimilate unreservedly into other cultural systems served only to exacerbate tensions between the members of host nations and the Jews. As a result, adherents of the main religions and cultures in countries in which Jews found themselves following the Diaspora viewed the transplanted newcomers with suspicion and distrust. Put alternatively, the Jews' unyielding allegiance to their faith and customs exposed them to cultural anti-Semitism.

In all fairness, members of most other belief systems around the world exhibit similar characteristics of loyalty and steadfastness, regardless of the environment in which they live. It is grossly inequitable, therefore, to direct a charge of stubbornness or egocentricity in such regard against Jews scattered as a result of the Diaspora, even though during such sojourns Jews would have intermingled with members of host nations for many years.

The following two observations by Louis Harap (1904-1989), the Jewish-American philosopher and scholar, and Eric Kandel (1929-), the Austrian-American neuroscientist and university professor of biochemistry and biophysics, help put the concept of cultural anti-Semitism in proper perspective.

Louis Harap defines cultural anti-Semitism as:

> ...that species of anti-Semitism that charges the Jews with corrupting a given culture and attempting to supplant or succeeding in supplanting the preferred culture with a uniform, crude, 'Jewish' culture.[12]

Eric Kandel characterizes cultural anti-Semitism as being based on "Jewishness" and as:

...a religious or cultural tradition that is acquired through learning, through distinctive traditions and education. Jews are viewed as possessing unattractive psychological and social characteristics that are acquired through acculturation.[13]

Additional forms of anti-Semitism mentioned by Louis Harap include *Social anti-Semitism* and *Ideological anti-Semitism.* Social anti-Semitism is the categorization of Jews as a socially inferior race, albeit a group of people who are pushy and undesirable. The consequence for the Jews is generally social exclusion. Ideological anti-Semitism relates to Jews as subversives and/or revolutionaries who seek to usurp a main culture or population and impose their convictions and thinking upon its members.

Two Additional forms of Anti-Semitism

Political Anti-Semitism

Political anti-Semitism derives from the belief that Jews seek national and/or global power or dominance. Some people embrace a perceived fear of the Jews' determination and resolve to succeed in multiple fields of endeavor, their propensity to survive terrible hardships and persecution, and their presumably higher than normal intelligence.

The question as to whether Jews are smarter than people of other ethnic persuasions has intrigued behavioral scientists and other developmental researchers for a long time. Jews, although they comprise only about two-tenths of one percent of the world's population, profess representation of a startlingly disproportionate number of the world's most intelligent, most accomplished, and most influential people. Among people of Jewish ancestry who have had a profound impact on humanity are the Biblical Patriarch Abraham, whose teachings and philosophy Jews, Christians, and Moslems consider sacred; the Old Testament prophet Moses, the lawgiver to Jews and Christians, and Jesus Christ and the apostle Paul, who founded and spread Christianity, a religious worldview that numbers more than one-third of the world's population among its adherents.

Jews have also played significant roles in shaping the modern world to large extent. In the 20th century alone, intellectual titans like the physicist Albert Einstein, the psychoanalyst Sigmund Freud, the philosopher and sociologist Karl Marx, the developers of the polio vaccine Jonas Salk and Albert Sabin, and the principal developers of the first atomic bomb, Felix Bloch, Niels Bohr, Otto Frisch, Robert Oppenheimer, Leo Szilard, and Edward Teller, all left indelible marks upon known history.

Friedrich W. Nietzsche (1844-1900), the German philosopher, cultural critic, philologist, and Latin and Greek scholar, whose work greatly influenced Western philosophy and modern intellectual history, staunchly opposed anti-Semitism. Historians attribute the following forthright statement to the German polymath.

> The whole problem of the Jews exists only in nation states, for here their energy and higher intelligence, their accumulated capital of spirit and will, gathered from generation to generation through a long schooling in suffering, must become so preponderant as to arouse mass envy and hatred. In almost all contemporary nations, therefore—in direct proportion to the degree to which they act up nationalistically—the literary obscenity of leading the Jews to slaughter as scapegoats of every conceivable public and internal misfortune is spreading.[14]

Nietzsche's upfront observation not only alludes to the baleful characteristics of political anti-Semitism and other forms of the degenerate mindset, but it also brings to the fore the unspeakable evil to which such predispositions led during the Second World War—the senseless, unmitigated slaughter of countless Jews.

Political anti-Semitism grew widely after the legal emancipation of the Jews in many European countries during the period spanning the late 18th century and the early 20th century, whereby Jews gained release from a number of social, cultural and political constraints. The freedom of Jews to participate in pursuits that beforetime were beyond their reach angered many non-Jews who had grown accustomed to relegating Jews to a status that encompassed less than first-class rights of domicile.

The contrast between the suggestion by racial anti-Semites (see above) that Jews are biologically inferior to so-called Aryans, and the belief, at least by some people given to social and political anti-Semitic sentiments that Jews are intellectually superior to other races, begs an explanation as to the bewildering nature of anti-Semitic reasoning in general. Biological racial inferiority, after all, especially if the concept proceeds from an evolutionary perspective, essentially suggests a deficiency in mental and/or intellectual acuity when measured against biological racial prominence.

The foregoing observation lends credence to the assumption that anti-Semitism, on the whole, is based on stereotypes and myths that target Jews, their religious practices and beliefs, and the Jewish State of Israel. The mindset, from its origins to its persistence over the centuries, confirms the implacable practice of scapegoating an ostracized group of people defined as the "other."

The New Anti-Semitism

The New Anti-Semitism is a more recent form of Jew-hatred that surfaced in the 1990s, and that accommodates socio-political musings of far-left and far-right scholars and allows the infusion of radical Islamic philosophy.

New anti-Semitism, in the main, manifests itself as opposition to Zionism and the existence of the State of Israel. Those who denounce new anti-Semitism say much of what amounts to criticism of Israel by individuals, groups, and organizations around the world is fundamentally demonization of the Jewish race and the Jewish State. Such a reality, they assume, along with the international resurgence of attacks on Jews and Jewish symbols, and the growing acceptance of anti-Semitic postulations in public discourse is a manifestation of the age-old sin of anti-Semitism in another form. Chapter Four, *Zionism – The Reestablishment, Development and Protection of the Nation of Israel* contains a detailed discussion about the concept and working of Zionism.

The French philosopher and writer Bernhard-Henri Levy (born 1948) efficaciously describes new anti-Semitism as follows:

> *It can operate on a large scale, convince, inflame hearts and minds, only by offering three shameful new propositions.*
>
> *1. Jews are detestable because they are assumed to support an evil, illegitimate, murderous state. This is the anti-Zionist delirium of the merciless adversaries of the re-establishment of the Jews in their historical homeland.*
>
> *2. The Jews are all the more detestable because they are believed to base their beloved Israel on imaginary suffering or suffering that at the very least has been outrageously exaggerated. This is the shabby and infamous denial of the Holocaust.*
>
> *3. In so doing, the Jews would commit a third and final crime that could make them still more guilty, which is to impose on us the memory of their dead, to completely stifle other people's memories, and to overshadow other martyrs whose deaths have plunged parts of today's world, most emblematically that of the Palestinians, into mourning. And*

here we come face to face with the modern-day scourge, the stupidity that is competitive victimhood.[15]

Levy goes on to intimate that unless anti-Semites succeed in popularizing the myth of the modern Jew as a vile and repugnant creature, the premise of anti-Semitism, on the whole, would tend to diminish. Anti-Semites acknowledge the usefulness of such a strategy, and in Levy's own words:

It (New anti-Semitism) has to be anti-Zionist, it must deny the Holocaust, and it must feed the competition of pain—or it will not thrive: The logic is implacable, despicable, but compelling.[16]

Demonstration of anti-Semitic feelings today sometimes assumes a circumlocutory nature. In other words, the unwarranted and widespread criticism of Israel and the State's supposed illegitimacy emboldens some people to feel justified in attacking Jews and Jewish institutions the world over for no reason other than to be part of a faddish Jew-hating movement.

Ronald Lauder, the President of the World Jewish Congress (WJC), laments the present surge in anti-Semitic behavior around the globe. The 73-year-old philanthropist and art collector, in a March 2017 interview with Michael Burleigh (1955-), British author and Nazi Germany historian, spoke concernedly about threats to, and attacks on synagogues and other Jewish institutions in his native America, and the desecration of Jewish graves in St. Louis, Missouri and other cities. Lauder pointed out that "Even in the US, the country with the strongest Jewish community in the diaspora, anti-Semitism is alive and kicking."[17]

Lauder underscored troubling concerns about developments in Hungary, France, and the United Kingdom whereby anti-Semitism resurfaced over recent years.

Lauder says that in Hungary, the notorious anti-Semite Miklos Horthy (1868-1957), who persecuted Jews for decades before Nazi Germany invaded Hungary, is memorialized in political discourse. Hungarians herald Horthy as a founder of the nation's far-right political constituency. In France, Lauder noted, while the National Front's Marine Le Pen "distanced herself from the morbid anti-Semitic obsessions of her father Jean Marie Le Pen," she nevertheless called for a ban of yarmulkes and kosher slaughter as part of a promise to curtail the public display of religious practices. Finally, in Britain, the Labor Party, which under the inspectorate of Jeremy Corbyn concurs with the predilections of groups with questionable missions, is presently a political affiliate of the Palestinian Solidarity Campaign (PSC)—this notwithstanding the fact there are only about 20,000 Palestinians in Britain. The PSC is the driving force behind the *Boycott, Divestment, and Sanctions (BDS)* movement.[18]

The BDS movement is a vile, misguided endeavor of recent derivation, the mission of which is to demonize and delegitimize Israel politically, economically, culturally, and ideologically. The promoters of the BDS movement make false analogies between democratic Israel and Afrikaner South America in an attempt to stigmatize and isolate Israel by likening it to an apartheid-like State. The BDS movement actively participates in infiltrating university campuses around the world and in disseminating its toxicant ideas to students everywhere, even in nations like the United Kingdom and the United States of America.

The author directs the reader to *Israel – Against All Odds (Volume II)*, Chapter Three - *The Boycott, Divestment & Sanctions (BDS) Movement* for a detailed discussion about the sinister, abhorrent anti-Semitic undertaking.

Some experts contend there has been an increase in anti-Semitic incidents in the USA over recent years. The Simon Wiesenthal Center, an international Jewish human rights organization headquartered in the USA, issued a statement on February 21, 2017, calling on the US Attorney General to establish a task force to address a recent rash of bomb threats against Jewish community centers across America. The organization's leaders also urged President Donald Trump to devise a plan to combat "surging anti-Semitism." Excerpts from the Center's statement, as reported in *The Times of Israel* on April 10, 2017, read as follows.

> *American Jewry is being targeted by extremists from multiple sources: On our nation's campuses, where incessant anti-Israel campaigns have created a climate of intimidation; in New York, home to the world's largest Jewish community, which reports a spike in anti-Semitic incidents...*
>
> *Further, social media is being deployed 24/7 by extremists to target and demonize individual Jews, entire communities, our faith and values. We need leadership from the top to effectively combat the hate."[19]*

A RECALCITRANT AMERICAN MEDIA – DISTORTING THE TRUTH & FUELING NEW ANTI-SEMITISM

Manfred Gerstenfeld (born 1937 in Vienna), is an Israeli author and considered one of the greatest authorities on anti-Semitism. Isi Leibler, the former chairman of the Governing Board of the World Jewish Congress, wrote in the *Jerusalem Post* in 2015 that "Gerstenfeld would today be considered the most qualified analyst of contemporary anti-Semitism with a focus on anti-Israelism." Gerstenfeld opines the rise in anti-Semitic incidents in the USA is due to the polarization of American society. In an exclusive interview with *JerusalemOnline*, Gerstenfeld volunteered the following opinion.

> *It is the general polarized atmosphere that causes anti-Semitism to flourish. In a quiet society, the anti-Semites are not aroused as much as they are in a polarized society. Bernie Sanders contributed to the polarized atmosphere. Trump contributed to the polarization and so did Clinton. So have the Democrats, the Republicans and don't forget Obama. Nobody has done so much damage to western values in recent decades as him. There was an outburst of anti-Semitism on the campuses under Obama.*[20]

Gerstenfeld points to media bias in America as the primary reason certain elements of the "new anti-Semitism" gained ground in the United States. Distorters of the news, for instance, try to pin the rise in anti-Semitic incidents on Donald Trump's election as President. Gerstenfeld says:

> *The media is not objective. They distort (news) in many ways. We know this because of CAMERA. They have done major work documenting how the New York Times distorts information on Israel. Once the information is proven to be distorted about Israel, it is also distorted about at least some other issues.*[21]

Yoram Ettinger, former Minister for Congressional Affairs to Israel's Embassy in Washington, DC, and former General Consul of Israel to the Southwestern United States shares Manfred Gerstenfeld's opinion that recent anti-Semitic incidents in the USA are not connected to the 2016 general election results. In an exclusive *JerusalemOnline* interview, Ettinger made the following remarks.

> *(Anti-Semitism) is part of an ongoing phenomenon throughout the world...One should not rush to the conclusion that it (anti-Semitism in the US) has to do with the election of a certain president in the US.*
>
> *...This threat has been with us for over 3,500 years— way before the Trump administration has been in Washington ... Therefore, we should focus on the strategic context. We should not delude ourselves into thinking that this (anti-Semitism) has to do with a particular phenomenon in the US.[22]*

Gerstenfeld singles out the *Black Lives Matter* movement, a so-called African-American civil rights/human rights awareness organization, which gained prominence during the Obama administration, as a major promoter of anti-Semitism in today's society.

> *They started a program for anti-Semitic things. They created a movement that supports BDS. Black Lives Matter is not going to desecrate a cemetery or murder Jews like some madman would, but it definitely contributes to the hate atmosphere. It is a movement that hides behind the humanitarian mask.[23]*

(See **Israel – Against All Odds (Volume II)**, Chapter Three - The Boycott, Divestment & Sanctions (BDS) Movement, for more on the controversial subject).

Many observers see the Black Lives Matter movement as a civil and/or humanitarian rights endeavor gone haywire, due more so than not to the sinister designs of some of its promoters who seek to inject racial undertones into issues better addressed by levelheaded investigation and assessment. Exceptions do not determine norms. Rather, norms determine exceptions, and isolated cases whereby race and/or bias may engender tragic consequences do not justify the relegation of every instance in which the life of a black individual is endangered or lost to the perpetration of a hate crime. Additionally, the rush by reckless black leaders to misrepresent the facts apropos to certain events serves only to exacerbate the issue.

A troubling aspect about the Black Lives Matter movement is the callous manner in which its advocates, hiding behind a façade of concern for black people, infiltrate traditionally neutral arenas of sport, politics, and religion, and infuse an unwelcome message of partiality and dislike. Whenever opportunists propagandize the so-called interests of a particular ethnic group under dubious circumstances, especially to the exclusion of the interests of people of other races, there will be a tendency, by default, to demonize one or more of the other races as xenophobic or prejudiced.

The Black Lives Matter movement, with its agenda of misconstruing anything with which it disagrees as a racial attack on black people, and its disgust for Jews draws troubling parallelism with another African-American movement, the pseudo-religious Nation of Islam organization. The Nation of Islam makes no pretense about its abhorrence for the nation of Israel and for people of Jewish ancestry.

Lamentably, very many otherwise decent, straight-thinking people, including many well-meaning black folks, allow themselves to be inveigled by the indiscretions of a malicious, misdirected alliance of troublemakers.

The bias in America's mainstream media, which perpetually slants toward liberal dissemination of information, can be nauseating to the traditionalist intellect. While the reality of a presumed rise in anti-Semitic incidents in the USA may be questionable, the age-old sin exists, locally and internationally, and a partial media relishes the opportunity to capitalize on the willingness of a credulous public to entertain news that fall even slightly outside the realm of accurate, but mundane circulation. Additionally, as intimated above, there seems to be a post-election trend by anti-Donald Trump activists to blame the incumbent leader for the so-called increase in anti-Semitic activity in America. The combination of the idiosyncrasies of a whimsical public with a witch hunt for transgressions by a polemical leader, whether such dislike is justifiable, provides a field day for those willing to engage in irresponsible, cesspool journalism.

Looking at the issue from another angle, divulging false news could have been a tactic to mislead the general public into acknowledging beforehand that the Democrats were sure winners of the 2016 American general elections, shattering the confidence of Republican voters and cajoling them into conceding victory to the Democrats even before the voting process ended. If that were the strategy, it failed miserably.

The labeling of Mr. Trump as an undesirable leader proceeds from partisan and one-sided broadcasting of the news. After all, during the 2016 electoral campaigns, liberal newspapers like the New York Times and the Washington Post, and partisan news agencies like CNN bombarded the public with poll results that put Hilary Clinton miles ahead of Donald Trump and repeatedly projected Mrs. Clinton as an imminent landslide victor. In the end, everyone, Republicans and Democrats alike, the latter plunged into utter confusion and disbelief, had to acknowledge such news was unrepresentative of the truth. The relentless post-election attacks on the new President fuels the belief in many people's minds that the

Democratic Party and its constituents are unable to recover from the shocking defeat in the 2016 general elections.

Indeed, the goal of the liberal media is not only to incriminate Donald Trump for the probable rise in anti-Semitism in America but to attack the Republican president from every conceivable front in the expectation of somehow forcing him out of office. An importunate accusation against the Trump administration revolves around is its supposed collaboration with the Russian government in meddling with the 2016 US general elections to enable a Republican Party victory. The Democratic Party refuses to abandon the ill-advised strategy nearly two years after Donald Trump's inauguration, even though the ploy's farcical, constantly reworked assumptions have repeatedly met with embarrassing refutation.

Trump's enemies spare no effort in delving into his past and amplifying decades old improprieties, some of which, although reprehensible, pale into insignificance in comparison to the indiscretions of former Democratic presidents—while they were in office! Names like William J. Clinton and John F. Kennedy immediately spring to mind. There was no demand to impeach either of the aforementioned individuals, yet Democrats and other anti-Trump elements clamor for Trump's removal and impeachment, in part because of sexually immodest behavior many years ago, long before he assumed the American presidency.

The foregoing observations about Donald Trump's quandaries notwithstanding, very many people think Trump is outspoken and highly effective, especially in connection with matters that impact American concerns at a national and international level, i.e. fixing America's economy, handling the JCPOA or Iranian nuclear deal, stymieing the threat of domestic and international terrorism, curtailing the infringement of immigration laws and regulations, and removing double standards relative to the dissemination of news by a liberally controlled media, among other considerations. Additionally, Trump's no-nonsense approach in dealing with autocratic leaders around the world, in particular, the rulers of North Korea, Iran, Syria, and Russia, who very many people see as threats to international peace and security, endear him as a strong, purposeful leader of the world's most powerful nation. Of course, the liberal media wastes no time in misrepresenting the majority of the foregoing issues in its incorrigible attacks on the Trump administration.

Were it that other politicians, especially Democrats, were more honest and forthright than hypocritical, and less obeisant to subterfuge and tokenism that cater to the idiosyncrasies of stroppy, immoderate voters. Were it that the double standards attendant to the dissemination of news in America were less pervasive, and the media reported on the indiscretions of Democrats and liberals as much as they did about Republicans and conservatives. Very many people would be aghast at such revelations!

Donald Trump unquestionably is prey to more hounding and harassment than any other US President in recent times. Even an occasional spur-of-the-moment tweet by the President or an innocent sartorial oversight by the First Lady provides fodder for insensitive critics with precious little else to do. Trump's supporters, meanwhile, are convinced the man's accomplishments as leader of America, although demonstrably more noteworthy than other US Presidents, are constantly trivialized in deference to unceasing, malicious hatemongering by Democrats and other people unable to come to grips with the fact that Trump's performance at the 2016 US general elections defied all odds and thrust his opponent Hillary Clinton's efforts into a political muddle.

The bias in America's media is further brought to the fore by the observations of Seth Frantzman, Ph.D., a Jerusalem-based commentator on Middle East politics, in a March 1, 2017 article in the sometimes controversial but widely read Algemeiner Journal, a New York newspaper covering American and international Jewish and Israel related issues.

Frantzman, in addressing multitudinous Internet articles and blogs, the writers of which purport to blame Donald Trump for the alleged rise in anti-Semitism in America, asks why such a phenomenon even exists. He dismisses the argument that anti-Semitism has grown since Donald Trump won the American general election and bemoans the likelihood that the staunchly liberal American press fields an agenda of misleading the public and protecting certain political elements from criticism. In such a regard, Frantzman questions why the 7,000 odd anti-Semitic incidents during the Barack Obama administration never made the news. Franztman notes there were 1,211 anti-Semitic incidents in Obama's first year in office. This was after four straight years of declining anti-Semitism. A tally of anti-Semitic incidents between 2009 and 2015 i.e. the years during which the Obama administration held office, reached more than 7,000, or more than double the number of incidents under the previous two regimes.[24]

Frantzman looks back almost a decade and asks where was the media in 2009, 2010, 2011, 2012, 2013, 2014, and 2015 when thousands of anti-Semitic incidents took place? There were, he alleges, 210 physical assaults on Jews, 3,900 threats against Jews and Jewish institutions, 2,900 incidents of vandalism, and 180 incidents of anti-Semitic activity on university campuses. Campus anti-Semitism was at its highest, so far, in 2015. Every six days in 2015, Frantzman says, there was an attack against a Jewish individual and the news ignored it. On average, anti-Semites made threats every day against Jews and Jewish institutions over the last eight years. Many did not make the news. Was the news about the 7,034 anti-Semitic incidents withheld from the public to shield the Obama administration from criticism, or because the American public had become desensitized to the phenomenon of Jew-hatred?[25]

Anti-Semitism is an age-old sin that shows no indication of disappearing from global society. The mindset assumes a multitude of forms, and even the anti-climax that historians refer to as the Holocaust, while it slowed the reprehensible practice, was not enough to eradicate the loathsome evil. As a matter of fact, newer forms of the transgression seem to be gaining ground rapidly. The world at large faces an ominous threat that may be impossible to overcome.

Chapter Two

A BRIEF HISTORY OF ANTI-SEMITISM

Now, when I hear that Christians are getting together in order to defend the people of Israel, of course it brings joy to my heart. And it simply says, look, people have learned from history.

Elie Wiesel (1928-2016) – Romanian-born American Jewish writer, political activist, Nobel Laureate, and Holocaust survivor.

JEWISH EXPULSIONS OVER THE CENTURIES

Throughout history, Jews suffered expulsions from places in which they settled, in some instances for many hundreds, even thousands of years, and never gained readmission to such lands. Jews always regarded the Land of Israel as their homeland, though throughout most of Jewish history very many of them could not live there.

Jews were first expelled from their homeland during the time of the Assyrian kingdom (734-724 B.C.) and the Babylonian kingdom (586 B.C.). Pagan Rome adopted the strategy of removing Jews from its capital cities, considering them rebellious and undesirable subjects. Mainstream Christian nations enforced the policy of banning Jews during the 4th century A.D. The strategy was to ostracize Jews from the rest of society and malign and degrade them with the intention of converting them to Christianity. Small-scale expulsions of Jews from Islamic countries in North Africa took place in the tenth century A.D.[1] The Roman emperor Tiberius legislated Jewish expulsion from Italy in 19 A.D., targeting all Jews who would not abandon their faith. In 50 A.D., the emperor Claudius expelled Jews from Rome. Jews were prohibited from living in Jerusalem and its immediate environs during the period between the Bar Kokhba Revolt (135 A.D.) and the siege of the city by Muslims in 638 A.D.

There were major expulsions of Jews from England in 1290. Jews could not reenter England until after 1650. The French threw Jews out of France in 1306 and 1394 and banned them from living in most of the territories until 1789. Historians estimate the number of Jews expelled from Spain and Portugal during the years 1492 to 1497 to be between 100,000 and several hundred thousand. Such expulsions removed the Jews from the Iberian Peninsula, located in the southwest corner of Europe and divided between Portugal and Spain. The expulsions triggered other ejections within the general region. During the time of the Black Death (1348-1350), Jews experienced evictions from various locations in Europe. Some of the "major expulsions," especially from predominantly Christian lands, removed people of Jewish ancestry from entire countries for extended periods of time.

Jews were unable to live in Russia from the 15th century until 1772 when they flooded the country from the annexed Polish-Lithuanian territories. There were concentrated Jewish expulsions from Moscow (Russia) in 1891, and Polish and Lithuanian Jewish groups were disallowed from living in numerous localities considered "out of bounds." Expulsions of short duration from the boundaries of entire countries also occurred, such as the removal of Jews from Lithuania in 1495. There were deportations from Germany and northern Italy during the 14th to 16th centuries. In some instances, such bans continued into the 18th century, like the expulsion from Prague from 1744 to 1752. During World War I, Russian authorities expelled over 600,000 Jews from Poland, Lithuania, and the Baltic countries to the deep interiors of Russia.

After its establishment in 1948, the State of Israel adopted the 1950 Law of Return restoring Israel as the Jewish homeland and making it the place of refuge for Jewish refugees at that time and into the future. The intent of the law was to encourage Jews to return to their homeland in Israel.

From 1933 to 1953, the British Mandate of Palestine outlawed Jewish immigration to Mandatory Palestine. European Holocaust (see below) survivors migrated to the allied controlled region of Europe after the Second World War. A Jewish exodus from Arab and Muslim countries took place between 1947 and 1972, whereby a Middle Eastern and North African Jewish population of close to 900,000 in 1948 dwindled to about 8,000 by the end of the period. People forced out of lands that were home to their ancestors for many centuries were forbidden to return. Approximately 600,000 of the expelled Jews resettled in Israel.

People use the history of the exodus as an argument both for and against a possible solution in connection with the Israeli-Palestinian peace negotiations. Pro-Jewish supporters equate the Jewish exodus as an equivalent to the 1948 Palestinian exodus and consider them true refugees while pro-Palestinian supporters disagree with such a determination.[2] The United Nations High Commissioner for Refugees (UNHCR) announced in February 1957 and in July 1967 that the Jews who fled from Arab countries "may be considered prima facie within the mandate of this office," and according to international law, bona fide refugees.[3]

The British Mandate of Palestine prohibited Jewish immigration to Mandatory Palestine during the years 1933 to 1957. The 1938 Evian Conference, the 1943 Bermuda Conference, and other attempts failed to resolve the problem involving Jewish refugees. Many German and Austrian Jewish refugees from Nazism emigrated to Britain where many were well treated, but many were not.[4] After World War II, eastern European Holocaust survivors migrated to the allied controlled part of Europe as the Jewish society to which most of them belonged did not exist anymore. They were many a time lone survivors consumed by the often-futile search for other family and friends, and often unwelcome in the towns from which they originally came. They were known as displaced persons (also known as Sh'erit ha-Pletah) and forced into displaced person camps, most of which ceased to exist by 1951. Föhrenwald, the last such camp, closed in 1957.

The Companies' Law, which became effective in Egypt in 1947, and that required that no less than 75 percent of employees of companies in Egypt to be Egyptian citizens, affected Jews adversely and drove many of them from the country since only about 20 percent of all Jews in Egypt were Egyptian citizens. Others, although in many cases born in Egypt and living there for generations, did not hold Egyptian citizenship.[5] Anti-Semitism grew rapidly in Egypt after the State of Israel came into existence in 1948. The Egyptian government declared emergency law on May 15, 1948, and forbade Egyptian citizens from leaving the country. Approximately 14,000 Jews left Egypt between 1948 and 1950.[6] During the Suez Crisis of 1956, authorities detained about 3,000 Egyptian Jews without charge in four detention camps. The government ordered thousands of Jews to leave the country within a few days. They were prevented from selling their property and could not take any capital with them. The deportees had to sign statements agreeing not to return to Egypt and agreeing to transfer their property to the administration of the government. The International Red Cross helped about 8,000 stateless Jews to leave the country, taking most of them to Italy and Greece. Israeli agents smuggled some Jews into Israel. The system of deportation continued into 1957.

Other Jews left voluntarily, after forfeiting their livelihoods, until only 8,561 remained per the 1957 census. The Jewish exodus continued until there were about 3,000 Jews left in 1967.[7]

Many Egyptian Jews left the country after the Six Day War in 1967. Egyptian authorities arrested, tortured and killed many of them. Spain and other foreign states came to the Jews' rescue. Jews in Libya, who numbered approximately 7,000, left in a mass exodus after the war. Less than 1,000 Jews still lived in Egypt in 1970. They received permission to leave but without their possessions. As of 1971, only 400 Jews remained in Egypt. As of 2013, only a few dozen Jews were left in the country.[8] Communist authorities forced thousands of Jews to leave Poland as a result of the 1968 Polish political crisis.

Jews fled Algeria as result of *Organisation armee secrete* (Secret Army Organization - OAS) violence during the Algerian War of 1954-1962. Many people feared the proclamation of independence would precipitate a Muslim outburst. By the end of July 1962, 70,000 Jews had left for France and another 5,000 for Israel. It is estimated some 80 percent of Algerian Jews settled in France. By 1969, fewer than 1,000 Jews remained in Algeria. By the 1990s, the numbers had dwindled to approximately 70.[9]

During the 1970s to 1990s, state-sponsored persecution in the Soviet Union prompted hundreds of thousands of Soviet Jews to flee, most of whom went to Israel and the United States.

ANTI-SEMITISM THROUGHOUT HISTORY

Historically, anti-Semitism began as a controversy over religious beliefs and later transformed and developed into a systematic program of racial, social, political, economic, and cultural excommunication. The heinous mindset progressed over many centuries into raw animosity and contempt for people of Jewish ancestry, and its practice instigated shameful episodes of persecution and carnage along the way. The evil that is anti-Semitism did not begin during the Nazi era when a degenerate German named Adolf Hitler, his Nazi regime, and their collaborators effected unheard of atrocities and murdered millions of Jews and other people opposed to Hitler's plan for world domination. It did not end after Hitler committed suicide, and the Nazis suffered a crushing defeat at the hands of allied forces. The iniquity called anti-Semitism continues today, and its reach permeates an unbelievable number of societies and cultures around the world. Hatred of people of Jewish ancestry was an ancient preoccupation, and anti-Semitism, as the mindset is now known, grew exponentially and today assumes a number of guises.

Anti-Semitism in the Ancient World

Abraham, the patriarch of the world's three major monotheistic religions (Judaism, Christianity, and Islam), relocated from his original homeland (probably the City of Ur in ancient South Mesopotamia) to the land of Canaan, a large ancient country located in present-day Lebanon, Syria, Jordan and Israel, around 1,000 years B.C. and birthed a new nation—the nation of Israel. Mesopotamia is a historical region in Western Asia situated within the Tigris-Euphrates river system, roughly corresponding today to most of Iraq, Kuwait, parts of Northern Saudi Arabia, the eastern parts of Syria, Southeastern Turkey, and regions along the Turkish-Syrian and Iran-Iraq borders.

It was accepted protocol during the time for newcomers to a region to adopt homegrown religions and to worship the idols of the kingdoms of the new territory. People indigenous to the various locations in which wandering Jews settled viewed the latter's refusal to worship their gods as rebellious. Such rejection led to resentment of the Jews by the people of the host prefecture.

People in pre-Roman times were unable to read or write, but records dating from the Roman era and subsequent civilizations reveal much anti-Semitic sentiment. The Romans tried, on different occasions, to exterminate the Jews who fell under their rule and remove all traces of Jewish culture from society. They considered Jews subversive and treacherous and viewed them with constant suspicion.

The Seleucid Empire, a Hellenistic state ruled by the Seleucid dynasty, existed from 312 B.C. to 63 B.C. Hellenization, or the historical spread of ancient Greek culture over foreign peoples conquered by Greeks or brought into their sphere of influence following the campaigns of Alexander the Great in the fourth century B.C., was an imperative constitutional requirement. Ancient Judea fell under the jurisdiction of the Seleucid Empire, and Jews, through the customary protocol, had to adopt pagan, or non-Jewish religious practices.[10] Non-compliance led to persecution.

Seleucid rulers outlawed Jewish sacrifices in 167 BC, banned Sabbaths and feasts, and made circumcisions illegal. Altars to Greek gods replaced Jewish dais, and the Greeks performed prohibited sacrifices on them. Hellenists placed the Olympian god Zeus on the altar of the Jewish Temple and forbade anyone to own or read the Jewish scriptures. An infraction such as the latter constituted a capital offense.

Anti-Semitism in the New Testament Era (A.D. 1 - A.D. 300)

Subsequent to the dawn of Christianity, a newer form of anti-Judaism emerged that encompassed the transference of blame for the Jews' rejection of Jesus Christ as the Messiah.

Prior to such a development, even after Christ's crucifixion, Christians and Jews coexisted peacefully for a couple hundreds of years as adherents of each worldview endeavored to practice their faiths in common regions. The Romans destroyed the Jewish Temple in A.D. 70 and scattered many Jews throughout the ancient world i.e., Israel, Asia, Greece, and Italy in continuation of the Jewish diaspora.

Gradually, the nexus between Jews and Christians began to weaken as Christianity became the official belief system within the Roman Empire. The conversion of Roman emperors to Christianity spurred a movement to convert Jews and Gentiles (people of non-Jewish ancestry) to the newer, expanding worldview. The Jews' reluctance to abandon their faith gave rise to animosity between the groups, and Christian leaders saw their refusal to acknowledge Jesus Christ as the Messiah as an endangerment to the nascent religion and to the Roman Empire.

In addition to the foregoing developments during the New Testament era, the misinterpretation of certain statements in some of the synoptic Gospels aided and abetted the rush by some Christian leaders to misjudge the Jews of Christ's time, and even more unwarrantedly, condemn and stigmatize Jews everywhere, for all time. Among the early church leaders up to 300 A.D. who misread and misconstrued New Testament scripture and consequently cast Jews as a sinister and criminal people were Justin Martyr (100-165 A.D.), Melito of Sardis (died c. 180), and Origen (185-254 A.D.).

The following New Testament passages are examples of scriptural statements that early Christians misread and misunderstood, and that Christians throughout the centuries used to stigmatize people of Jewish ancestry in connection with Christ's trial, condemnation and crucifixion.

You belong to your father, the devil, and you want to carry out your father's desires. He was a murderer from the beginning, not holding to the truth, for there is no truth in him. When he lies, he speaks his native language, for he is a liar and the father of lies. – (John 8:44, New International Version (NIV)

> When Pilate saw that he was getting nowhere, but that instead an uproar was starting, he took water and washed his hands in front of the crowd. "I am innocent of this man's blood," he said. "It is your responsibility!"

> All the people answered, "His blood is on us and on our children!" – (Matthew 27:24-25, New International Version (NIV)

> For you, brothers and sisters, became imitators of God's churches in Judea, which are in Christ Jesus: You suffered from your own people the same things those churches suffered from the Jews who killed the Lord Jesus and the prophets and also drove us out. They displease God and are hostile to everyone. – 1 Thessalonians 2:14-15 New International Version (NIV)

> Woe to you, teachers of the law and Pharisees, you hypocrites! You build tombs for the prophets and decorate the graves of the righteous. And you say, 'If we had lived in the days of our ancestors, we would not have taken part with them in shedding the blood of the prophets.' So you testify against yourselves that you are the descendants of those who murdered the prophets. Go ahead, then, and complete what your ancestors started!

> You snakes! You brood of vipers! How will you escape being condemned to hell? Therefore I am sending you prophets and sages and teachers. Some of them you will kill and crucify; others you will flog in your synagogues and pursue from town to town. And so upon you will come all the righteous blood that has been shed on earth, from the blood of righteous Abel to the blood of Zechariah son of Berekiah, whom you murdered between the temple and the altar. Truly I tell you, all this will come on this generation. – Matthew 23:29-36, New International Version (NIV)

The author directs the reader to Chapter Three - *The Shameful Sin of Christian Anti-Semitism* for an analysis of the forgoing scriptural passages, a debunking of the inference about the exclusive guilt of Jews for Christ's death, and for a more detailed discussion about the foregoing, contentious subject.

It is conceivable that as both Judaism and Christianity proceeded from Old Testament precept and practice—Christianity with a few tangential extrapolations—early Christians strove to establish the validity of the newer religion by assuming it supplanted the older worldview.

Anti-Semitism during the Middle-Ages - Worldwide

The ascent to power by Constantine the Great in 306 A.D. precipitated the issuance of laws that severely constrained the rights of Jews as citizens of the Roman Empire. Anti-Semitism continued to grow during the Middle Ages as constituents of the Roman Empire instituted a multitude of legalistic restrictions against people of Jewish ancestry in lands that fell under their jurisdiction.

The *Latin Codex Theodosianius*, and the *Latin and Greek Codex of Justinian* contained most of the imperial laws that affected Jews from the time of Constantine the Great. The *Codex Theodosianius* (*Theodosian Code*) was a compilation of the laws of the Roman Empire under the Christian emperors from 312 A.D. onward. Theodosius II and his co-emperor, Valentinian III, commissioned the compilation of the aforesaid laws, which they published in 438 A.D.

The Codex Justinianus (*The Code of Justinian*) was a part of the *Corpus Juris Civilis*, the codification of Roman law ordered early in the 6th century A.D. by Justinian I, an Eastern Roman (Byzantine) emperor in Constantinople. The Code went into effect in 534 A.D. The codes and the *Laws of Constantine the Great* and the *Laws of Constantius* served to impose serious constraints on the rights of Jews and their participation in the precincts of religious, social and political activity.

The ***Crusades*** were defensive wars against centuries of Muslim aggression and barbarism i.e. from the time of the worldview's founder and leading prophet Muhammad to the late 11th century. The crusades were necessary to liberate the Holy Land from ruthless Mohammedan pillagers and land grabbers. Pope Urban II, in 1095, appealed to the Christians of Europe to take up arms and defend their territories, which they undertook to do with unbridled religious and nationalistic enthusiasm. There were nine crusades, the last one taking place in 1291, during which the Christians lost control of the City of Jerusalem.

Traditional Islam teaches that Christian and Jewish constituents who oppose the worldview must be destroyed and their lands confiscated. Christianity was the dominant religion during the time Mohammed waged war against Mecca in Saudi Arabia in the 7th century. Christianity was the official belief system of the Roman Empire and the faith encompassed the entire Mediterranean, including the Middle East, its original birthplace. The Christian world, it follows, was a chief target for the earliest caliphs, and would remain so for Muslim leaders over the next millennium.

Islamic trespassers directed their efforts against Christian nations shortly after Mohammed's death. They were hugely successful and gained control of countries like Palestine, Syria and Egypt, which beforetime were predominantly Christian territories. By the 8th century, Muslim intruders had conquered all of Christian North Africa and Spain. The Seljuk Turks overran Asia Minor (modern Turkey) in the 11th century, a region that had been Christian since the time of the New Testament apostle Paul. The old Roman Empire, which modern historians refer as the Byzantine Empire, whittled down to little more than the nation of Greece. The emperor of Constantinople, Alexios Komnenos, faced with the prospect of his empire's total eradication, sent word to the Christians of Europe requesting their assistance in aiding their Eastern brothers and sisters. Thus, Christian guardians undertook the crusades.

Christians in the 11th century were not paranoid lunatics bent of confiscating Muslim territories and "corrupting" a so-called wholesome Mohammedan culture—a claim that borders on the imbecilic—they had to attempt to stem a Muslim expansion that was being carried out by the sword, a venture steeped in the dogma of a religion born and bred in war and bloodshed. Muslims had already stolen two-thirds of the old Christian world. Christianity as a faith and a culture was in dire danger and Christians had no other recourse but to defend themselves or be subjugated by Islamists. The Crusades represented such a defense.

The foregoing notwithstanding, some of the Christian crusaders, in their fervor to recover the Holy Land from Islamic rule, fell victim to a kind of primitive militarism that hindered their judgment and, in acquiescence to misplaced anti-Semitic predispositions, proceeded to kill Jews unreservedly. Such actions were unwarranted and in unmistakable contradiction of the Christian Gospel. Reckless and misguided Christian crusaders tainted the annals of Christendom with the blood of very many people of Jewish ancestry during the Crusades. The Rhineland massacres in locations along the Rhine River in Western Germany in 1096 was a shameful exhibition of anti-Semitic violence that claimed the lives of thousands of Jews.

Around the middle of the 14th century, the *Bubonic Plague,* or *Black Death*, one of the most devastating pandemics in human history, spread throughout the Mediterranean and Europe. During 1346 and 1353, the plague resulted in the deaths of an estimated 75 to 200 million people in

Eurasia, reaching its peak in the years 1346-1353.[12, 13] Scholars reckon the Black Death killed 30-60 percent of Europe's total population.[14]

The Bubonic Plague left in its wake, widespread religious, social and economic unrest, which was to impact the course of European history. Superstition and ignorance were the order of the day, and tense, fearful people searched for explanations for the unprecedented decimation of their fellow men, women and children and the untold suffering they had to endure. Someone, or some group of people had to be at fault.

The Jews were a convenient target!

With a plethora of myths and stereotypes already to their discredit, Jews were lambasted by desperate, hatemongering non-Jews who blamed them for poisoning wells and spreading the plague. This notwithstanding the fact very many Jews themselves were dying from the disease.

To compound the trials and tribulations of Jews in Europe and the Roman Catholic world in general, anti-Semites directed various other fabricated claims of sinister practices that led to the slaughter of hundreds of thousands of innocent men, women and children. Among the more preposterous accusations against Jews in the Middle Ages were the *Blood Libel* and *Host Desecration* charges. The "blood libel" contention stated that Jews killed Christian children and used their blood in religious rituals during Jewish holidays. [15, 16] The "host desecration" charge revolved around the alleged mistreatment or malicious use of a consecrated host—the sacred bread used in the Eucharistic service of the Divine Liturgy or Mass. Christians and other non-Jews in the Middle Ages accused Jews of stabbing, tormenting and/or burning the host or wafer in attempts to revisit the agonies of Christ's passion on the host and on Christ himself. The desecrated host allegedly would ultimately shed blood, speak or even fly away.[17]

Anti-Judaism continued to grow during the Middle-Ages and by the 16th century had mushroomed from the hatred of Jews because of their refusal to convert to Christianity, to animosity for Jews as a race. Anti-Judaism effectively became "anti-Semitism," even though scholars did not coin the term until late in the 18th century in Germany.

Martin Luther (1483-1546), the German theologian and founder of the Protestant Reformation, and John Calvin (1509-1564), the French theologian and Reformation leader, along with other church leaders, played principal roles in fostering dislike for Jews as a group of people. Luther's *Of the Jews and Their Lies,* written in 1543, was a virulent anti-Semitic tirade that served to incense and inflame the minds of 16th century

Christians and other non-Jews toward hounding, persecuting and murdering countless Jews.

See Chapter Three - *The Shameful Sin of Christian Anti-Semitism* for more detailed discussions about the blood libel, host desecration, and Protestant Reformation topics.

As the years progressed, Jews experienced increasing political, economic and social inequity and discrimination, and the eventual deprivation of their legal and civil rights. Their oppressors relegated them to living in ghettos under appalling conditions, particularly in Germany and Poland during the World War II years.

The *Jewish Badge* was a mark of dishonor and social inferiority that anti-Semites compelled Jews to wear in order to identify them as a group of people set apart from Christians and other non-Jews.

The practice of wearing identifying badges became prevalent in the 13th century, even though its origins date back as far as the 8th century, when caliphates and other Muslim rulers mandated that Christians and Jews in Middle Eastern countries identify themselves as "People of the Book," whose belief in the God of Abraham predated the founding of Islam. Consequently, under the caliphate, wearing the marks of identification served a two-fold purpose i.e. they signified a "dhimmi" (protected religion) status for Jews and Christians and simultaneously labeled them socially inferior to Muslims.[18]

During the Middle-Ages, European rulers persisted with edicts requiring Jews to identify themselves by wearing clothing or markings that distinguished them from Christians and other non-Jewish people. They popularized various types of badges or markings in England, including a badge in the form of the Tablets of the Law (the Ten Commandments). Jews wore marks or badges of identification in French, Spanish and Italian territories in the early 13th century. In German-speaking Europe, the required mark was a Judenhut (or "Jew's Hat") i.e., a cone-shaped pointed headdress.

The charge to wear a "Jewish badge" or other identifying mark persisted over the centuries leading up to the French Revolution in the 18th century and Jewish emancipation in the 19th century, after which the practice disappeared in Western Europe.

The Nazis reinstated the objectionable custom in the 20th century.

17ᵗʰ Century Anti-Semitism – Worldwide

Poland/ Lithuania

Jews in the Polish-Lithuanian Commonwealth (the Kingdom of Poland and the Grand Duchy of Lithuania—after 1791 the Commonwealth of Poland), which was a dualistic state ruled by a common monarch, suffered immensely due to a number of devastating conflicts during the mid-to-late 17ᵗʰ century. The loss of Jewish lives amounted to hundreds of thousands while the Commonwealth itself lost over a third of its population i.e. over three million people.

A major conflict that occurred during this time was the Khmelnytsky Uprising, a Cossack rebellion during the years 1648 to 1657. Bohdan Khmelnytsky (1595-1657), a Polish Hetman (political leader) led an uprising against the Commonwealth and its rulers. Khmelnytsky subsequently took control of the eastern and southern regions (today's Ukraine). An estimated 18,000 to 100,000 Jews perished as a result of the rebellion.[19, 20]

United States of America

European immigrants were responsible for the introduction of anti-Semitism to American society as early as the 17th century. Peter Stuyvesant (1610 -1672), the Dutch Governor of New Amsterdam, a 17th-century Dutch settlement established at the southern tip of Manhattan Island (renamed New York in 1664), sought to prevent Jews from settling in the city.

The American government severely constrained the political and economic rights of Jews during the Colonial Period i.e. 1609-1763. Jews obtained legal rights, including the right to vote, only after the onset of America's Revolutionary War (1775-1783).

18th Century (The Age of Enlightenment) - Anti-Semitism in Europe

The *Age of Enlightenment* (Age of Reason) was an intellectual and philosophical movement that dominated the disciplines of conception, analysis, and application in Europe during the 18th century, and advocated reason as the primary source of authority and legitimacy. Proponents of the movement sought to advance ideas that revolved around themes like liberty, progress, tolerance, constitutional government, and the separation of church and state. Historians generally place the Enlightenment age between 1715, the year of Louis XIV died, and 1789, the beginning of the French Revolution.

While the Age of Enlightenment presumably fostered pursuits that embodied a diverse number of magnanimous ideals, such standards apparently did not apply to people of Jewish ancestry as they did others. Governing authorities subjected Jews to various oppressive and unfair laws, and many forms of dehumanizing treatment in places like Prussia (now part of Germany), Germany, Bohemia (now the Czech Republic), Russia, Poland, Austria, and France, among other places.

Anti-Semitism did not die with the onset of the Age of Enlightenment, it remained alive and even grew. The following leaders figured prominently in the growth and persistence of anti-Semitism in eighteenth-century Europe—*Frederick II of Prussia* (1712-1786); *Archduchess of Austria Maria Theresa* (1717-1780); the *Empress of Russia Catherine II* (1729-1796), and *Voltaire* (Francis-Marie Arouet (1694-1778), the French Enlightenment writer and historian.

Modern Anti-Semitism (Worldwide) - 19th Century Onward

Anti-Semitism gained further ground during the 19th century with the introduction of various claims about Jewish conspiracies to seize control of Germany, Europe, and eventually the world.

Agitators like the German politician Wilhelm Marr (1819-1904), mentioned earlier in this chapter, whose thesis *Victory of Judaism over Germanism* (1879) dealt with the theory that Jews were conspiring to run the state and should be excluded from citizenship, helped instill a newer form of anti-Semitic dislike in the minds of people.

In 1903, Russia's czarist secret police published *The Protocols of the Elders of Zion* (also called *The Protocols of the Meetings of the Learned Elders of Zion*), a forged collection of documents pointing to a Jewish plan for taking over the world by controlling the press and the economy from a global standpoint. The American industrialist Henry Ford assisted in spreading the noxious propaganda by publishing hundreds of thousands of the Elders of Zion text and distributing them across the USA during the 1920s.

The Alfred Dreyfus affair, which revolved around a Jewish captain in the French army unfairly accused in 1894 of selling military secrets to the Germans—charges that were later dismissed—helped confirm how deeply entrenched anti-Semitic feelings were in France. Subsequent inquiry revealed French Officers of the General Staff wanted to pin the "crime" on a Jew from the outset.

19ᵗʰ & 20ᵗʰ Centuries - Anti-Semitism in Russia

The Jews of Russia endured three ruinous waves of pogroms, each of which was progressively more devastating than the previous one. The persecutions took place between the years 1881 and 1884, in 1903 and 1906, and in 1917 and 1921. Additionally, Jews in Poland faced outbursts of violence after the country regained independence in 1918, and Romanian Jews experienced similar onslaughts from 1921 onward.

1881 - 1884

The pogroms in the 1880s against Russian Jews grew out of misperception and uncertainty that followed the assassination of Czar Alexander II by members of the revolutionary organization Narodnaya Volya on March 31, 1881. Malicious anti-Semites circulated the rumor that Jews had killed the czar and the government had sanctioned acts of vengeance against them.

The first pogrom took place in April of 1881 in the town of Yelizavetgrad (Kirovogard) in Ukraine. The violence spread to the provinces of Kherson, Taurida, Yekaterinoslav, (Dnepropetrovsk), Kiev, Poltava, Chernigov, and Odessa. There was a halt in the pogroms after those carried out in the spring and summer of 1881, although sporadic attacks occurred in various parts of the country. Most of the pogroms occurred in southern and eastern Ukraine.

An abrupt wave of pogroms erupted in the towns of Rostov and Yekaterinoslav and their environs in the spring of 1883. The authorities summarily quelled the outbreaks of violence. The final significant pogrom occurred in Nizhni in June 1884, whereby mobs attacked the Jews of the Kanayino quarter, killing nine people and engaging in much looting of property. Authorities arrested and tried numerous rioters and jailed many of them.

The pogroms in the 1880s marked a turning point in the history of Russian Jewry and the attitude of the government toward these people considered social, religious and moral pariahs. The Russian authorities embarked on an agenda of maltreatment and discrimination aimed at removing Jews from economic and public offices. There began mass Jewish immigration from Russia to the United States of America and other countries.

A notable reaction to the first wave of Russian pogroms was the beginning of a nationalist and Zionist movement among Russian Jews. The pogroms initiated a motivation toward meaningful, albeit gradual, positive change not only for Russian Jewry but also for Jewish people everywhere.

1903 -1906

The second wave of pogroms in Russia took place from 1903 to 1906, and to a large extent developed during an atmosphere of uncertainty and confusion following the Russian revolution of 1905. The Russian government, engaged in a fierce struggle against the revolutionary movement, adopted a strategy of assigning the press free rein to demonize Jews and cast guilt for the nation's woes on the already ostracized group. The objective was to redirect the anger the masses felt for the government toward the Jews and effectively upbraid the latter for the development of the revolutionary movement.

The first of the second wave of pogroms took place in the city of Kishinev, the provincial capital of Bessarabia on the southwestern border of imperial Russia. The deaths of a Christian Ukrainian boy and a girl prompted Kishinev's most popular newspaper, the *Bessarabetz* (meaning "Bessarabian") to level charges of murder against the Jewish community. The Jews, the periodical claimed, used the children's blood in the preparation of matzo for Passover.[21]

The perceived abomination of the "blood libel" accusations, along with the prodding by Kishinev's Russian Orthodox bishop, triggered a bloody pogrom against resident Jews. The attacks on the Jews began on April 19, 1903, after churchgoers had attended services on Easter Sunday, no less, and continued for two days. The mayhem left 47 Jews dead, 92 seriously wounded, and 500 less seriously injured. Jew haters destroyed 700 houses and pillaged 600 stores or businesses.[22]

The Kishinev pogrom stirred international ire. Jewish youth subsequently formed a self-defense movement, with its organizers emerging from Zionist socialist parties and the General Jewish Labor Bund in Lithuania, Poland and Russia. Numerous additional pogroms followed the initial attacks on Jews. The forgoing pogroms included a major one in Odessa, then part of the Russian Empire, in October 1905, during which ethnic Russians, Ukrainians, and Greeks murdered over 400 Jews, wounded thousands, and damaged or destroyed over 1,600 Jewish properties.[23]

During pogroms in Bialystok and Siedlce in 1906, police and military forces played a direct role in the slaughtering of the victims. It is execrable that in most instances governmental authorities were instigators of the pogroms and collaborated with law enforcement officials in terrorizing and killing innocent people simply because they were of Jewish ancestry.

The 1903-1906 pogroms in Russia served as a wake-up call for the Jews of Europe and stimulated the formation of organized self-defense and self-preservation movements. The continuing volatile environment in which Jews found themselves helped hasten their relocation to Palestine via the Second Aliyah during 1904-1914, and the development of the Hashomer society in Israel, an association of Jewish guards created in 1909 to defend Jewish settlements in the region.

1917 to 1921

The third rash of pogroms befell the Jews during the years 1917 to 1921 and assumed a range and enormity that far exceeded the two earlier waves of attacks i.e. in the 1880s and early 1900s. The pogroms occurred in the wake of revolutions and the Polish-Soviet War of 1919-1921 in Eastern Europe.

The Soviets, following the atrocities by recalcitrant Red Army members who murdered many Jews during their retreat from the German army in the Ukraine in the spring of 1918, instituted strict protective measures aimed at defending the Jews and simultaneously prosecuting and punishing pogromists. Harsh penalties, including execution, applied to guilty individuals, and the authorities castigated and disbanded whole army units.

Units of the Ukrainian Army, as it withdrew in the spring of 1919 from Kiev, an area occupied by the Red Army, carried out pogroms in Berdichev, Zhitomir and their outlying areas. An attack at Proskurov (now Khemlnytskyi) on February 15, 1919, was especially brutal. In just three and a half hours, soldiers murdered at least 1,500 Jews [24] (up to 1,700 by other estimates [25]) and wounded more than 1,000 including women, children and the old.[25] The next day Ukrainian soldiers killed 600 more Jews in the neighboring townlet of Felshtin (Gvardeiskoye).

The pogromists who participated in the atrocities evaded prosecution and punishment, an omission on the part of the authorities that prompted the Ukrainian soldiers to feel they had free license to murder Jews. The anarchism that prevailed in the Ukraine in 1919 led to the formation of various groups or gangs of peasants that challenged the Red Army. The commanders (atamans) of the gangs sometimes exercised jurisdiction over large regions. Jews suffered extensively at the hands of the peasants, who terrorized, robbed and killed them. Nikifor Grigoriev, a Ukrainian paramilitary leader noted for switching loyalty to different sides during the country's civil war, engineered pogroms in about 40 communities during the summer of 1919 and caused the deaths of about 6,000 Jews.[26]

During the fall of 1919, the White Army (an arm of the White Movement), under the command of Anton Denkin, a leading general of the White Movement in the Russian Civil War, executed a series of pogroms in its advance from the northern Caucasus into deeper Russia. The White Army was an offshoot confederation of anti-communist forces that fought the Bolsheviks (Reds) in the Russian Civil War (1917-1923). The officers and soldiers of the army, the latter's objective which was to restore the old regime, envisioned their mission as one that should "strike at the Jews and save Russia." They attacked Jews unrestrainedly wherever and whenever they could. One of the most heinous of such assaults took place in September 1919 in Fastiv, when about 1,800 men, women, and children met their deaths, and about 8,000 died during the following year from wounds or epidemics.[27]

Members of the White Army engaged in pogroms in other regions of Russia also, i.e. Siberia, Mongolia, and Belorussia; many such attacks being the systematic destruction of entire communities. The Red Army seized control of Ukraine during 1920-1921, and the well-armed anti-Soviet mobs continued their assaults against the Jews. More and more, the pogroms adopted a guise of vengeance, such as the March 25, 1919 carnage in Tetiev, a city in the Kyiv region in Ukraine, whereby 4,000 Jews out of a population of 6,000 lost their lives, and the entire townlet was burned to the ground.[28] Providentially, it seemed that the limitations of the military might of the pogromists bent on the total annihilation of the Jews, preempted a "holocaust" of Ukrainian Jewry.

The sustained incidence of pogroms against the Jews in Ukraine during 1917-1921 gave rise to the formation of numerous Jewish self-defense organizations, including the renowned "Jewish Militia for War against Pogroms" of Odessa. Such organizations were successful to some extent but were unable to counter the dreaded efficiency of the military units or larger armed gangs.

An accurate assessment of the magnitude of the scope of the Ukrainian pogroms in Russian during the civil war years and the number of people killed admittedly would be a daunting task. According to Simon Dubnow (1860-1941), the Jewish historian, writer, and activist, 60,000 Jews died and several times that number were wounded. There were close to 890 major pogroms and 350 minor ones. Other estimates include the Jewish historian Elias Heifetz's suggestion of 120,000 victims in *"The Slaughter of the Jews in the Ukraine in 1919"*—the reproduction of a book published before 1923.[29] The Jewish rights activist, humanitarian, sociologist and author, Yiddish Nahum Gergel (1887-1931), put the number of people killed in the Ukrainian pogroms at between 50,000 and 60,000.[30] The Russian born Jewish historian Elias Tcherikower (1881-1943) fielded a similar figure of 50,000 to 60,000 victims of the Ukrainian pogroms.[31]

The pogroms of 1917-1921 left European Jewry, and world Jewry as well, in a state of shock and unbelief. Acknowledgment of the devastation of the pogroms, while it encouraged many Jews to embrace the Red Army and the Soviet regime, also galvanized the Jews in their desire to create of a common homeland and an independent Jewish nation. Such ambition led to the founding of the Zionist movement, and other endeavors such as the He-Halutz enterprise, which was a Jewish youth movement that trained young people for settling in the Land of Israel, and the Haganah organization, a Jewish paramilitary undertaking in the British Mandate of Palestine (1921-1948), which later became the core of the Israel Defense Forces (IDF).

Mid 20th Century Anti-Semitism - The Holocaust (Eastern Europe, Germany)

The Holocaust (Hebrew-*Shoah*) was the mid-20th century mushrooming of anti-Semitism or Jew-hatred that had festered for many centuries around the world since Biblical times.

During the Holocaust, which took place during the years 1941-1945, Adolf Hitler's Nazi regime and World War II collaborators with the German nation slaughtered six million Europeans of Jewish ancestry or two-thirds of the nine million Jews who lived in Europe. The victims included 1.5 million children. Another five million non-Jewish people met their deaths at the hands of Nazi madmen and other savage perpetrators of the worst genocide in history. The hitherto unprecedented acts took place in Nazi Germany, Poland, and German-occupied territories.

The author devotes an entire chapter to the Holocaust later in the book, as even a remotely comprehensive discussion of the dreadful subject necessitates much research and analysis. He directs the reader to Chapter Five - *The Holocaust*, for a somewhat lengthy narrative on the topic. Suffice it to say that the following statements/observations by or on behalf of the Roman Catholic Church, an establishment long caught up in a

51

maelstrom of perceived Semitic indifference as opposed to Semitic commiseration relative to Holocaust atrocities, allude to the tragedy's enormity and its ineffaceable impact upon human history.

A Vatican statement of March 12, 1998, read as follows:

> *This century has witnessed an unspeakable tragedy, which can never be forgotten—the attempt by the Nazi regime to exterminate the Jewish people, with the consequent killing of millions of Jews. Women and men, old and young, children and infants, for the sole reason of their Jewish origin, were persecuted and deported. Some were killed immediately, while others were degraded, ill-treated, tortured and utterly robbed of their human dignity, and then murdered. Very few of those who entered the (concentration) camps survived, and those who did remained scarred for life. This was the Shoah.[32]*

Pope John Paul II, speaking to 60 theologians and clergy from around the world at a Vatican symposium held during October 30-November 1, 1997, tendered the following reflection.

> *...erroneous and unjust interpretations of the New Testament regarding the Jewish people and their alleged culpability have circulated for too long... and "contributed to a lulling of consequences" at the time of World war II, so that, while there were "Christians who did everything to save those who were persecuted, even to the point of risking their own lives, the spiritual resistance of many was not what humanity expected of Christ's disciples."[33]*

Pope Francis, speaking at the Major Temple in Rome on January 17, 2016, delivered a well-received speech on Holocaust remembrance. Excerpts from Francis' speech follow:

> *During their history, the Jewish people have had to experience violence and persecution, even to the extermination of European Jews during the Holocaust...Six million individuals, simple because they belonged to the Jewish people, were victims of the most inhuman atrocities perpetrated in the name of an ideology that sought to replace god with man.[34]*

> *On October 16, 1943, over a thousand men, women and children in the Jewish community of Rome were deported to Auschwitz...Today I wish to offer a particularly heartfelt*

remembrance: their sufferings, their anguish, their tears must never be forgotten. And the past should serve as a lesson for the present and for the future.[34]

The Holocaust teaches us that the utmost vigilance is always necessary, so as to intervene immediately in defense of human dignity and peace...I would like to express my closeness to each witness of the Holocaust still living, and I address a special greeting to those of you who are here today.[34]

Post-Holocaust Years - Contemporary & New Anti-Semitism

The Holocaust and its concomitant demonstrations of ruthlessness and barbarism marked a high point of anti-Semitic expression. The Holocaust, however, was not the culmination of anti-Semitic attitude or behavior. The unspeakable evil that is anti-Semitism, in its various forms, continued in the aftermath of the Holocaust, which lasted for decades after the Second World War. It continues today, and gains with each passing day. Sadly, the world is unwilling to learn from what should be one of history's most compelling lessons.

Immediately after the Holocaust, when the abhorrent truth about the Nazi concentration and extermination camps became public knowledge, there was a widespread feeling of empathy for the Jews, even if it were only superficial in some instances, and a distaste for anti-Semitic predispositions. The Catholic Church straddled on the peripheries of a seemingly subjective position relative to the professed guilt of Jews for Christ's death, promulgated the Nostra aetate (Latin: *In Our Time*) or the *Declaration on the Relation of the Church with Non-Christian Religions* on October 28, 1965, by Pope Paul VI. Among departures from previous, entrenched opinions about Hindus, Buddhists, and Muslims, the Catholic Church declared that the long-heeded allegation of "Jewish deicide" was indiscriminate, and even though some Jews were responsible for Jesus' death, the charge could not be leveled against all Jews during Christ's time or at no other time. The declaration also decried all forms of anti-Semitism.

Contemporary anti-Semitism, although it assumes some forms that seem to differ from more traditional versions of the sinister mindset, nevertheless stems in the main from the age-old "deicide (God killer)" and "blood-libel" allegations, and an alleged obsession by Jews to dominate the world. Modern anti-Semites, for instance, claim Jews are selfish and are disinterested in the social, economic and political goals of host countries,

53

and they simultaneously wield a disproportionate measure of clout in such spheres.

In recent years, as a remembrance of the Holocaust's shocking events dimmed and widespread animosity toward the Jewish State of Israel regained ground, anti-Semitism experienced an upsurge. Jew hatred has seen a renewal as anti-Semites rail at Israel and its purported mistreatment of Palestinians, the latter who claim most of the Jewish nation's one-sixth of one percent of the Middle Eastern territory. It is irrelevant to many people that Arabs and Muslims own or "occupy" ninety-nine and five-sixths of the entire Middle Eastern region. Due to motives that are bereft of all semblance of justice and fair play, Arabs and Muslims feel over ninety-nine percent is not enough. They must have it all!

The contempt for Israel as a socio-political state, and rancor for Jews in cultural and economic contexts give rise to what scholars refer to as "the new anti-Semitism." Anti-Semites, especially those of Muslim descent, who are party to the "new anti-Semitic" attitude (a) oppose Zionism, or the desire by Jews to return to their original homeland in Israel, (b) hold Jews in disdain and (c) refuse to recognize the statehood of the Israeli nation.

ARAB/MUSLIM ANTI-SEMITISM (7TH CENTURY ONWARD) – THE MIDDLE EAST

Arab/Muslim anti-Semitic practices began as far back as 622 A.D. when Muhammad, the founder of Islam embarked on a quest to conquer pagan Arab nations in the Arab deserts and peninsulas. Muhammad established a precedent for conversion—death or servitude whereby the will or opinion of non-Muslims met with total disregard as Muslim armies overran one territory after another. Muhammad cunningly intertwined obsessive religious precept with military might and successfully subjugated many nations, whether the rulers and people he pursued were ambivalent or confrontational.

Seventh Century A.D. - The Dhimma Directive

In 629 A.D., Muslim forces conquered the Jewish stronghold of Khaybar, an oasis some 95 miles to the north of Medina (ancient Yathtib). The battle lasted for a month and a half. The Khaybar Jews conceded defeat under an agreement i.e. the *dhimma*, set in place by Muhammad. The "dhimma" allowed the Jews to continue to inhabit the land and cultivate their crops as long as they forfeited half of their produce. Muhammad reserved the right to terminate the agreement at any time and expel the Jews from the territory in which they resided.

Additionally, Jews in lands overrun by Muslims were required to pay *Jizya* or jizyah (Arabic) tax, which was a per capita yearly tax historically levied by Islamic states on certain non-Muslim subjects or dhimmis permanently residing in Muslim lands under Islamic law.[35] Dhimmis were relegated to an inferior status under Islamic rule. They suffered various social and legal inequities such as prohibitions against bearing arms or giving testimony in courts in cases involving Muslims.[36]

Fez Massacres, 1033, 1276, 1465

In 1033 A.D, following their conquest of the city from the Maghrawa tribe, the forces of Tamim, chief of the Zenata Berber Banu Ifran tribe, one of the main tribes of Arabia, perpetrated a bloodbath of Jews in Fez, then the capital city of Morocco. Tamim's forces killed over six thousand Jews, appropriated their belongings, and captured the Jewish women of the city. The killings took place in the month of Jumaada al-Akhir 424 AH (May-June). [37] There were further massacres in Fez in 1276 A.D. and 1465 A.D. The 1276 carnage ended after the Emir intervened.[38] Many Jews died in the 1465 Moroccan revolt, during which the last Marinid sultan's rule ended. The Marinid dynasty was a Sunni Muslim caliphate that ruled Morocco from the 13th century to the 15th century.

Granada Massacre, 1066

The *Granada Massacre* took place on December 30, 1066, when a Muslim mob assailed the royal palace in Granada, in Andalusia, Spain, and murdered the Jewish vizier Joseph ibn Naghrela. The intruders subsequently massacred much of the Jewish population of the city. The 1906 Jewish Encyclopedia states, "More than 1,500 Jewish families, numbering 4,000 persons, fell in one day."[39]

Yemen – The Mawza Exile, 1679 - 1680

Scholars consider the *Exile of Mawza*, or the expulsion of *Yemenite Jews to Mawza* (1679-1680), the single most distressing event experienced collectively by the Jews of Yemen.[40] The Yemenite king, Imam al Madhi Ahmad, exiled Jews who lived in just about all the towns and cities throughout Yemen to a dry and uninhabitable region of the country named

Mawza. Many Jews died during their trek to, and during their stay at the hot and arid terrain.

Jews who resided in a small number of communities in the far eastern locations of Yemen i.e. Nihm, al-Jawf and Khawlan, escaped the Imam's cruel sentence after the Arab patrons associated with these communities refused to follow the Muslim leader's directives.[41]

The Muslim authorities told the Jews to return to their former places of abode after a year of exile, the main reason for such a recall being the need for the Jews to carry out their customary tasks and labors for the indigenous Arabs who had banished them in the first place. The Arabs, during the period of the exile, felt deprived of the goods and services produced by the Jews.

The Damascus Affair, 1840

The *Damascus Affair* revolved around the disappearance of a French monk and his servant in 1840 in Damascus, the largest city in Syria. City officials immediately instituted a ritual murder charge against thirteen notable members of the Jewish community in connection with the missing individuals. Ottoman authorities imprisoned and tortured the accused Jews. The consuls of England, France and Germany as well as Ottoman authorities, Christians, Muslims and Jews participated, directly and indirectly, in the prosecution of the Jews implicated in the crime.[42] The incident drew widespread international attention. Arabs and Muslims, and other ethnic and religious groups as well carried out numerous pogroms against Jews in the Middle East and North Africa following the Damascus affair.

The results of the legal proceedings produced the unconditional release and recognition of the innocence of the prisoners, four of whom had died in prison. The courts also issued of a *firman* (edict) intended to halt the spread of blood libel or ritual murder accusations in the Ottoman Empire.

(Chapter Three - *The Shameful Sin of Christian Anti-Semitism* contains additional details about the Damascus Affair)

1920, 1921 and 1929 Palestine Riots

The *1920 Nebi Musa riots* or *1920 Jerusalem riots* occurred in the British controlled section of the Occupied Enemy Territory Administration shortly before the area became Mandatory Palestine. The riots took place in and around the Old City of Jerusalem and lasted from April 4th (Easter Sunday) to April 7th, 1920. The uprising derived its name from the Nebi Musa festival, which celebrants observed every year on Easter Sunday. The unrest signaled rising Arab-Jewish tensions at the time.

The *1921 Jaffa riots* took the form of a series of violent disturbances in Mandatory Palestine on May 1st to May 7, 1921. The unrest began as a quarrel between two Jewish groups but escalated into attacks by Arabs on Jews during which many people died. The riots began in Jaffa and spread to other parts of the country.

The *1929 Arab riots* in Palestine, also known as the *1929 Massacres*, was the culmination of a longstanding dispute between Arabs and Jews over access to the Western Wall in Jerusalem. The riots, in the main, consisted of attacks by Arabs on Jews and the destruction of Jewish property. The riots lasted for seven days from August 23rd to August 29th. Arabs killed 133 Jews and injured 339 others, while 110 Arabs lost their lives and 232 suffered non-fatal injuries. The majority of the Arabs died due to the intervention by the British police while the latter tried to quell the disturbances.[43, 44] The August 1929 uprisings resulted in the evacuation of seventeen Jewish communities.[45]

The Farhud Riots, 1941

The *Farhud riots* in June 1941 in Baghdad, Iraq, were violent outbreaks against Jews immediately following the British victory in the Anglo-Iraqi War. The riots ensued after the defeat of the pro-Nazi government of Rashid Ali al-Gaylani, an ally of Adolph Hitler's Nazi regime. Rashid Ali's supporters alleged the Jews assisted the British in bringing down the Muslim government.

Casualties of the Farhud riots included 180 Jews who died and 1,000 who suffered injuries. Up to 300-400 non-Jewish rioters lost their lives as law enforcement officers attempted to stem the violence.[46] There was widespread looting of Jewish properties and the destruction of 900 Jewish homes.[47]

MIDDLE EASTERN ANTI-SEMITISM – HOLOCAUST YEARS

The Middle East experienced much uproar and instability during the Holocaust years. Britain proscribed Jewish immigration to the British Mandate of Palestine. Such a decree naturally angered Jews in the Middle

East especially, and just about everywhere else. The *Jewish Lehi*, also known as "Fighters for the Freedom of Israel," a Zionist paramilitary organization founded by Avraham ("Yair") Stern, a noted Zionist leader, assassinated Lord Moyne, the British Minister Resident in the Middle East in 1944. The Jewish Lehi's primary objective was to facilitate unrestricted Jewish immigration into Palestine and expedite the formation of a Jewish State.

Amin al-Husayni (the *Mufti of Jerusalem*—a position created by the British Mandate authorities) was a Sunni Muslim cleric in charge of Jerusalem's Islamic holy places, including the Al-Aqsa Mosque. The Mufti orchestrated a pro-Nazi coup in Iraq, which led to pogroms against about 150,000 Iraqi Jews. Amin-al-Husayni was an Arab nationalist and Muslim leader in the British Mandate of Palestine. Al-Husayni violently opposed Zionism and was an ardent supporter of Hitler's Nazi regime.[48, 49]

The Jews, in the aftermath of the failed coup and the hostilities generated by the war with Israel in 1948, became targets for violence, persecution, boycotts, confiscations and near complete expulsion in 1951.

Anwar Sadat (1918-1981) – The British government jailed Anwar Sadat, the third President of Egypt (1970-1981), for conspiring with the Nazis during World War II. Sadat was a young Arab leader at the time, and his resolve to aid the Nazis jeopardized the lives of many of Egypt's 75,000 Jews as the decision left them at the mercy of the Germans and Arab jihadists. Later, as President of Egypt, Sadat, along with the then-Israeli President Menachem Begin, signed an Egyptian peace treaty between the two countries, which had been sworn enemies since the 1948 Arab-Israeli War. Both leaders received the Nobel Peace Prize in 1978 for orchestrating the treaty.

The treaty was extremely unpopular in most of the Arab world and the wider Muslim world.[50] Enraged Islamists assassinated Anwar Sadat on October 6, 1981.

MIDDLE EASTERN (MUSLIM & ARAB) ANTI-SEMITISM – POST HOLOCAUST YEARS

The Arab-Israeli conflict, which refers to the political tension, military conflicts and territorial and other disputes between a number of Arab/Muslim nations and Israel, engendered a rise in animosity toward Jews all over the Middle East. The conflict finds its source in the growth of both Zionism and Arab nationalism during the latter part of the 19th century.

Over the years since the outset of the Arab-Israeli conflict, hundreds of thousands of Jews have been displaced from Arab and Muslim Middle Eastern countries they had inhabited for over two thousand years. After the War of Independence in 1948-1949, over 850,000 Jews fled persecution or were expelled by Muslims from such countries. Between 1948 and 2000, the Jewish population in Middle Eastern and North African countries dwindled from around 900,000 to under 50,000.[51] The Egyptian government, reacting to the Suez Crisis of 1956, ejected almost 25,000 Egyptian Jews, seized their property, and railroaded another 1,000 or so to prisons and detention camps.

The *Palestinian-Israeli* conflict is an ongoing war between the Jewish nation of Israel and Palestine, the latter region that comprised ancient Judea and Samaria and known today as the West Bank. Palestinian and/or Arab/Muslim contention is that the areas belong to those who consider themselves "Palestinians" and not Israelis or Jews. The popular, widely accepted allegation is that Israelis or Jews occupy the area illegally. The Palestinian-Israeli conflict is a major dispute between the two nations and commands international attention and embodies far-reaching regional (Middle Eastern) and global implications. Anti-Semitic behavior by non-Jews impacts the conflict in no uncertain manner. The subject is dealt with in its entirety in a separate chapter i.e. *Israel – Against All Odds (Volume II)* Chapter Two – *The Israeli-Palestinian Conflict.*

The *Zabdani Mountains (Syria) slaughter* relates to the torture, rape, and mutilation of four Syrian Jewish young women whose bodies border police discovered in a cave in the Zabdani Mountains northwest of Damascus on March 2, 1974. Sisters Fara Zeibak, 24, Lulu Zeibak, 23, Mazal Zeibak, 22, and their cousin Eva Saad, 18, had contracted with a gang of smugglers to help them flee from Syria to Lebanon and then to Israel. The police also discovered the remains of two Jewish boys. Natan Shaya, 18, and Kassem Abadi, 20, who they determined were victims of an earlier butchery. [52]

Syrian authorities, in a final act of disrespect and cold-bloodedness, deposited the bodies of the murdered young men and women in sacks in front of their parents' homes in the Jewish ghetto in Damascus.[53]

WESTERN ANTI-SEMITISM – NEW TESTAMENT TIMES ONWARD

Anti-Semitism in Europe during the Middle Ages was largely religious in nature. Christian anti-Semitism, as a matter of fact, dates back to the time of the early Church and began as early as the first century A.D. The mindset derived from the "deicide" or god-killing" charges whereby many Christians blamed Jews everywhere, for all time, for Christ's crucifixion. There were countless instances of full-scale persecution of Jews in many locations in Europe in the form of blood libels accusations, expulsions, forced conversions and massacres.

The author directs the reader to Chapter Three - *The Shameful Sin of Christian Anti-Semitism*, for a thorough discussion on Christian and Western anti-Semitism.

APARTHEID & SOUTH AFRICAN ANTI-SEMITISM – 20th CENTURY

The Nazi movement that took root in Germany during the early 1930's served as a means of deep motivation for many Nationalist Party leaders in South Africa, and a considerable number of Afrikaner people as well. Afrikaners are a Southern African ethnic group descended from predominantly Dutch settlers first arriving in the country in the 17th and 18th centuries. Proponents of Afrikaner nationalism, a political ideology that originated in the late nineteenth century and that found strong influence in anti-British sentiments, saw an anticipated fall of the British Empire on an international stage as a significant boost for the rise of a new era of Afrikanerdom, whereby a Republic of South Africa or a nation independent of British reins would fulfill a dream of social, political and economic autonomy. Any enemy of Britain, the latter that stood at loggerheads with Nazi Germany, became a representational ally of Afrikaner nationalists.

Hendrick Frensch Verwoerd (1901-1966), the grand architect of the engineering and implementing of the racial policies of apartheid that hallmarked legalistic racial classification and mandatory racial segregation in South Africa, held the position of Prime Minister from 1958 to 1966. Verwoerd helped establish the Republic of South Africa in 1961, thereby bringing to fruition, the Afrikaner vision of an independent republic for South Africans.

Years before, in 1936, Verwoerd protested the admission of Jewish refugees from Nazi Germany to South Africa. Later, promoters of the Aliens Amendment and Immigration Bill of 1939 sought to suppress all Jews, who they claimed were cunning and manipulative and planned to overwhelm and supplant Protestants in the business world.

The Pre-Apartheid Era

Jews in South Africa suffered much under the anti-Semitic policies of the ruling National Party of Daniel F. Malan (1874-1959), the Prime Minister of South Africa from 1948 to 1954. Malan himself was a champion of Afrikaner nationalism and embraced the anti-Jewish philosophies of the Nazis.

The primary objective of the Aliens Act of 1937 was to curtail Jewish immigration to South Africa as people of Jewish ancestry fled Nazi Germany due to anti-Semitic repression. The legislation, introduced by the United Party government led by Prime Minister James Barry Hertzog, also intended to restrict and regulate immigration and exercise control over resident aliens in general.[54]

Promoters of The Aliens Amendment & Immigration Bill of 1939 sought to suppress all South African Jews, who they claimed planned to overwhelm Protestant business owners, and who were a danger to society because of their treachery and tendency to mislead and control others. Jews, it was said, entertained a grand plan to spread Communism worldwide.

The South African Gentile National Socialist Movement was a pseudo-religious, political and racial organization whose mission was to combat and destroy the alleged "perverse influence of the Jews in economics, culture, religion, ethics, and statecraft, and to reestablish European Aryan control in South Africa for the welfare of the Christian peoples of South Africa." [55] The misrepresentation of the Christian Gospel and its message of universal comradeship in the foregoing agenda was nauseating, to put it mildly.

The Apartheid Era

Jews, although they were considered Europeans, found it difficult to assimilate into white South African society and encountered much discrimination.

The 1956 Treason Trial dealt with the prosecution of the South African civil rights activist Nelson Mandela and a group 155 other anti-apartheid leaders. The courts dismissed the majority of the cases over the period of the trial, which lasted until 1960. A November 1957 rewording of the indictment by the prosecution reduced the number of defendants to a definitive 30 individuals. Many Jewish men and women were among those arrested, which led to accusations about a Jewish conspiracy to overthrow the white South African government and a scheme to introduce communism. The Jewish men and women included the anti-Apartheid campaigners Joe Slovo, Ruth First, Ben Turok, Leon Levy, and Lionel Berstein. The courts dismissed the charges against the group, the members of which faced prosecution again in 1960 at the Rivona Trial, a more involved hearing that revolved around accusations of treason and sabotage.

The Rivona Trial (1963-1964) culminated in the conviction of Nelson Mandela and other anti-apartheid and anti-Semitism leaders of sabotage against the South African government. The convicted defendants received life sentences at the Palace of Justice in Pretoria. [56] The Rivona Trial gleaned its appellation from the term Rivona, the name of a suburb of Johannesburg, where governmental authorities arrested activist leaders on July 11, 1963, at the Liliesleaf Farm, owned by the Zionist Arthur Goldreich. The authorities reportedly found incriminating documents at the farm. Jewish leaders who were part of the Rivona Trial included Goldreich, Denis Goldberg, Harold Wolpe, James Kantor, and Lionel Bernstein.

The Afrikaner Weerstandsbeweging (Afrikaner Resistance Movement or AWB) is a South African separatist political and paramilitary organization, often referred to as a white supremacist group.[57] Founded in 1973, the AWB identifies itself with far-right neo-Nazism and patterns its public image after Adolf Hitler's National Socialist Party, complete with fascist regalia and a singularizing emblem that resembles the swastika used by the Nazis during World War II. The AWB advances its mission as one dedicated to secessionist Boer-Afrikaner nationalism and the creation of an independent Boer-Afrikaner republic (Volkstaat/Boerrestaat) in South Africa. The organization was the subject of much discourse during the 1980s and 1990s as the then white South African governmental leaders contemplated sharing political power with black people.[58]

The Post-Apartheid Era

Anti-Semitism remained an active component of South African society long after the Apartheid era. The following incidents attest to the continuance of the odious, anti-Jewish perpetrations of various anti-Semites over the years since apartheid lost its foothold in Africa's largest country.

1. In May 1998, Radio 786, a Cape community radio station, managed by a Muslim organization and catering to a predominantly Muslim audience, aired a program denying the reality of the Holocaust. Consequently, the South African Jewish Board of Deputies instituted legal

proceedings against the disrespectful sponsors of Radio 786, who refused to retract, and/or apologize for the hateful, uncorroborated claim.[59]

2. The World Conference against Racism (WCAR), also known as Durban I, took place at the Durban International Convention Center in Durban, South Africa from August 31 to September 8, 2001. The United Nations oversaw the conference.

The conference addressed several controversial issues, including reparation for slavery, and so-called Israeli bias. The language of the final Declaration and Program for Action was highly controversial and strongly disputed by many participants. The United States of America and Israel withdrew from the conference after protesting the suggestion in a draft document equating Zionism with racism.[60]

A non-governmental organization (NGO) forum held around the same time as the Durban I conference produced a Declaration and Action Program of its own, which authorities did not consider an official conference document. The latter document contained anti-Israel language similar to that presented at the WCAR conference, but that officials subsequently excluded. The NGO Forum was replete with attacks on Israel and anti-Israel demonstrations.

The NGO Forum came to a discomfiting end in the wake of the myriad of anti-Semitic sentiments, the latter with which many participants disagreed. The September 11, 2001 (World Trade Center-WTC) terrorist attacks in New York, USA, whereby thousands of people lost their lives through the despicable acts of radical Islamists, relegated the anti-Semitic and racial undertones that hallmarked the WCAR and NGO conferences to a status of cellar importance, and essentially nullified the volatility of the tense atmosphere that prevailed during the meetings.

Two other WCAR conferences followed the Durban I meeting—a 2009 Durban II conference in Geneva, which ten western nations boycotted, and a 2011 Durban III conference in New York, USA, supposedly to commemorate the WTC terror attacks, which drew wide criticism and that fourteen western countries refused to attend.

The author directs the reader to *Israel – Against All odds (Volume II)*, Chapter One - *The United Nations & Israel – A History of Discrimination* for more information on the three Durban (WCAR) conferences.

3. Fatima Hajaig (b. 1938), a South African politician with the ruling African National Congress (ANC) and former Deputy Minister of Foreign Affairs under President Kgalema Motlanthe, is known for making disparaging comments about Jews and Israel.

Hajaig, in December 2008, criticized Israel's actions in Gaza during a meeting with the Jewish State's ambassador. An official complaint by Israel to the South African Embassy in Tel Aviv ensued, in which the Israelis claimed Hajaig insulted Elias Inbram, the Israeli Embassy Ethiopia-born spokesman, whom she apparently presumed attended the meeting as a form of tokenism because he was black.[61]

On January 14, 2009, at a COSTAU rally in Lenasia Gauteng, a Johannesburg suburb with a predominantly Muslim population, Hajaig, herself a Muslim, again bared her anti-Semitic sentiments when she said:

> The control of America, just like the control of most Western countries, in is the hands of Jewish money, and if Jewish money controls their country then you cannot expect anything else.[62]

Hajaig's loathsome statement mentioned above was met with much condemnation and disgust from various political and social representatives from many quarters, including the South African President Kgalema Motlanthe, Foreign Affairs Minister Nkosazana Dlamini-Zuma, the South African Jewish Board of Deputies, and the South African Human Rights Commission.

Hajaig later apologized for her pitiable outburst, but it seemed that many people did not think her apology was genuine. Also, much harm to the socio-political relationship between Israel and South Africa by then had already been done.

4. In 2013, Marius Fransman, The African National Congress' (ANC) Western Cape leader, made the contemptible allegation that ninety-eight percent (98%) of land and property owners in Cape Town was "white" and "Jewish." Research into the claim showed it to be false.[63]

Anti-Semitism or Jew hatred has existed for many centuries i.e. from ancient times during the Hellenistic Seleucid Empire (312 B.C to 63 B.C.), through New Testament times, the Middle Ages, the 17th and 18th centuries, and in the 19th century and beyond. Modern anti-Semitism effectively began in the 19th century and the nauseating mindset bourgeoned into what is known today as the Holocaust, which took place during the Second World War in Europe. Anti-Semitism remains an obsessive inclination today and many Jew haters advocate a form of anti-Semitism called the "New Anti-Semitism," which is animosity directed at Jews as a collective whole and at Israel as a Jewish state. (See Chapter One – *Anti-Semitism: A Global Hatred in Many Forms*, for a brief discussion about the "New Anti-Semitism."

Chapter Three

THE SHAMEFUL SIN OF CHRISTIAN ANTI-SEMITISM

We Gentiles owe our life to Israel. It is Israel who has brought us the message that God is one, and that God is a just and righteous God, and demands righteousness of his children. It is Israel that has brought us the message that God is our Father. It is Israel who, in bringing us the divine law, has laid the foundation of liberty. It is Israel who had the first free institutions the world ever saw. When our own unchristian prejudices flame out against the Jewish people, let us remember that all that we have and all that we are we owe, under God, to what Judaism has given us.

Lyman Abbott (1835-1922) - Early 19th Century American Preacher and Journalist

Preamble

Lest the reader is caught up in the throes of semantic ambiguity, it is mute to mention that the term "Christian Anti-Semitism" is an oxymoron. An oxymoronic phrase, as commonly known, is a combination of contradictory or incongruous words. It follows, from the perspective Biblical or Christian demeanor, especially where it appertains to Christ's philosophy of love for one's enemies, and more particularly in the case at hand—the attitude of non-judgment—no one can be a Christian and an anti-Semite at the same time. The foregoing observation notwithstanding, over the centuries the transgression of anti-Semitism in the ranks of Christendom has left an ineradicable blemish on the chronicles of the greatest belief system the world has ever known.

Many Christians today are either unenlightened about the long history of Christian anti-Semitism or they choose to labor under some manner of denial of the abhorrent tradition. Also, most modern-day Christian believers unwittingly accede to a theological premise about Jews that proceeds from centuries of distortion and misrepresentation of the true

Christian Gospel. Christian Church leaders, over the centuries, sought to infuse Christ's Gospel with various repugnant anti-Semitic doctrines and teachings that spawned a contemptuous hatred for people of Jewish ancestry, so much so as to lead to the slaughter of millions of them.

Christian anti-Semitism, like any form of animosity toward Jews, becomes an integral component of a mindset of widespread disdain and abhorrence of such people. It is reprehensible that Christian believers, who more than any other collective group of adherents of a religious worldview should share a Biblically enunciated comradeship with people of Jewish ancestry, would adopt the role of Jew haters and inveigle people of non-Christian persuasions to follow suit.

This chapter, because it addresses an issue that requires an analysis of Biblical doctrine in the refutation of the egregious mindset that is Christian anti-Semitism, represents a slight departure from the composition of the rest of the book. In other words, the discussion is mainly theological and necessitates the presentation of various scriptural quotations, which are pointedly pro-Christian. The author consequently courts the reader's indulgence.

The nature and gravity of some of the utterances of early Church Fathers and other Christian leaders throughout history, which the author uses in this chapter to bolster his argument against Christian anti-Semitism, may discommode some readers. However, it is by citing such declarations and denouncing them in no uncertain manner that the author mounts a defense of the true Christian Gospel.

It is regrettable that people who consider themselves Christians, and Christian leaders also, would pervert the Christian Gospel and debase it from a message of love and inclusion into one of detestation and ostracism. The statements in this chapter by "Christian anti-Semites," and as intimated above, one can never simultaneously be a Christian and an anti-Semite, are in diametric contradiction of Christ's teachings and essentially are expressions of discomfiture to the Christian faith. The premise of Christian anti-Semitism, therefore, embodies false theology and are contrary to all facets of Christ's Gospel.

In the following subsections, the discussion focuses on (a) a presentation of a *historical* perspective of Christian anti-Semitism, (b) a *Biblical* perspective of Christian anti-Semitism (c) a *theological* perspective of Christian anti-Semitism and (d), a *practical* perspective of Christian anti-Semitism.

CHRISTIAN ANTI-SEMITISM - AN HISTORICAL PERSPECTIVE

The Christ Killer & Deicide Charges

Scholars of comparative religion trace the origin of Christian anti-Semitism to the earliest years of the Christian Church. The loathsome mindset fed on a repulsive belief termed "collective guilt," which grew leaps and bounds over the centuries. "Collective guilt" refers to placing the responsibility for Christ's trial and crucifixion on the Jewish people and charging them with the crime of "deicide," or the killing of a god. [1] Early church leaders contended the transgression was unprecedentedly heinous as it was God himself, or God the Son whom the Jews murdered.

The anti-Semitic slur "Christ-killer" used by mobs to incite violence against Jews contributed to many centuries of pogroms and the murder of Jews during the Crusades, the Spanish Inquisition, and during the Holocaust. [2] At the Second Vatican Council (1962-1965), the Roman Catholic Church under Pope Paul VI repudiated belief in collective Jewish guilt for the crucifixion of Jesus. [3] The Church declared that the accusation could not be made "against all the Jews, without distinction, then alive, nor against the Jews of today."

The concepts of "collective guilt" and "deicide" gave rise to an era of hatred and resentment for Jewish people that has persisted for over 2,000 years and does not show marked signs of attenuation in the present age. The pronouncements presaged the vile sin of Christian anti-Semitism, and also served as catalysts for some of history's most sinister misdeeds during its gloomiest periods, including the unmitigated carnage of over six million Jews in Germany and Europe by the Nazis and their allies during World War II.

There are three central elements associated with the Christ-killer or deicide allegation. Misguided Christians have utilized such accusations over the centuries to castigate and dehumanize people of Jewish ancestry.

The first component of the Christ-killer or God-killer charge is that Jews are exclusively guilty for the crucifixion of Jesus Christ. The foregoing notion is indelibly ingrained in the minds of countless Christian believers around the world, so much so that the roles of the Romans and other non-Jewish participants in the horrifying incident are robotically obfuscated. Accordingly, Jews and only Jews are responsible for Christ's death.

The second component of the deicide contention is that all the Jewish people of Christ's day were guilty of his death. Every Jew living at the time of Christ shared the blame for his crucifixion. Every Jew in Judea, every member of the Sanhedrin, and every Jew who was part of the crowds present in Jerusalem when the Jewish and Roman authorities condemned Christ to death was responsible for the frightful deed. A Jew in Rome who had never heard of Jesus of Nazareth, an Asia Minor Jew who never lived in Israel, and even a Jew of Galilee who had been a member of one of the young Rabbi's deferential audiences was one of his "killers." Further, there is the intimation that all Jews who did not recognize Christ as the Messiah helped to kill him and therefore were guilty of his murder.

The third aspect of the Christ-killer allegation is that Jewish people are perpetually guilty for Jesus' crucifixion and death. Such a position effectively convicts all Jews, of all time, as Christ-killers, and guilty of one of the darkest deeds in history. Any Jewish individual living today, for instance, who do not accept Christ as the Messiah and Savior of humankind, is responsible for Jesus' death on the cross, to the exclusion of similar judgment of any non-Jewish man or woman.

Of a truth, some Christians, hopelessly enveloped by a distorted Gospel message, believe no Jewish individual may obtain salvation unto eternal life because of perpetual guilt for Christ's death.

The foregoing observations about the "Christ-killer" or deicide charge are not meant to classify all Gentile or non-Jewish people, particularly Christians, as anti-Semites. It is brought to the fore to alert uninformed or misinformed people about the iniquitous and prejudicial allegation, and the sinister and shameful ways anti-Semites, including Christians, used it against people of Jewish ancestry over the centuries. While in recent years many mainstream Christians have withdrawn from their position of accusing Jews of being extemporaneously responsible for Christ's death, many continue to avow the charge.

The Blood Libel and Host Desecration Accusations

Christian leaders leveled a number of revolting accusations against Jews around the mid-twelfth century A.D. Two of these malicious claims revolved around the blood libel and host desecration myths.

The blood libel charge originated in Norwich in eastern England in 1144 A.D. Theobald, a Jewish monk who converted to Christianity, spread the rumor that Jews kidnapped a Christian child, tied him to a cross, stabbed him in the head to replicate Jesus' crown of thorns, killed him, emptied his body of its blood, and used the blood as an ingredient in making matzos (unleavened bread) for use during Passover. Apparently, someone discovered the body of a boy named William in the woods outside Norwich. Theobald also said Jewish leaders assembled in each year in Narbonne, France to decide in which city a Christian child would be killed and sacrificed. Although many of the Norwich townsfolk did not believe the monk's story, a number of people prejudiced against Jews formed a cult that sought to venerate the dead child and elevate him to a form of sainthood. The boy subsequently became known as Saint William of Norwich. People made pilgrimages to his tomb, and some even claimed that appeals to the saint produced miracles.[4]

Pope Innocent IV (1195-1254 A.D.) enjoined an official inquiry into the blood libel accusation in 1247. Investigators determined that the myth was perpetration by malicious, so-called Christians aimed at persecuting Jews. Other popes after Innocent IV declared the Jews guiltless of the blood libel charge. However, accusations against Jews continued unchecked, and many faced trial for the alleged trespass over ensuing centuries. Some paid with their lives. Eventually, Czar Alexander 1 of Russia pronounced the blood libel contention a myth. This notwithstanding, Christians did not desist from charging Jews of killing and sacrificing Christian children and using their blood during Passover observances. Professor William Nicholls, a former minister in the Anglican Church and the founder of the Department of Religious Studies at the University of British Columbia, said "...there are more than 150 recorded cases of the charge (against Jews) of ritual murder (around the world), and many led to massacres of the Jews ..."[5]

The blood libel rumor spread throughout the Christian world in the Middle Ages and persisted for many centuries. In 1840, local residents accused the members of a Jewish community in Damascus, Syria, of abducting and killing a Christian priest. Authorities tortured several prominent Jews in attempts to obtain confessions of guilt. A reckless and incensed mob destroyed a synagogue and its Torah scrolls. Muslims in Syria and the Middle East, and around the world as well, combined the blood libel "sin" with traditional anti-Jewish sentiments born of Islamic indoctrination, and used such antipathy to hound, persecute and massacre people of Jewish ancestry.[6]

Atrocities stemming from the blood libel myth continued into the twentieth century. In 1913, Ukrainian authorities charged a Jew named Menahem Mendel Bellis with ritually killing a Christian child and discarding its body near a brick factory in Kiev. Bellis' trial was nothing short of astonishing, as numerous high-standing Russian intellectuals testified that Jews routinely attacked Christians and used their blood in disgusting rituals. Although the courts eventually acquitted Bellis of the charges against him, the Russian media spared no effort in repeatedly broadcasting and disseminating horrifying anti-Semitic allegations for public consumption.[7]

In 1928 in Massena, New York, USA, after a four-year-old girl went missing, a rumor surfaced that local Jews kidnapped and killed her. Enraged crowds gathered outside the Massena police precinct to confront the town's rabbi, who the lawmen summoned to answer questions about Jewish ritualistic practices. Searchers later found the child alive and unharmed.[8, 9]

The host desecration complaint against Jews, unlike the blood libel accusation, disappeared in the Middle Ages. The myth originated in the 11th century. This notwithstanding, two incidents that took place during the 1990s were probably a revival of sorts. In two Roman Catholic cathedrals, one in Canada and other in Mississippi, USA, people believed to be Satanists masquerading as parishioners attended Mass but did not consume the "host" or wafer served. They instead took the host from the church and used it in satanic rituals.

The wafer or "host" is thought by Roman Catholics to change into Christ's actual flesh or body, in a similar manner as the wine dispensed during the mass becomes his blood. Protestants (non-Catholic Christians) do not subscribe to the belief that the host or wafer, or wine transmutes into Jesus' body and blood.

The host desecration allegation was an offshoot or variation of the "blood libel" claim, whereby instead of killing a child, Jews supposedly desecrated the host. They allegedly committed the iniquitous act in several ways. Sometimes they pushed pins into the host or wafer or trampled the host underfoot. At other times, Jews stabbed the host with a knife until blood, presumably Jesus', oozed out of it. Yet at other times, Jews supposedly nailed the host itself, in a symbolic depiction of Christ's crucifixion. The theologian and scholar William Nicholls (see earlier in the subsection) states in his book, Christian Antisemitism: A History of Hate that "...100 instances of the (host desecration) charge have been recorded, in many cases leading to massacres (of Jews) ..."[10]

The blood libel and host desecration accusations against Jews became so entrenched in the minds of Christians, and Muslims as well, by the Middle Ages that people of Jewish ancestry became prime targets for uncurbed harassment and summary annihilation. Vindictive, ill-advised believers misrepresented Holy Week—which Christians observe during the days leading up to Christ's arrest, trial, and crucifixion, and is one of the holiest phases in the Catholic/Christian calendar—and transformed it into a time of horror for Jews. Jews would stay indoors to avoid meeting Christians during Holy Week, for fear of being attacked and killed for inherent guilt in the alleged murder of Christ.

Early Church Founders and the Propagation of Anti-Semitism

A number of early church fathers, in clear contradiction of the message of the New Testament, promulgated the view that people of Jewish ancestry were reprehensible, idolatrous, unrighteous and worthy of hellfire. It is execrable that this contempt and disdain for Jews fostered by pioneers of Christendom gradually became intertwined with the original Gospel message and gave rise to a prostituted version of God's Holy Word that many Christians of today find acceptable. The following early Church founders were responsible in no small way for the importunate evil that came to be known as "Christian anti-Semitism."

Justin Martyr (100-165 A.D.) – Justin Martyr was a founder of Replacement Theology, or Supersessionism, the teaching that the Christian church replaced the nation of Israel regarding the plan, purpose, and promises of God. Martyr, in his *"Dialogue with Trypho"* (Trypho was a Jew), made the following reckless and unjustifiable remark.

> *For other nations have not inflicted on us and on Christ this wrong to such an extent as you have, who in very deed are the authors of the wicked prejudice against the Just One, and us who hold by Him. For after that you had crucified Him, the only blameless and righteous Man...through whose stripes those who approach the Father by Him are healed...when you knew that He had risen from the dead and ascended to heaven, as the prophets foretold He would, you not only did not repent of the wickedness which you had committed, but at that time you selected and sent out from Jerusalem chosen men through all the land to tell that the godless heresy of the Christians had sprung up, and to publish those things which all they who knew us not speak against us. So that you are the cause not only of your own unrighteousness, but in fact of that of all other men.[11]*

Melito of Sardis (died c. 180) was the Bishop of Sardis near Smyrna in western Anatolia (a part of Modern Turkey) and a great authority in early Christianity. In his *Homily On The Passion*, written sometime between 160 A.D. and 170 A.D., Melito of Sardis wrote:

> An extraordinary murder has taken place in the center of
> Jerusalem...And who has been murdered? And who is the
> murderer? ...The One who hung the earth in space is Himself
> hanged; the One who fixed the heavens in place is Himself
> impaled; the One who firmly fixed all things is Himself firmly
> fixed to the tree. The Lord is insulted; God has been
> murdered; the King of Israel has been destroyed by the right
> hand of Israel.[12]

Origen (185-254 A.D.) – Origen was one Christianity's most influential writers. He was a philosopher and theologian, and many consider him one of the most innovative thinkers of his time. Origen nevertheless was unabashedly anti-Semitic and had no qualms about broadcasting his contempt for Jewish people, as evidenced in the following excerpt from The Writings of Origen.

> On account of their unbelief and other insults which they
> heaped upon Jesus, the Jews will not only suffer more than
> others in the judgment which is believed to impend over the
> world, but even have already endured such suffering. For
> what nation is in exile from their own metropolis, and from
> the place sacred to the worship of their fathers, save the Jews
> alone? And the calamities they have suffered because they
> were a most wicked nation, which although guilty of many
> other sins yet has been punished severely for none as for those
> that were committed against our Jesus.[13]

John Chrysostom (349-407 A.D.), Archbishop of Constantinople, and regarded as the "greatest preacher of the early church," was another anti-Semite. Chrysostom used his eloquence and effective preaching style to foment widespread hatred for Jews. He termed them "assassins of Christ." The following venomous tirade appears in Chrysostom's Orations against The Jews.

> The Jews sacrifice their children to Satan. They are worse
> than wild beasts. The synagogue is a brothel, a den of
> scoundrels, the temple of demons devoted to idolatrous cults,
> a criminal assembly of Jews, a place of meeting for the
> assassins of Christ, a house of ill fame, a dwelling of iniquity,
> a gulf and abyss of perdition. The Jews have fallen into a
> condition lower than the vilest animal. Debauchery and
> drunkenness have brought them to a level of the lusty goat
> and the pig. They know only one thing: to satisfy their
> stomachs, to get drunk, to kill, and beat each other up like

stage villains and coachmen. The synagogue is a curse, obstinate in her error, she refuses to see or hear, she has deliberately perverted her judgment; she has extinguished with herself the light of the Holy Spirit...I hate the Jews because they violate the Law. I hate the synagogue because it has the Law and the prophets. It is the duty of all Christians to hate the Jews.[14]

Chrysostom's stance against the Jews affected deep negative and horrible sentiments among Christians. His sermons and homilies became part of the educational criteria adopted by Christian colleges and seminaries, and regrettably, over ensuing centuries, received endorsement as parallels of the Christian Gospel. Historians contend Chrysostom's anti-Semitic rants served as an impetus for the Nazis in the 1930s to attempt to validate the systematic annihilation of the entire Jewish race.

Augustine of Hippo (354-420 A.D.), also known as Saint Augustine, was an early Roman African Christian theologian and philosopher whose ideas greatly influenced the expansion of Western Christianity and Western philosophy.

Augustine developed "the Witness theory" about the atypical role of Jews as perennial wanderers in a global environment. Augustine's theory proceeded from a bewildering interpretation of Psalm 59:11, which reads, "Slay them not, lest my people forget: scatter them by thy power; and bring them down, O Lord our shield." Jews, Augustine claimed, were drifters, and cursed by God and dispersed across the earth to live in misery as a testimony to the evil they perpetrated in delivering Christ to the Roman authorities to be crucified. Augustine contended God condemned Jews, as murderers of their Jewish brother, Jesus, to suffer and traverse the earth as a perpetual witness to divine judgment and to Christian truth.[15]

Augustine perceived a kind of parallel in his "witness theory" whereby God's condemnation of the Jews to wander the earth as a result of their crucifying Christ was akin to the Old Testament story about Cain being banished from his home into exile for slaying his brother Abel.

Augustine's construal of Psalm 59:11 is discreditable, and quite likely sprung from his acquiescence to the anti-Semitic mindset that prevailed among many Christian scholars of his day, and among earlier pioneers of the Church as well. While Augustine did not advocate violence against Jews, like contemporary anti-Semitic church leaders like John Chrysostom, and later theologians like Martin Luther, his animosity toward Jews and his dislike for them were unmistakable. Augustine's sway on Western Christendom and Western philosophy was so powerful that countless

Christian believers readily accepted his "witness theory" deliberation and sought to endorse such dogma for approval by succeeding generations. Augustine's appalling distortion of the Holy Scriptures remains an enduring conviction in the minds of many deluded Christians today.

The Medieval Period

Christian anti-Semitism continued to grow unchecked in the centuries following the era of the early church fathers. A number of Christendom's premier campaigners incorporated intense anti-Semitic messages in their writings and sermons and induced countless otherwise well-meaning believers to nurture virulent and hostile sentiments toward anyone of Jewish ancestry. By the 11th century, the societal footing of Jews almost everywhere was at an unprecedented nadir. Jews could not assume public offices, could not own real estate, and effectively could not build synagogues or practice their religion.

Saint Thomas Aquinas (1225-1274), the Italian priest considered the Catholic Church's greatest theologian, and the foremost classical proponent of natural theology laid the foundation of modern Christian doctrine. Aquinas' views on the Jewish people appear in his *Summa Theologica,* probably his most famous body of writings. Although Aquinas did not advocate violence against the Jewish people for the role they might have played in the death of Jesus Christ, his intimation as to their guilt in Christ's arrest, torture and crucifixion left no room for doubt in the mind of even the casual observer. Aquinas proposed the doctrine of "affected ignorance," which suggested that the Jewish leaders of the time handed over Christ to Pontius Pilate and the Romans fully cognizant of the fact that the young rabbi was the Promised Messiah. An extract from Part III of Summa Theologica reads:

> It must, however, be understood that their (the Jews) ignorance did not excuse them from crime, because it was, as it were, affected ignorance. For they saw manifest signs of His Godhead; yet they perverted them out of hatred and envy of Christ; neither would they believe His words, whereby he avowed that He was the Son of God...Yet we may hold that they are said to have known also that He was verily the Son of God, in that they had evident signs thereof: yet out of hatred and envy, they refused credence to these signs, by which they might have known that He was the Son of God.[16]

Aquinas' "affected ignorance" concept is in stark contradiction of New Testament doctrine about the role and responsibility of the Jews in Christ's

74

death. The teachings of the apostle Paul, in particular, put to naught Aquinas' misinformed conclusion about the blameworthiness of the Jews. Paul taught that the Jews were effectively culpable of "invincible ignorance" in that Almighty God farsightedly prevented them from determining that Jesus Christ was the Messiah. To such an effect, Romans 11:25-26 (NIV) contains the following statement:

> I do not want you to be ignorant of this mystery, brothers and sisters, so that you may not be conceited: Israel has experienced a hardening in part until the full number of the Gentiles has come in, and in this way all Israel will be saved. As it is written: "The deliverer will come from Zion; he will turn godlessness away from Jacob.[17]

In addition to the scriptural absurdity of Saint Aquinas' "affected ignorance" pronouncement, such disputation that in itself should invalidate any semblance of authenticity or truthfulness, there remain a few fundamental inconsistencies with the theory.

Firstly, the Jewish leaders of Jesus' time did not believe that he was the Promised Messiah. They thought he was an impostor or some kind of zealot given to blasphemy. The Jews were awaiting the appearance of the Messiah, and if they felt Jesus were he, why did they not acknowledge him as the promised Redeemer?

Secondly, it is patently logical to presume the Jews were awaiting the appearance of a Messiah who would set them free from Roman oppression, quite likely in a militaristic manner. Jesus came as a humble, donkey-riding teacher, and although the reception he received when he entered the city of Jerusalem a week before he died was loud and frenzied, the people turned against him after they realized he was a man of peaceful means. The Jewish leaders did not want such an individual as the Messiah or as a liberator.

Thirdly, Aquinas' contention that the Jews "...saw manifest signs of His (Christ's) Godhead; yet they perverted them out of hatred and envy of Christ...Yet we may hold that they are said to have known also that He was verily the Son of God..."[18] is unreasoned. The Jews, although they were aware of Jesus' ability to perform extraordinary feats or miracles, did not ascribe them to divine dispensation, but instead accused Christ if being in league with the devil. Luke 11:15 (NIV) says, "But some of them said, 'By Beelzebul, the prince of demons, he is driving out demons.'"

Aquinas' "affected ignorance" concept, notwithstanding the absence of straightforward advocacy of violence against Jews, served as a catalyst for anti-Semitic sentiments for centuries after the church leader introduced the idea in the mid-thirteenth century.

The Reformation Period

Martin Luther & the Doctrine of Replacement Theology

Martin Luther (1483-1546) was a German theologian and religious reformer considered by many to be one of Christianity's most influential figures. Luther was a chief progenitor of the Protestant Reformation movement and succeeded in reformulating certain tenets of Christian belief that resulted in the division of Western Christendom between Roman Catholicism and newer Protestant traditions. The Reformation Period or the Protestant Reformation or simply the Reformation, was a schism in the universal Christian church whereby Protestant reformers, led by Luther, broke away from established Catholicism during the 16th century in Europe.

The Reformation represented a widespread theological revolt in Europe against what many people felt were abuses by the Roman Catholic Church and the institution's totalitarian control of the universal Christian establishment. Out of the Protestant Reformation sprang unswerving opposition to the unbiblical practices of the Catholic Church, especially its claim of papal infallibility and apostolic succession, the latter that teaches the line of Roman Catholic Popes threads through the centuries going back to the time of the apostle Peter to the current pope. This continuous, uninterrupted chain of authority, Roman Catholics assert, translates into the absolute authenticity of the Roman Catholic Church as the only true church and confirms the Pope as the preeminent leader over all churches everywhere.

While the Reformation occasioned a tenable and meaningful departure from Roman Catholic precepts and practices that were contradictory to true Biblical doctrine, it also gave rise to one of Protestantism's most controversial contrivances, namely, the doctrine of Replacement Theology.

Replacement Theology or *Supersessionism* promotes the view that the New Testament Church or the universal Christian Church supersedes, replaces, or fulfills Israel's place and role in God's plan for the eventual redemption of mankind. In Christianity, supersessionism is a theological view on the current status of the church in relation to the Jewish people and Judaism. [19] It holds that the Christian Church succeeded the Israelites as the definitive people of God, [20, 21] and the New Covenant replaced or superseded the Mosaic covenant. From a supersessionist's "point of view, just by continuing to exist (outside the Church), the Jews dissent." [22] Such a view directly contrasts with dual-covenant theology, which states that the Mosaic covenant remains valid for Jews.

The author submits that Replacement Theology is not a Biblical doctrine but is an ill-judged attempt at falsifying the Holy Scriptures and simultaneously fostering anti-Semitism. More disquieting is the pervasive, deleterious impact the teaching has had on Christians in general over the centuries since Luther first presented the notion. The German theologian's revolutionary idea about the Christian Church replacing Israel as Almighty God's archetypical nation on the global stage of spiritual deliverance served only to exacerbate an existing mindset of entrenched contempt and disrespect for Jews propagated by earlier pioneers of the faith like Justin Martyr, Origen, John Chrysostom, and Thomas Aquinas.

Martin Luther, at the outset of his replacement theology proposition, extended a gesture of kindness and concern to people of Jewish ancestry. In the book, *That Jesus Christ was Born a Jew* (1523), he voiced the following sentiments.

> ...I hope that if one deals in a kindly way with the Jews and instructs them carefully from Holy Scripture, many of them will become genuine Christians and turn again to the faith of their fathers, the prophets and patriarchs.

> ...Since they dealt with us Gentiles in such brotherly fashion, we in our turn ought to treat the Jews in a brotherly manner on order that we might convert some of them.

> ...When we are inclined to boast of our position we should remember that we are but Gentiles, while the Jews are of the lineage of Christ. We are aliens and in-laws; they are blood relatives, cousins, and brothers of our Lord...as Saint Paul says in Romans 9:5, 'God has also demonstrated this by his acts, for to no nation among the Gentiles has he granted so high an honor as he has to the Jews.'[23]

Unfortunately, Luther's seeming fondness for the Jews stemmed from his envisioning their acceptance of the New Testament Gospel and their subsequent conversion to Christianity. This did not take place as he anticipated, and in a grotesque change in attachment, Luther developed an intense abhorrence of Jews. The following excerpt from On the Jews and

Their Lies, one of Luther's last literary works, bares his utter dislike for Jews in general and incites uninhibited hostility toward them.

> If I had to baptize a Jew, I would take him to the river Elbe, hang a stone around his neck and push him over with the words 'I baptize thee in the name of Abraham'...What then shall we do with this damned, rejected race of Jews?...I shall give you my sincere advice: first to set fire to their synagogues or schools and to bury and cover with dirt whatever will not burn, so that no man will ever again see a stone or cinder of them...Second, I advise that their houses also be razed and destroyed...We ought to take revenge on the Jews and kill them...We are at fault for not slaying them.[24]

The forgoing diatribe of loathing and repugnance directed toward Jews, and that proceeded from one of Christendom's most prominent leaders no less, numbs even a barbarous intellect. Further, it is appalling that Martin Luther's twisted ideology, and the warped teachings of other Christian leaders before him, persisted over ensuing centuries and gave rise to the abhorrent anti-Semitic mentality that served as a precursor to one the darkest periods in history—the Holocaust years in Germany during the Second World War—whereby the Nazis and their allies systematically slaughtered over six million European Jews.

Luther expressed antagonistic views toward Jews and urged non-Jews to destroy Jewish homes and synagogues, confiscate the money of Jews, and curtail their liberty. Condemned by virtually every Lutheran denomination, Luther's odious statements and their influence on antisemitism contributed to his controversial status.[25]

Apologists for Martin Luther and his life's work argue that the philosopher's ideas had little or no impact on the Nazi mindset. Such a contention is open to much dispute, however, as evidence of Luther's influence on at least some of the German populace, and the Nazis themselves, is undeniable. Historian Marc H. Ellis states that Julius Streicher (1885-1946), a premier Nazi propagandist and publisher of a number of anti-Semitic newspapers, was presented by officials of the city of Nuremburg with a copy of Martin Luther's *On the Jews and Their Lies* in 1937. [26] Ironically, Streicher stood trial in Nuremburg after the Second World War. His accusers condemned and executed him for his role in the slaughter of millions of Jews.

John Calvin (1509-1564) was a French theologian, pastor and reformer in Geneva during the Protestant Reformation, a time (1517-1648) when a schism in Western Christianity initiated by Martin Luther (see above) took place. Early Protestant reformers in 16th-century Europe, along with Calvin himself, introduced major changes in mainstream Christian thought that was critical of certain teachings of the Catholic Church.

Calvin, like Martin Luther and other critics of people of Jewish ancestry, railed against the Jews. In his work *A Response to Questions and Objections of a Certain Jew*, Calvin wrote:

> Their (the Jews) rotten and unbending stiffneckedness deserves that they be oppressed unendingly and without measure or end and that they die in their misery without the pity of anyone.[27]

The Second World War & Nazism

Extrapolating on the histrionics of Nazi proponents like Julius Streicher and other German fascists like Adolf Hitler, Heinrich Himmler, Reinhard Heydrich, Joseph Mengele, and Adolf Eichmann, to name a few, it is plain to see that hatred for the Jewish people mushroomed to unprecedented levels with the onslaught of Nazism under Adolf Hitler. Although Nazi ideology progressed from racial and social disdain for the Jews rather than from religious anti-Semitism, Hitler and other German leaders capitalized upon the Christ-killer accusation and utilized it in a vastly successful strategy to incite the German Christian populace to resent and persecute its Jewish neighbors. The Nazi dictator cunningly manipulated the alleged Jewish guilt for killing Christ in a largely effective scheme to win German Christians over to his diabolical plan to effect the widespread annihilation of Jews in Europe.

The notorious *Sturmer Press*, a leading player in the Nazi propaganda initiative, published a reading primer titled *Don't Trust a Fox in The Meadow* and *Don't Trust a Jew by His Word* in 1936. Reprobate, misguided educators used the book to teach children how to read. An excerpt from the book reads as follows.

> 'From the beginning, the Jew has been a murderer,' so says Jesus Christ. And when the Lord Jesus had to die, He did not know of any other nation that could torture Him, so he chose the Jew. That is why the Jews imagined they are the Chosen People.[28]

The Sturmer Press and other propagandist entities used the Christ-killer or deicide charge in many creative but sinister ways to inculcate deep anti-Semitic sentiments in the minds of young, impressionable German Christian children. Hitler himself opined:

I believe today that I am acting in the sense of the Almighty Creator. By warding off the Jews I am fighting for the Lord's work.[29]

Unfortunately, casting blame on Jews for the death of Jesus remains a pervasive attitude among many Christians today. There exists the preponderance of thought that Jewish people who do not believe in Jesus Christ as the Messiah are guilty of his death. Many mainstream Christian teachers and disseminators of Christ's Gospel impress upon their audiences that the New Testament squarely places the blame for Jesus' death on Jews, for all time. Such a tactic is opprobrious and reeks of an objectionable misrepresentation of the Christian Gospel.

CHRISTIAN ANTI-SEMITISM – A BIBLICAL PERSPECTIVE

Not many people are familiar with or care to try to understand New Testament teaching about human responsibility for the death of Jesus. Such a lack of witting or unwitting comprehension might serve as a major catalyst for the promulgation of anti-Semitic sentiments among countless people, including many professed, otherwise well-meaning Christian believers. In order to analyze the Holy Scriptures effectively in this regard, one must ponder Christ's predictions about his crucifixion and the roles of the various players juxtaposed in the carrying out of what many people consider history's single most consequential misdeed.

Christ's Prediction about His Death & a Cycle of Guilt

In Mark 10:33-34 (BSB), Jesus said to his disciples:

> *Look, we are going up to Jerusalem, and the Son of Man will be betrayed to the chief priests and scribes. They will condemn Him to death and hand Him over to the Gentiles, who will mock Him and spit on Him and flog Him and kill Him. And after three days he will rise again.*[30]

Three aspects of guilt come to the fore upon examination of the foregoing statement by the charismatic leader of the small band of itinerant Jewish—yes, Jewish communicators of a revolutionary religious message.

Firstly, Christ spoke about the individual who would betray him and hand him over to chief priests and lawmakers. The act of treachery would occur in the Garden of Gethsemane at the foot of Mount Olives in Jerusalem. Jesus and his disciples were in the garden during the night before his crucifixion when Judas Iscariot, one of the young rabbi's own followers, entered the locale and pointed out his master to the Jewish authorities. Judas traveled and preached with Jesus for three years prior to the fateful night on which he betrayed him. Judas Iscariot essentially shouldered the first component of guilt for the death of Jesus.

Secondly, Mark 10:33-34 mentioned: "the chief priests and scribes" who would try and condemn Jesus and deliver him to the Gentiles or Romans. The term "chief priests and scribes" refers to the Sanhedrin, the Jewish presiding council during the New Testament period. As a matter of fact, the Sanhedrin did conduct a trial or "grand jury" kind of investigation during the night of Jesus' arrest, although a full forum was not in attendance. Joseph of Arimathea and Nicodemus, two members of the council, objected to any legal or obligatory decision-making by the gathering as the full complement of members was lacking, and also disagreed with the rest of the council members' determination that Jesus was guilty of one or more capital offenses. The foregoing notwithstanding, the members of the Sanhedrin who were present that night condemned Jesus, through manipulation of the legal system and distortion of the truth. They trumped up charges against the young Rabbi, including the damning accusation of blasphemy and allowed false testimony in condemning him to death. The "chief priests and scribes," like the deceiver Judas Iscariot, were guilty of the death of Christ.

Thirdly, the Gentiles about whom Jesus spoke in the prediction about his death were also participants in the horrid events that culminated in his trial and crucifixion. The Sanhedrin handed over Jesus to the Roman authorities who, along with the governor Pontius Pilate, put an end to the innocent rabbi's life. Pilate, notwithstanding his initial reluctance to condemn Christ to death, likely felt he was simply ridding Rome of another Jewish troublemaker. The Roman inspectorate, and Roman citizens, no doubt, considered Jews, in general, to be a rebellious people bent on refusing to acquiesce to Roman rule, which was in about its 90th year around the time of Jesus' crucifixion. The Romans assumed control of the region in 63 B.C.

It is clear that Jesus, in Mark 10:33-34, identified three parties to be blamed for his death i.e., one of his own followers, a number of Jewish leaders, and the Romans, or Gentiles. Why, after Christ's crucifixion, did the guilt for his death swing from the antagonists identified by Christ himself in the Holy Scriptures, to one such antagonist or group of people i.e., the Jews? More worryingly, why is the blame not directed at only the Jews who were present at the locations of the events leading up to the crime, and at the scene of the misdeed itself? Why are all Jews, living during the time of Jesus, and ever since that time, across the world, charged with his murder?

Christ's Prediction about His Death & a Conspiracy of Guilt

In Chapter 4 of the Book of the Acts of the Apostles, it reads:

> *Indeed Herod and Pontius Pilate met together with the Gentiles and the people of Israel in this city to conspire against Your holy servant Jesus, whom you anointed.*[31]

There is the inference of a scheme in the foregoing passage to hound, accuse and condemn Christ to death. The conspirators, identified in greater detachment below, were as follows.

Herod Antipater – Herod Antipater, also known as Herod Antipas (born before 20 B.C.-died after 39 A.D), was the pro-Roman half-Jewish king of the Galilee and Perea regions. Herod was the son of the infamous Herod the Great, who ruled Israel during the time Jesus was born. Herod the Great undertook extensive building projects throughout Judea. The New Testament identifies Herod the Great as the ruler who orders the massacre of very many children around the time of Christ's birth.[32, 33, 34]

History portrays Herod Antipas as a cunning and selfish individual, given to scandalous behavior. Jesus himself referred to Herod as, "...that fox" (Luke 13:32, NIV). John the Baptist reprimanded Herod for marrying his own sister-in-law, Herodias. Herodias, craving revenge, requested during a celebration at the king's palace that the ruler have the Baptist beheaded. Matthew 14:1-13 records the performance of this foulest of deeds.

Pilate, after he realized Jesus was a Galilean, sent him to Herod Antipater for judgment because the town of Galilee fell under the king's jurisdiction. Herod, as the holy Scriptures imply, probably feared somehow Jesus was John the Baptist returned to life (Mark 6:14), or perhaps he wanted to meet the young Jewish rabbi, about whom people spoke so much. Luke 23:8 states that Herod Antipas hoped Jesus would perform some kind of miracle to confirm rumors about his ability to do the extraordinary.

The New Testament records that Jesus did not comply with Herod's request for a miracle or sign, nor did he respond to the profusion of inquiries the Roman ruler directed at him. Herod and his soldiers subsequently mistreated Jesus, mocked him, clothed him in a robe and sent him back to Pilate. Herod could have set Jesus free, but instead remanded him to the Roman governor, not troubled in the least about the possible consequences for the Jewish teacher. Accordingly, Herod established his own guilt in Christ's death by rendering the decision.

Pontius Pilate - Pontius Pilate was the Roman Governor of Judea from 26 A.D. to 36 A.D. Historians submit that Pilate was one of the most brutal Roman rulers ever to assume office. Among the governor's more outrageous perpetrations were (a) installing standards bearing the image of Emperor Tiberius in the Jewish temple area in Jerusalem, (b) hanging golden shields inscribed with the names of Roman deities on Mount Zion, which he removed only after the emperor commanded they be taken down, to avoid an insurrection, (c) appropriating the Jewish temple revenue to construct an aqueduct, again almost causing a riot. Further, Luke 13:1 states that Pilate murdered Galileans as they worshiped at the temple, and mixed their blood with their sacrifices.

Pontius Pilate, like most Romans, considered Jews rebellious and bothersome and had no qualms about putting them to death. The Roman government, recognizing that Pilate was too brutal and merciless, recalled him to Rome in 36 A.D.[35]

Rewinding the historical chronometer, one sees that Sejanus, a prominent administrator of Emperor Tiberius, appointed Pilate proconsul of Judea. The emperor had elevated Sejanus, then his most trusted subordinate, to a position second-in-command only to himself. Sejanus practically ruled the Roman Empire while Tiberius retreated to a life much removed from a portfolio in public office. Sejanus, historians say, subsequently entertained a grandiose scheme to overthrow Tiberius and make himself "Caesar" or emperor. Pontius Pilate, meanwhile, became one of Sejanus' loyal underlings, although not necessarily a party to the plot to overthrow Tiberius.

Tiberius discovered Sejanus' traitorous plan and ordered his arrest. The emperor condemned Sejanus and executed him. Subsequently, just about everyone close to Sejanus fell under suspicion of being a traitor to Rome. Pontius Pilate was among the suspects.

Fast forwarding events to the time of Jesus' trial around 30 A.D., the Jewish leaders who thrust Jesus before Pilate said to the governor, "If you let this Man go, you are no friend of Caesar" (John 19:12). There is a veiled implication in such a statement. The phrase was more of a caution than an appeal. The term "no friend of Caesar" had come to refer to anyone who was a traitor to Rome, or the emperor. The expression's semantics no doubt stemmed from the incidents involving Sejanus, the ambitious and disloyal administrator who attempted to overthrow Emperor Tiberius, but who failed and met his death. Sejanus' unprecedented dare and subsequent downfall helped engender an atmosphere of intense distrust and apprehension.

The members of the Sanhedrin effectively were warning Pontius Pilate that they would expose him as a traitor to Rome if he did not condemn Jesus Christ to death. Pilate realized his association with the disgraced Sejanus made him susceptible to prosecution and possible execution. Pilate's hesitation or indecisiveness to condemn Christ as recorded in the New Testament was not due to a concern for the young rabbi's welfare and wellbeing, or because of he was contemplative about being just. He wished to preserve his office as Governor and more particularly, his own life. In submitting to the Sanhedrin's demands, and his own selfish preoccupations, Pilate sentenced to death, a man he knew was innocent. Pontius Pilate was a co-conspirator in the scheme to kill Christ and was guilty of a terrible misdeed.

Christ himself alluded to Pilate's blameworthiness when he addressed the governor saying, "The one who handed me over to you is guilty of a greater sin." (John 19:11, NIV). The implication here is if there is a "greater sin," there must be a "lesser sin." Pilate committed the "greater sin" in participating in the trial of Christ and sentencing him to die.

A Number of Gentiles – The Gentiles involved in the crucifixion of Christ were the Roman soldiers. They comprised a party to the group of conspirators who engineered the despicable scheme to put the young rabbi to death. The soldiers exacted horrendous punishment on Jesus before finally killing him. They mocked Jesus, flogged him mercilessly, tore his flesh with a specially designed whip into which they embedded bits of metal and pieces of broken glass. They then nailed him to a cross.

The Romans customarily crucified people, especially Jews, whom they looked upon with derision and resentment. As far as they knew, they were simply killing another Jewish troublemaker. The Romans' guilt in Jesus' death is unmistakable.

A Number of Israelites – Some "people of Israel" were among the conspirators who devised a plan to accuse, try, condemn and crucify Jesus Christ. The Israelites included the Jewish leaders of the Sanhedrin and the crowd of Jewish people who called for Christ's crucifixion and shouted, "Crucify Him!" (Luke 23:21) The Jewish leaders sought to preserve their social standing and financial position, and as a result, fabricated charges against Jesus and delivered him to the Roman authorities. The devious, calculating Jewish leaders swayed the throng of people who stood immediately outside Herod's palace in Old Jerusalem to cry out for Christ's blood.

Contrary to misinformed claims by anti-Semitic revisionists, not all the Jewish people in Jerusalem during the time of Christ's trial, condemnation and crucifixion were guilty of the heinous crime. There is nothing in the Holy Scriptures to indicate that everyone living in the city or in the proximate area where the pre-crucifixion events unfolded, was in attendance on that fateful day, notwithstanding the ludicrous presumption that simply being a Jew was enough justification for guilt. Besides, there were many Jewish people, directly and indirectly, involved in the heartrending goings-on during the time who did not support the decision to crucify Jesus. Among them was Simon of Cyrene, who helped Jesus carry his cross, the disciples of Jesus, many people who believed the rabbi's message of repentance, forgiveness, and salvation, the women who followed him to Calvary where he paid with his life, and even the Sanhedrin members Nicodemus and Joseph of Arimathea. In essence, some Jewish people, not all Jews, participated in Christ's killing.

Christ's crucifixion was not a uniquely Jewish transgression. It was a universal crime and involved Jews and Gentiles.

The Misconception of Perpetual Jewish Guilt for Christ's Death

Matthew 27:25 (NIV) reads, "All the people answered, 'Let His blood be on us and on our children.'" Many scholars of religion point to the forgoing scriptural verse as validation of continual or perpetual guilt borne by Jews for Christ's death. How appropriate or justifiable is such a presumption?

Firstly, the venting of one's emotions, whether such feelings are rational and/or defensible, and calling for chastisement on oneself and/or other parties in one's accepting responsibility for an act done or left undone, does not necessarily impute guilt to the other parties. Nor does such jeremiad translate into culpability or suffering simply because of the utterance of a curse upon someone, or the dispensing of an imprecation of some kind.

The intimation that all Jews, past, present, and future, are guilty of Christ's death is a charge mired in inanity and utter disregard for Biblical veracity. The Matthew 27:25 passage properly indicates that the

85

consequences of sin may be borne by subsequent generations (Exodus 20:5), but the blame appertaining to a sinful act or omission falls on the individual or individuals who commit the transgression. The Old Testament prophet Ezekiel, to such an effect, wrote:

> The one who sins is the one who will die. The child will not share the guilt of the parent, nor will the parent share the guilt of the child. The righteousness of the righteous will be credited to them, and the wickedness of the wicked will be charged against them. – Ezekiel 18:20 (NIV)

The scriptural statement was made by one of Almighty God's prophets some six hundred years before the time of Christ's crucifixion, and before the bitter, misguided rabble present at the young rabbi's trial and condemnation called for his blood to be upon them and their children. The prophet Ezekiel's divinely enthused wisdom negates and puts to naught, any assumption of perpetual guilt on the descendants of sinners, and more specifically, invalidates the suggestion that the descendants of the Jews who were directly or indirectly involved in condemning Christ to death should shoulder guilt for the crime.

The guilt of sin attaches to the sinner alone, even though his or her perpetration may adversely affect his loved ones. The banking executive, for instance, who embezzles money would face prosecution and incarceration. He or she also may have to make restitution to his or her victims. The defrauder answers for his or her wrongdoing, as would be expected. However, his or her family and other loved ones may suffer also, not because of any kind of imputed sin or guilt, but because of circumstantial contingency. They may undergo mental and/or emotional stress or experience financial hardship because of the banker's indiscretions.

Secondly, it is a clear misconstrual of the facts to claim the crowd of Jews that called for Jesus' blood represented the entire Jewish nation. Revisionist scholars labor to convey the impression that the full complement of Jewish residents of Jerusalem and its environs was present at Christ's trial and condemnation. Christ's trial before Pontius Pilate took place early in the morning i.e., around 6 a.m. John 19:14 (NASB) reads, "Now it was the day of preparation for the Passover; it was about the sixth hour. And he said to the Jews, "Behold, your King!" It seems reasonable to assume that not many people attended the event. The chief priests and elders, who persuaded the crowd to demand Jesus' death, probably selected a special group of people to support their perverted agenda. Such people quite likely included impostors, false witnesses, and embellishers of the truth.

86

Additionally, the Praetorium of the Antonio Fortress, where Jesus' trial took place, could not accommodate more than 100-200 people at one time. It is therefore markedly unlikely the crowd that cried for Christ's blood to fall upon them and their children, as recorded in Matthew 27:25, could have encompassed the entire Jewish nation.

Thirdly, as mentioned earlier, simply admitting guilt and calling a curse upon oneself and/or his or her relations or descendants do not result in the transference of blame on innocent parties, especially into posterity. Matthew 27:25, in reporting the people's frenzied call for the young rabbi's blood to fall upon their descendants, does not confirm any incidence of theological truth. In other words, the crowd's demand that guilt for Christ's crucifixion be assigned to their children is as useless as Pontius Pilate's attempt to exonerate himself of guilt for sentencing the rabbi to death by washing his hands publicly and declaring himself innocent (Acts 4:27).

Matthew 27:25 records correctly, what the intolerable throng said when it wished guilt for their actions to fall on their children. The statement does not confirm the conveyance of blame on the children of the mob's members or on all Jews at the time of Christ's crucifixion. It certainly does not lend credence to the absurd inference that Jews everywhere, for all time, are guilty of Christ's death.

The Book of Acts contains an accurate account of what took place during a meeting that included Pontius Pilate, Herod, the Israelites, and the Gentiles. The scriptural passage clearly points to a conspiracy by several individuals and groups, not by a specific group i.e. the Jews.

> Indeed Herod and Pontius Pilate met together with the Gentiles and the people of Israel in this city to conspire against your holy servant Jesus, whom you anointed. Acts 4:27-28 (NIV)

The Misconception of National Jewish Guilt for Christ's Death

Revisionist scholars frequently quote the following Biblical passage as scriptural validation of national Jewish guilt for Jesus' condemnation and crucifixion.

> For you, brothers and sisters, became imitators of God's churches in Judea, which are in Christ Jesus: You suffered from your own people the same things those churches suffered from the Jews who killed the Lord Jesus and the prophets and

also drove us out. They displease God and are hostile to everyone. – Thessalonians 2:14-16 (NIV)

It is regrettable that ostensibly intelligent and methodical researchers and historians would choose a superficial interpretation of the foregoing Biblical passage and conclude the Apostle Paul sought to promote the idea that all Jews, and only Jews, should bear the blame for killing Jesus Christ.

Paul's statement addresses a parallel between the goings on in certain Gentile churches and in certain Jewish churches. Thessalonian Gentile believers were being mistreated by other Gentiles and Paul likened them to people in Judean churches who likewise suffered at the hands of Jewish leaders. The comparison could not refer to all Jews and perceived guilt for killing Christ since the members of the Judean churches were themselves Jews.

Additionally, the term "the Jews" in the scriptural passage does not refer to all Jews, but a particular group of them i.e. the Jewish leaders or the Sanhedrin of Jesus' day. Such a determination proceeds from the fact that only high-ranking Jews figured in the activities to which Paul alluded in his statement. As a matter of fact, John 11:49-50 speak about the Jewish leaders plotting Christ's death; Luke 23:2 and 23:10 record the Jewish leaders accusing the young rabbi before Pilate and Herod, and Matthew 27:20 and Mark 15:11 recount members of the Sanhedrin inciting the crowd against Jesus, resulting in the mob calling out for his crucifixion.

One observes yet another parallel in the comparison between 1 Thessalonians 2:14-16 and other Biblical passages that refer to the misdeeds of people who held positions of high office, or more particularly, the chief priests and Pharisees of Jesus' time and not all people of Jewish heritage.

In the parable of the vine-growers (Mark 12:1-12; Matthew 21:33-46; Luke 20:9-19), the owner of the vineyard sends his servants, one after another, to collect revenues due to him. The vine-growers kill the servants and withhold money that does not belong to them. The vineyard owner finally sends his own son, whom the vine-growers also murder. The logical sequence of events implies that the vineyard owner goes himself with able assistants and destroys the wicked vine-growers. Matthew 21:45; Mark 12:12, and Luke 20:19 report that after the chief priests and Pharisees heard Jesus' parable, they knew he referred to them when he spoke about the evil vine-growers.

The following scriptural passages speak about Christ's condemnation of the Pharisees and other high-ranking Jews.

Woe to you, teachers of the law and Pharisees, you hypocrites! You build tombs for the prophets and decorate the graves of the righteous. And you say, 'If we had lived in the days of our ancestors, we would not have taken part with them in shedding the blood of the prophets.' So you testify against yourselves that you are the descendants of those who murdered the prophets. Go ahead, then, and complete what your ancestors started!

'You snakes! You brood of vipers! How will you escape being condemned to hell? Therefore I am sending you prophets and sages and teachers. Some of them you will kill and crucify; others you will flog in your synagogues and pursue from town to town. And so upon you will come all the righteous blood that has been shed on earth, from the blood of righteous Abel to the blood of Zechariah son of Berekiah, whom you murdered between the temple and the altar. Truly I tell you, all this will come on this generation. – Matthew 23:29-36 (NIV)

Matthew 23:29-36 makes it clear that Jesus was rebuking the hypocritical Jewish leaders whose ancestors were guilty of killing God's prophets. He was bringing to the fore, the fact that the Jewish leaders of his time persisted in committing evil by hounding and persecuting those sent by God to preach his Holy Word and lead people to him. Jesus spoke about the Jewish leaders incurring God's wrath and causing the destruction of Jerusalem.

1 Thessalonians 2:14-16 echoes a sentiment similar to the one contained in Jesus' statement in Matthew 23:29-26 i.e. the Jewish leaders who killed God's prophets inspired their descendants to persecute the Messiah (Jesus Christ) and his followers. Further, leaders of the Thessalonian Gentile churches chose to "imitate" perverse leaders of Jewish churches who brought about suffering on their own Jewish countrymen.

Some scholars are wont to take away the idea that Paul, himself a Jew and once a rancorous antagonist of Christian believers and a proactive persecutor of Christ's followers, eventually understood how reprehensible it was to pursue and torment non-Jews. Such a realization might have translated into a kind of vengeful remorse and hence Paul's seemingly vituperative and vindictive position against his countrymen who remained opposed to Christ's revolutionary Gospel. The ostensibly condemnatory tone of Paul's New Testament statements, therefore, might have been reflective of his apparent disgust for orthodox Jews, and as some suggest, albeit incorrectly, his condemnation of Jews in general for Christ's death.

While some of the forgoing deliberations might seem understandable to the middling, uninformed intellect, they are disputative with the merited unanimity that the Holy Bible, including the New Testament, which contains the Apostle Paul's letters to the various nascent Christian churches, are representative of Almighty God's Holy and inerrant Word. The Bible cannot be tainted by human predilections.

In conclusion, therefore, it seems safe to assume that Paul, in making the statement contained in 1 Thessalonians 2:14-16, referred to the Pharisees and other Jewish leaders during the time of the early Church, and not the entire Jewish nation. Consequently, the inference of national Jewish guilt for Christ's death is an aberrant notion that is scripturally unsound and that falls outside the ambit of befitting theological inspection.

A Misunderstanding of Christ's Forgiveness on the Cross

Luke 23:34 (NIV) reads, "Father, forgive them, for they do not know what they are doing." Biblical scholars refer to the foregoing saying of Jesus on the cross as "The Word of Forgiveness." [36] It is theologically interpreted as Jesus' prayer for forgiveness for the Roman soldiers who were crucifying him and all others who were involved in his crucifixion.[37]

The previous statement, if anything, should serve toward helping to exculpate the Jews and Gentiles who actively participated in Christ's condemnation and crucifixion, in as much as the sin they committed at Calvary was unspeakably evil. Indeed, many scholars of comparative religion correctly interpret the statement as a heartfelt entreaty by Jesus, in the final minutes of his earthly life, for the forgiveness of those who, directly and indirectly, were putting him to death. Other religious scholars, however, in what has to be an exercise in calculated illogicality, claim that Jesus' request for pardon referred only to the Romans or Gentiles, and not the Jewish people. Is such an argument a valid one?

Some theologians contend that the Jews, especially those present at Jesus' crucifixion, knew they were crucifying the Messiah or one who was God incarnate. Such knowledge, they maintain, firmly incriminated the Jewish leaders and Jews everywhere. Christ's petitioning his Father to forgive those who were killing him, therefore, could relate only to the Romans or Gentiles. The Jews involved in Christ's condemnation and crucifixion, and Jews everywhere, incautious scholars suggest, were unpardonably guilty for Jesus' death, as are Jews of all time.

Jesus, contrary to the unreasoned postulation by revisionist scholars that his prayer on the cross at Calvary was on behalf of only the Romans, prayed for the forgiveness of all caught up in the terrible events of the few days leading up to his crucifixion. He prayed for the soldiers who mercilessly whipped him, put a crown of thorns upon his head and nailed him to the cross. He prayed for the Jewish leaders and crowds of people who persuaded Pontius Pilate to sentence him to die and then stood at the cross, mocking him and laughing at him as he hung on the tree, bloodied and battered beyond recognition. Jesus prayed for Jew and Gentile, to the exclusion of no one. He did so with his dying breath!

The apostle Peter, after he healed the crippled man at the temple, lent sure credibility to the supposition that Christ, as he was dying on the cross, prayed to Almighty God to forgive the Jews and Gentiles for putting him to death. Acts 3:17 (NIV) reports that Peter, addressing a group of Jews at the portico of Solomon in the temple compound, said, "Now, fellow Israelites, I know that you acted in ignorance, as did your leaders."

Irrational scholars who posit that the Jews involved in Christ's trial, sentencing and eventual execution, knew exactly what they were doing and consequently must shoulder the full burden of guilt for his death, are misinformed and mistaken. Notwithstanding their inextricable envelopment in the young rabbi's death, the Jewish leaders did not consider Jesus the Messiah. As a matter of fact, they felt beyond all doubt Christ committed blasphemy by claiming he was equal with God. They did not know they were killing someone who was an embodiment of God. To such an effect, the apostle Paul says, in 1 Corinthians 2:8 (NIV) that "None of the rulers of this age understood it, for if they had, they would not have crucified the Lord of glory." It is evident the term "the rulers of this age" referred to the Jewish leaders of Jesus' time.

Jesus, while on the cross and while he suffered unspeakable physical and emotional agony, still cared enough for sinful humankind to ask his Father in heaven to forgive his tormentors and killers, who included Jews and Gentiles. His petition was one of genuine concern and compassion. It is regrettable that over 2,000 years later, very many professed followers of the Galilean miracle worker who they worship as the Son of God refuse to acknowledge the validity and importance of Christ's prayer to Almighty God; a petition that symbolizes everything the Redeemer of the world stood for, and still epitomizes to this day—unconditional love for humankind and a willingness to give his all for his children!

91

CHRISTIAN ANTI-SEMITISM – A THEOLOGICAL PERSPECTIVE

Some scholars of comparative religion neglect or fail to acknowledge a factor of indispensable consequence in Jesus' trial, condemnation and crucifixion—a theological upshot without which the very message of Christ's Gospel and the entire Biblical premise of salvation would lose their meaning.

The immediate subsection of this chapter revolves around a theological analysis that encompasses divine and supernatural considerations as enunciated in the Holy Bible. The author alerts the reader to a departure from the mainly secular theme of this book's discussion and apologizes for any inconvenience occasioned.

The Holy Bible, including the Old Testament and the New Testament, comprises God's infallible Word and originated from divine inspiration. The Book is historical and prophetic and describes an omnipotent, omniscient and omnipresent deity's perfect plan for humankind's redemption from sin, and a means whereby every human being may avoid an eternity of unimaginable suffering and torment. The crux of such a plan revolves around the death and resurrection of Jesus Christ, God's only Son.

Even if imprudent theologians are correct in heaping blame for Christ's death on Jews alone, and they are sorely amiss in doing so, there is the explicable premise of God's sovereign plan holding sway over events he predestined from the beginning of time. While it is true the members of God's creation are moral agents endowed with the capacity to choose between good and evil, or right and wrong, it is theologically expedient to expect an all-knowing and all-powerful God who wants to reconcile a wayward creation unto himself to implement a program that accommodates at least certain pre-determined outcomes. Christ's death and resurrection were two such facets of a foreordained strategy.

It follows that the preordained plan involving Christ's death and resurrection would engage the actions of people who, although guilty of participating in the events at hand, nevertheless did what they did in accordance with God's ascendant expectations. Therefore, while the Jews and Gentiles shared the guilt of Christ's death; and not Jews alone, as deluded scholars claim, they were ill-fated players in a supernatural or divine decree that necessitated Christ's crucifixion and subsequent resurrection, which provided the only means by which sinful humankind could obtain salvation unto eternal life.

The apostles Peter and John, upon their release by the chief priests and elders who imprisoned them in Jerusalem for preaching about Jesus, returned to their brethren, who joined together in prayer to God. The Book of Acts records the prayer, which outlines the conspiracy of human guilt for Christ's death, and also states that those who killed Christ...

> ...did what your (their) God's power and will had decided beforehand should happen. – Acts 4:28 (NIV)

Peter made a similar observation when he preached to a crowd on the Day of Pentecost.

> This man (Jesus) was handed over to you by God's set purpose and foreknowledge. – Acts 2:23 (NIV)

That God, owing to his eternality and supernatural nature, had a plan of redemption for his fallen creation even before the time of Adam and Eve's disobedience in the Garden of Eden, is a foregone conclusion. He knew, before the creation of the universe and the making of humankind in his own image that he would one day send his Son to die on the cross as atonement for people's sins. The Old Testament prophet Isaiah spoke about Jesus' crucifixion 800 years before it took place. Isaiah's prophecy serves to confirm the fact that the Holy Bible is God's unfailing, divine revelation, and God, and only God, could devise a foolproof plan of redemption for lost sinners, and very significantly, predestine such an agenda within faultless parameters. Isiah's statement reveals in part, one of the Holy Bible's most important prophecies, which scholars refer to as the "suffering servant" prophecy and that alludes to the long-awaited Messiah.

> Yet it was the LORD's will to crush him and cause him to suffer, and though the LORD makes his life an offering for sin, he will see his offspring and prolong his days, and the will of the LORD will prosper in his hand. – (Isaiah 53:10, NIV)

Another Biblical passage that infers God, from eternity past, preplanned his Son would die on the cross for humankind's sins, appears in Revelation 13:8 (NIV), in which the divinely inspired sage who wrote the chapter refers to the Messiah, Jesus Christ as "the Lamb that was slain from the creation of the world."

Jesus willingly gave up his life on the cross because he was aware of his Father's plan. He knew he would suffer indescribable pain and agony, but he cared so much for wayward humankind that he obeyed his heavenly Father's will. Jesus was the Son of God and the Messiah of all peoples, and he could have forgone the terrible fate that awaited him. He could have summoned legions of angels to come to his aid, and also vanquish his tormentors and killers, but he chose not to do so.

The Book of John reads:

> No one takes (My life) from Me, but I lay it down of My own accord. I have authority to lay it down and authority to take it up again. This command I received from my Father. – (John 10:18, NIV)

Jesus accepted his Father's will regardless of the apprehension and distress he felt. The Book of Matthew records the agony Christ experienced. It reads:

> Going a little farther, he fell with his face to the ground and prayed, "My Father, if it is possible, may this cup be taken from me. Yet not as I will, but as you will. – (Matthew 26:39, NIV)

God sent his one and only Son to die for the sins of humankind...for all humankind! Jesus' death on the cross was an atoning sacrifice for Jews and Gentiles alike because all are guilty of sin and willful separation from Almighty God. The Old Testament, particularly its mention of sacrificial offerings, and the New Testament confirm that God's plan, from eternity past, was to reconcile his wayward creation with himself via the death and resurrection of the Messiah.

God's decision to choose the Jewish people as a unique nation to spearhead his plan for sinful humankind's redemption is representative of his sovereign will and divine purposefulness. God could have selected any other people as his chosen nation, and Jesus could have been incarnated as say, an Asian or a Filipino or an African, and his message of salvation unto eternal life would still have been rejected by his kinsmen. Also, they would not have accepted his sacrifice on the cross as atonement for their sins. God chose the Jewish nation, however, and the Messiah's crucifixion and subsequent resurrection served as a means for all, Jews and Gentiles, to approach God's Throne of Grace in seeking forgiveness and obtaining eternal life in a place called Paradise.

The fact that some Jews who rejected Christ's message participated in his condemnation and crucifixion should not be surprising. Had he come to earth as a member of any other ethnic persuasion, some members of such a group would have been involved in denouncing and killing him.

CHRISTIAN ANTI-SEMITISM – A PRACTICAL PERSPECTIVE

It is regrettable so many people who profess to be followers of Jesus Christ either exist in a state of denial of the deicide or Christ-killer charge and the church's history of anti-Semitic activity, or forthrightly maintain Jewish people, on the whole, are guilty of Christ's condemnation and death, and that hatred and persecution of such people is justifiable in one way or another, notwithstanding evidence to the contrary.

In deference to proper theological, and more particularly, accurate Biblical interpretation, there are three approaches through which to repudiate the reprehensible transgression of Christian anti-Semitism born of the deicide allegation. The three perspectives find their root in trustworthy Christian practicality and serve to engender positive and meaningful changes in the demeanor of so-called Christians who persist in blaming Jews for Christ's death and in ostracizing them from an environment that should be inclusive of all people who wish to approach Almighty God's Throne of Grace.

Recognition of the falsehood of the deicide allegation should encourage errant Christians everywhere to embrace the following three attitudes toward change.

Firstly, all must accept their responsibility for Christ's death. Jesus died because everyone sinned—Jew and Gentile. All of God's creation, including the most virtuous people throughout history, fell short of the Creator's holy standards and required the involvement of a Savior and Redeemer to be reconciled to their Maker. Jesus Christ satisfied such an intercessory obligation and suffered humiliation, torture, torment, and death for the sake of all humankind. All people, of all time, everywhere are therefore guilty of Jesus' murder.

God would have sent his Son to die even if only one man or woman had sinned. The Messiah had to give up his life on the cross for the sins of humankind, regardless of the attendant number of sinners. The foregoing notwithstanding, the Holy Bible states in the Book of Romans:

> There is no difference between Jew and Gentile, for all have sinned and fall short of the glory of God, and all are justified freely by his grace through the redemption that came by Christ Jesus. – (Romans 3:20-25, NIV)

In other words, there is, and there was, no one who ever lived and who was without sin except Christ, such sin being inherited by all, good and bad, through the original sin committed by Adam and Eve in the Garden of Eden.

Jesus did not die because the Jews and Gentiles (Romans) killed him. He gave his life willingly for all people everywhere, of all time. He died in order to implement his Father's redemptive plan to save the wayward, sinful members of a creation gone astray.

Secondly, the committed Christian ought to recognize the enormity of the Christ-killer charge and its inexcusable corollary of anti-Semitic sentiment. The baleful proposition of blaming Jews, and Jews alone, for Christ's death, must be denounced in no uncertain terms. Reliable polls indicate that among Christians worldwide, anti-Jewish feelings are increasing. In Europe, the rise is dramatic. Christian anti-Semitic attitudes in Middle Eastern nations are also very high, even though the number of Christians in most of these countries dwindled significantly over recent decades because of persecution and excommunication.

True Christian believers shoulder the responsibility of expressing unequivocally, their kinship with Jewish people, and their love for them in protesting the age-old antipathy known as anti-Semitism.

Thirdly, and very importantly, Christians must proclaim the good news of Christ's Gospel. Merely acknowledging Jesus' death on the cross is meaningless if the focus remains on his maltreatment at the hands of wicked people and on his suffering and agony. An outlook such as the foregoing is akin to the resignation that Christ was simply another Jewish man who met his death at the hands of the Romans. The good news contained in the Christian Gospel is that out of the more than 100,000 Jewish men crucified by the Romans under Pontius Pilate's inspectorate, only one rose from the dead—Jesus Christ!

Jesus' resurrection, upon which the Christian believer must center his or her attention more than on his crucifixion, even though the latter event is inseverably connected to the former, is confirmation that he is indeed God incarnate. The Book of Romans reads:

> Who through the Spirit of holiness was appointed the Son of God in power by his resurrection from the dead: Jesus Christ our Lord. – (Romans 1:4, NIV)

It is of paramount importance the Christian acknowledges Jesus is no longer on the cross, or in the tomb. While the cross symbolizes the greatest sacrifice ever made on behalf of humankind, its real power lies in the fact that the individual whose killers nailed him to it is not there, nor is he in the tomb of stone in which his disciples laid him. He fulfilled his promise to his Father and now sits on his right hand in heaven after paying the price for the sins of everyone, for all time. He bore the punishment meant for the entire human race. The offer of eternal life in a place called Paradise is open to all—Jews and Gentiles alike—who would repent, seek forgiveness and accept Christ's ransom for their souls through his death and resurrection.

The Boycott, Divest and Sanctions Movement (BDS)

The Boycott Divest and Sanctions movement (BDS) is a global campaign to delegitimize and demonize Israel. Ever since the early 2000's, organized campaigns around the world sponsored and advocated the "boycott, divestment and sanctions" (BDS) against Israel. The BDS movement is pro-Palestinian and widely supported by Arab and Muslim Middle Eastern nations, and many organizations in Europe and the USA as well. Contrary to the claim by many detractors, the BDS movement is undeniably anti-Semitic.

The BDS movement demands the "divestment" of university, municipal, church, union and other investment portfolios from companies that the movement's advocates claim "aid Israel's occupation" of Palestinian territory. BDS supporters also encourage the "boycott" of Israeli products, professionals, professional associations and academic institutions, and artistic performances in Israel and abroad. BDS campaigns promote a biased and simplistic approach to the complex Israeli-Palestinian conflict and present the controversy over territorial and nationalist claims as accruing to only one party—Israel. The BDS campaign does not support Israeli-Palestinian peace efforts. Instead, the movement jeopardizes the effecting of a solution to the conflict.

The author lists the Boycott, Divestment and Sanctions (BDS) movement in this chapter about Christian anti-Semitism, albeit at the very end, because of the participation by many Christian churches and other Christian-oriented organizations around the world in helping to propagandize and advance the movement, which is aimed at marginalizing Israel and punishing the Jewish nation for fabricated offenses. *Israel – Against All Odds (Volume II),* Chapter Three – *The Boycott, Divestment, and Sanctions (BDS) Movement* contains a more detailed discussion about the BDS movement.

Chapter Four

ZIONISM – THE REESTABLISHMENT, DEVELOPMENT & PROTECTION OF THE NATION OF ISRAEL

Israel was not created in order to disappear – Israel will endure and flourish. It is the child of hope and the home of the brave. It can neither be broken by adversity nor demoralized by success. It carries the shield of democracy and it honors the sword of freedom.

John F. Kennedy - President of the United States of America (1961-1963)

An Overview

Zionism is the national movement of the Jewish people that has as its ultimate objective, the reestablishment of a Jewish homeland in the territory defined as the historic Land of Israel. Many scholars consider the territory to encompass the Land of Canaan or the Holy Land, or Palestine, the latter name coined by the Romans in 135 A.D. after the Emperor Hadrian's soldiers defeated Simon bar Kokhba's Jewish armies.[1]

The Jewish diaspora culminated in the dispersion of Israelites, Judahites, and Jews from their ancestral homeland (the Land of Israel) and their forced relocation to various countries around the world. Beginning with the *Assyrian exile* in 733 B.C., and continuing with the *Babylonian exile* in 597 B.C., and the *Roman exile* that began around 70 A.D. and ended around 135 A.D. when the emperor Hadrian ruled, Jews were an expatriated people without an ancestral home or a national state.

The Zionist movement, in the main, emerged during the late 19th century as a response by Ashkenazi Jews to growing anti-Semitism in Europe. Ashkenazi Jews had emigrated during the Middle Ages to what are today's Germany and northeastern France, and until modern times

98

followed the dictates of Yiddish culture and Ashkenazi prayer customs. "Ashkenazi" today more or less refers to a subset of Jewish religious practices, embraced over time, rather than to an inflexible ethno-geographic demarcation, the latter that disappeared over the course of many years.

Incidents such as the Alfred Dreyfus affair, whereby French authorities unfairly accused a young French-Jewish artillery officer of channeling French military secrets to the German Embassy in Paris and convicted him of treason, created a sharp and lasting division in the Third French Republic from 1894 until its resolution in 1906. The Dreyfus affair gave rise to a number of anti-Semitic incidents in France as malicious non-Jewish observers rushed to judgment and infused the specter of Jewish conspiracy and manipulation into the matter. In the end, the courts found all the accusations against Dreyfus to be without merit and dismissed them forthwith.

The Dreyfus affair is often seen as a modern and universal symbol of injustice [2] and remains one of the most notable examples of a prototypical miscarriage of fairness and impartiality. The widespread bias against Jews in Europe, as evidenced by the fallout ensuing from the shameful Alfred Dreyfus affair in France, and numerous anti-Jewish pogroms in the Russian Empire served as a catalyst for change.

Theodor Herzl (1860-1904), an Austro-Hungarian journalist, political activist, and writer, is considered the founder of the Modern Zionist Movement, which essentially emerged in the late 19th century. Herzl created the World Zionist Organization and advocated Jewish migration to Palestine in the hope of developing a Jewish state. Other notable Zionists, even before Herzl's time, were Yehuda Bibas (1789-1852), a Sephardic rabbi, Zvi Hirsch Kalischer (1795-1874), an Orthodox Jewish rabbi, and Judah Alkalai (1798-1878), another Sephardic Jewish rabbi. The publication of Herzl's 1897 book, *Der Judenstaat* (*The Jewish State*), essentially launched the Zionist movement. The mission of the movement was to encourage Jews to relocate or return to the Land of Palestine, which at the time, fell under Ottoman occupation. Herzl's eloquent conclusion in his book, *The Jewish State*, included the following statement.

> *I believe that a wondrous generation of Jews will spring into existence. The Maccabeans will rise again. Let me repeat once more my opening words: 'The Jews who wish for a State will have it. We shall live at last as free men on our own soil and die peacefully in our own homes. The world will be freed by our liberty, enriched by our wealth, magnified by our*

greatness. And whatever we attempt here to accomplish for our own welfare, will react powerfully and beneficially for the good of humanity' [3]

Until 1948, Zionism had as its chief goals, the reestablishment of Jewish self-government in the Land of Israel, the Aliyah or ingathering of exiled people of Jewish ancestry, and the deliverance of Jews worldwide from the anti-Semitic discrimination and persecution directed against them during their diaspora or displacement across the globe. Israel gained statehood in 1948, and since then the Zionist movement has undertaken to promote and defend Israel, and to respond to and neutralize threats to the Jewish nation's continued existence and security.

Protracted anti-Semitism in pre-World War II Europe spiraled into the horrors of the Holocaust during the war and helped put to naught the Zionist cause that had taken root in the late 19th century. Jewish life was all but destroyed in Central and Western Europe. The Zionist movement subsequently modified its mission to address the creation of a Jewish national state.

Zionists employed resourceful forethought in forming an alliance with Great Britain to facilitate Jewish emigration from Europe to Palestine. Many Jews welcomed the opportunity to flee areas in the Russian Empire where anti-Semitism was rampant. The coalition between the Zionists and Great Britain was not without complexity as advocates came to acknowledge the ramifications of the Jewish movement for Arabs living in Palestine. The Zionists, however, persisted and their efforts to create a Jewish state met with success when Israel acquired statehood on May 14, 1948, and the Jewish People's Council declared the country the homeland of the Jewish people. The United States and the USSR subsequently recognized the legitimacy of the new State.

Notwithstanding the acknowledged objective of Zionism being the establishment, development, and protection of a Jewish state in the Palestine region, or the ancestral home of Jews, the movement also espoused, as a tangential mission, the assimilation of Jews into modern society in foreign countries that became their homes. Many Jews who fled to foreign countries chose to remain attached to their Jewish identity and way of life and shunned modernistic trends. "Assimilationist" Jews, or those who promoted assimilation into the modern world, pursued and encouraged total integration into European society, even at the expense of the abandonment of traditional Jewish culture.

The cultural synthesis was a less extreme form of assimilation and required only moderate changes in Jewish culture and customs. The concept, although it enabled enough transformation through which Jews might relate socially and politically to non-Jewish populations, did not call for the relinquishment of Jewish roots. Cultural synthesis emphasized both a need to maintain traditional Jewish values and faith and a need to conform to a modernist society, for instance, in complying with work days and rules.[4]

The United Nations General Assembly (UNGA) passed a resolution (3379) in 1975 that classified Zionism as a "form of racism and racial discrimination." UNGA repealed the resolution in its 1991 meeting by replacing Resolution 3379 with Resolution 4686, after considerable pressure from the United States of America, which led to a final vote of 111 to 25, with 13 abstentions. The following developments probably impacted the global political mood and set the stage for a rethinking of the previously enacted Resolution 3379.

(a) The end of apartheid in South African in the early 1990s, and the Soviet Union's political climate in the 1990s.

(b) The Gulf War (enabled via a United Nations resolution), which took place in 1991. The conflagration caused a division in the Arab world.

(c) Israel making its attendance at the Madrid Conference* contingent on a repeal of Resolution 3379.

*The Madrid Conference of 1991 was a peace conference, held from October 30 to November 1 in Madrid, Spain. Hosted by Spain and co-sponsored by the United States and the Soviet Union, the conference constituted an attempt by the international community to revise the Israeli-Palestinian peace process through negotiation and required participation by the Israelis, Palestinians, as well as representatives from Arab countries, including Jordan, Lebanon, and Syria.

Critics of Zionism claim the movement promotes the segregation of peoples who instead should seek peaceful coexistence. Also, in the context of the ongoing Arab-Israeli conflict, disparagers of Zionism liken the movement to a system that fosters apartheid and racism. The author addresses the forgoing misguided reproaches and other unwarrantable admonitions toward the end of this chapter.

It is eminently practical to assume the Zionist movement has been a success, despite impassioned and continued opposition from the supporters of anti-Semitic behavior around the world. The number of Jewish people living in Israel rose steadily since the movement began in the late 18th century. By the early 21st century, more than 40 percent of the global Jewish population resided in Israel, by far the highest compared to any other country. The foregoing developments are unmatched by any other Jewish political undertaking in the past 2,000 years.[5]

ZIONISM – ITS HISTORY & UNDERLYING PRINCIPLES

The central goal of Zionism was to create a Jewish state that would progress toward a Jewish nation in which Jews were a majority, rather than scattered disenfranchised minorities in a diasporic existence in various parts of the world.

Theodor Herzl (1860-1904), the Zionist movement's most prominent advocate, realized that anti-Semitic practice was a reality in every society in which Jews existed as a minority. He strongly felt the only way Jews would be relieved of the horrors of anti-Semitic maltreatment was to detach themselves from their oppressors and create a separate nation for themselves in which they could live and progress under self-rule.

Herzl envisioned two possible destinations to inhabit and develop— Argentina and Palestine but evinced a preference for Argentina because of its vast and sparsely populated terrain and warm climate. He, however, conceded that Palestine might be the better choice due to the historic ties of Jews to the region.[6]

Zionism taught that Jews in the Diaspora were condemned to a substandard existence and could not achieve full growth individually and nationally, especially as it impacted the historical Jewish religious and communal identity. Diasporic life was therefore undeserved and improper. The concept of "Aliyah" (migration, ascent) to the Land of Israel, on the other hand, resonated with the call in the Jewish Torah (Old Testament Scriptures) for a grand regathering of God's children from foreign lands, and indeed, was the undergirding theme of the Zionist mission.

The preferred language of Zionists was Hebrew, a Northwest Semitic language native to Israel, and spoken by over nine million people worldwide.[7] The contention was the Hebrew language developed in a free society in ancient Judah and was modified and modernized to fit everyday life. The Yiddish language, the historical tongue of the Ashkenazi Jews, was sometimes shunned by Zionists, owing to its presumed development during a period of European persecution whereby Jews suffered extensively at the hands of anti-Semites during the 9th century in Central Europe. Many Jews, after they relocated to Israel, abandoned the languages of their adopted or diasporic countries. Many of them changed their names to ones that reflected their Hebrew ancestry in one way or another.

Zionists chose the Hebrew language not only for ideological reasons but because its use made it expedient for the citizens of the new state to adopt a common language, which helped to strengthen the political and cultural relationships therein.

The Israeli Declaration of Independence, or the Declaration of the Establishment of the State of Israel, proclaimed on May 14, 1948, lists the following elements of the Zionist mission.

- The Land of Israel was the birthplace of the Jewish people. Here their spiritual, religious and political identity took shape. Here they first attained statehood, created cultural values of national and universal significance and gave to the world the eternal Book of Books (the Holy Bible)

- After being forcibly exiled from their land, the people kept faith with it throughout their dispersion and never ceased to pray and hope for their return to it and for the restoration in it of their political freedom.

- Impelled by this historic and traditional attachment, Jews strove in every successive generation to reestablish themselves in their ancient homeland. In recent decades, they returned in masses.[8]

Zionism & the Rebirth of a Nation

Jews have inhabited the Palestinian region continuously for over three thousand years. After the Romans conquered and subjugated them in the first century, and destroyed the Holy Temple, Jews chose to remain in the region. The Romans changed the name of the Jewish homeland i.e. the Land of Israel or Judah in the region known as Canaan, to *Palestina* (Palestine) in an effort to mock the Israelis by likening them to an ancient enemy known as the Philistines. The term "Palestine' referred to Jews and the Jewish homeland until the mid-20th century. Subsequent to 1948, when the newly formed Jewish State re-adopted the name "Israel,' the term "Palestine" faded in usage as a reference to the Jewish homeland and by the early 1970s became associated exclusively with Arabs.

The Jews who stayed in Palestine after the Roman conquest encountered many hardships, but through dedication and perseverance, experienced periods of plenty as well. Also, Jews who had been exiled returned in waves of immigration from time to time. By the latter 19th century, Jews comprised the largest ethnic and religious group in Jerusalem and subsequently became the city's largest population overall.[9]

The foregoing observations notwithstanding, Jews suffered unceasing oppression in their own homeland, and their numbers fluctuated depending on the idiosyncrasies of the rulers who exercised jurisdiction over them through the centuries.

In the 18th and early 19th centuries, the Jewish community in Eastern Europe and other parts of the world faced seemingly insurmountable challenges in the form of exorbitant taxes, widespread discrimination, and persecution. Anti-Semitism or Jew hatred, in its various forms, also became unbridled in most Middle Eastern Arab and Muslim countries, the latter which by the end of the 20th century, comprised 99 5/6th percent of the entire region. Effectively, Israel's land mass today amounts to about 1/6th of one percent of the Middle East. Arabs and Muslims, in collaboration with the transplanted nation of Palestine, also want this comparatively infinitesimal piece of terrain. This is inexcusable greed and covetousness at their zenith. Long before this time, by the end of the 18th century, Jews had found themselves at the bottommost level of despair and wretchedness, even in the homeland of their ancestors. They were desperate people. The following two statements, disturbing to the sane and civilized intellect, relay the travail and torment Jews faced at home and abroad.

> Between 1881 and 1906, Jews in Russia were slaughtered, their homes and towns were destroyed, and their women were raped. In Kishinev, "The mob was led by priests and the general cry, 'Kill the Jews' was taken up all over the city. The Jews...were slaughtered like sheep... Babies were literally torn to pieces by the frenzied and bloodthirsty mob."[10]

> Like a miserable dog without the owner, he (the Jew) is kicked by one because he crosses (a Muslim's) path, and cuffed by another because he cries out—to seek redress he is afraid, lest it bring worse upon him; he thinks it better to endure than to live in the expectation of his complaint being revenged upon him.[11]

Out of the Jews' worldwide, sorry plight, the Zionist movement was born!

Waves of Aliyah

"Aliyah" (ascent) is the Hebrew term for the immigration of Jews from the diaspora i.e. foreign lands to which they were exiled, to the Land of Israel (*Eretz Israel* in Hebrew). The definition of *Aliyah* is "the act of going up" for instance, toward Jerusalem or the Land of Israel. The concept of Aliyah is one of the basic tenets of Zionism. The State of Israel's Law of

Return gives Jews and their descendants an automatic right regarding residency and Israeli citizenship.

Millions of Jews lived in the diaspora for many centuries. *Aliyah,* or the return of Jews to their homeland of Israel or Palestine, became a nationalistic ideal for the Jewish people, although it was not effectively fulfilled until the development of the Zionist movement in the late nineteenth century. The large-scale immigration of Jews to Palestine began in 1882.[12] Since the establishment of the State of Israel in 1948, more than three million Jews have moved to Israel.[13] As of 2014, Israel and the Palestinian territories together contained 42.9 percent of the world's Jewish population.[14]

Prior to World War II (1939-1945), there were five separate waves of immigration of Jews from a diasporic world to the Land of Israel. The five "Aliyahs" were as follows:

1. *1st Aliyah* (1882-1903) – Twenty-five thousand (25,000) socialist and religious Jews sought to flee persecution and/or to reestablish a homeland. The majority of the victimized Jews lived in Russia, Romania, Kurdistan, and Yemen.

2. *2nd Aliyah* (1904-1914) – Forty thousand (40,000) Jews subjected to persecution and harm escaped from Russian and Poland, recreated their nationhood and dignity, and achieved their socialist ideals.

3. *3rd Aliyah* (1919-1923) – Thirty-five thousand (35,000) Jews returned to the Land of Israel after escaping oppression and impoverishment in Russia (53%), Poland (36%), Lithuania, Romania, Western and Central Europe (11%). They rebuilt their society and realized their socialist goals.

4. *4th Aliyah* (1924-1928) – Sixty-seven thousand (67,000) Jews left Poland for Israel to avoid persecution and poverty.

5. *5th Aliyah* (1929 – 1939) – Two hundred and fifty thousand (250,000) Jews fled Germany, Austria, and other countries as a result of rampant discrimination and anti-Semitism.

Zionism - The Modern Revival (Late 19th Century to early 20th Century)

Jews in Palestine staged a revival during the mid-1800s. They relocated from cities in the region and purchased land and built farms, villages, and schools. Jewish philanthropists from around the world played a significant role in empowering the Jews in Palestine to become self-sufficient and develop their own communities. Sir Moses Montefiore (1784-1885) was a notable such benefactor. Montefiore was born to an Italian Jewish family and held prominent social and political positions in England. He donated large sums of money to promote economic development, education, and healthcare among the Jewish communities in the Land of Israel during the mid-19th century. Montefiore founded the Mishkenot Sha'ananim (Peaceful Habitation) community in 1860 in the New Yishuv, the first area of Jewish settlement in Jerusalem outside the Old City walls.[15]

The Lovers of Zion (*Hovevei Zion, Hibbat Zion*, Hebrew) collectively referred to a variety of organizations that became active in 1881 to respond to the anti-Jewish pogroms that plagued Jews in Europe and the Middle East at the time. Scholars consider "The Lovers of Zion" the forerunners and foundation-builders of modern Zionism. Many of the initial groups originated in Eastern European countries in the early 1880s with the objective of encouraging Jewish relocation to Palestine and setting up agricultural and other communities. There was heavy immigration to Palestine during the years 1882 to 1914. Historians recognize Leon Pinsker (1821-1891) a physician and Zionist pioneer and activist, as the founder and leader of the Hovevei Zion movement.

Many of the Jews who immigrated to Palestine from European and Middle Eastern countries in the late 19th and early 20th centuries were socialists who anticipated introducing Western political ideas and other noninterventionist concepts to the new society they envisaged. They felt their homeland would be reestablished through resilience and hard physical labor. The mission was to spearhead a renaissance of Jewish culture and restore Jewish dignity, self-sufficiency, and independence.

The terrain the Jews proposed to develop was under-populated, and much of it was infertile. The region was an impoverished section of the Ottoman Empire. Estimates put the area's population in the early 1880s in the range of 280,000 to 400,000 people. Many of the inhabitants were recent immigrants, who lacked unity and were without any semblance of ethnic or national identity.[16] The loyalties of the people were spread among the religious groups of the ruling Ottoman Empire, their clans and their local communities. An entry under "Palestine" in the Encyclopedia Britannica, 11th edition, 1911, pg. 600 states, "The area included such an assortment of ethnic groups that over 50 different languages were spoken."

The expanse of land that the returning Jews and those already resident in the region decided to inhabit, notwithstanding its deplorable condition and the innumerable challenges it presented to even the most resilient of pioneers, is described in a June 1921 interim report on *Palestine to the League of Nations.* An extract from the report reads as follows:

> *The country was...and is now, underdeveloped and under-populated...There are...large cultivable areas that are left untilled. The summits and slopes of the hills are admirably suited to the growth of trees, but there are no forests. Miles of sand dunes that could be redeemed, are untouched.*[17]

The greater portion of the land the Jews bought was swampland and/or uncultivable sand dunes. The price paid for the land was exorbitant, notwithstanding its immediate uselessness. The absentee landlords were only eager to hand over possession of unusable terrain to the Jews, especially for significant sums of money. The following statements contained in the *Hope Simpson Report* and the *Peel Commission Report* help confirm the aforementioned observations.

> *They (Jews) paid high prices for the land, and in addition, they paid certain occupants of those lands a considerable amount of money which they were not legally bound to pay. (Hope Simpson Report, 1930)*[18]

> *Arab claims that the Jews have obtained too large a proportion of good land cannot be maintained. Much of the land now carrying orange groves was sand dunes or swamps and uncultivated when it was bought. – (Peel Commission Report, July 1937)*[19]

Early Jewish pioneers worked diligently and unceasingly to transform vast areas of wasteland and malarial swamps into cultivable land. Through foresight and painstaking labor, they reforested hillsides and created towns and villages. The following are extracts from official reports about the progress made by early Jewish settlers in the Palestine region during the late 19th and early 20th centuries.

> *Nobody knows of all the hardships, sickness and wretchedness they (the early Zionists) underwent. No observer from afar can feel what it is like to be without a drop of water for days, to lie for months in cramped tents visited by all sorts of reptiles, or understand what our wives, children, and mothers go through...No one looking at a completed building realizes the sacrifice put into it.*[20]

> *Jewish agricultural colonies...developed the culture of oranges...They drained swamps. They planted eucalyptus trees. They practiced, with modern methods, all the processes*

of agriculture...Every traveler in Palestine...is impressed by...the beautiful stretches of prosperous cultivation about them. [21]

Zionism - The Modern Revival (Early to Mid-19th Century)

The *League of Nations,* an intergovernmental organization founded in 1920 as a result of the Paris Peace Conference that ended the First World War, and the first international organization commissioned to maintain world peace, created, along with Britain, the *Palestine Mandate* as the Jewish national home in September 1923. The Palestine Mandate, or British Mandate for Palestine, covered territories of the Ottoman Empire i.e., the *Ottoman Empire sanjaks* of *Nablus, Acre,* the Southern part of the *Vilayet of Syria,* the Southern portion of the *Beirut Vilayet,* and the *Mutasarrifate of Jerusalem,* prior to the *Armistice of Mudros.* The territories today are the State of Israel, the West Bank, the Gaza Strip, and Jordan.

The Palestine Mandate followed the acknowledgment by the League of Nations and Britain of the exponential growth of the Jewish population in the region, and the enormous progress the inhabitants achieved prior to the World War 1 period. The Jewish population increased from 42,000 in 1890 to 83,000 in 1915. [22] The Jews, by the early 20th century, had succeeded in various ventures that hallmarked a flourishing, progressive society. They formulated a rich culture, revived the Hebrew language, patterned socialist communes and created villages, towns, and complementary institutions. The following two statements corroborate the foregoing achievements.

> *The British Government was impressed by the reality, the strength and the idealism of this (Zionist) movement. It recognized its value in ensuring the future development of Palestine.[23]*

> *During the last two or three generations, the Jews have recreated in Palestine a community...This community (has) its town and country population, its political, religious and social organizations, its own language, its own customs, its own life.[24]*

The Mandate period lasted nearly two decades, up to 1948, when Israel acquired statehood. During this time, Jews in the Palestine region persisted with innovative agricultural programs, including purchasing and restoring otherwise uncultivable land and planting trees. It was estimated that by 1935, the Jewish National Fund had planted over 1.7 million trees.[25]

Zionists were also successful in various other areas of growth and development concomitant with a modernized, progressive society. There was industrial advancement and urban and social changes that facilitated the emergence of higher education, the arts, labor unions, and political parties. The Jews also built hospitals and various social institutions.

A leading facet of the Zionist mission was to coexist peacefully with the Arab/Muslim population in the Palestine region. Jews anticipated the restoration and cultivation of the land, along with other improvements to everyday life, would benefit all the region's inhabitants. Many Arabs reciprocated such sentiments and goals, and such an understanding encouraged the immigration of Arabs from nearby countries. Historians reckon about 25 to 37 percent of immigrants to Israel (Palestine) before the nation acquired statehood were Arabs, not Jews. Approximately 100,000 Arabs relocated from neighboring countries to Israel between the years 1922 and 1946. The number of Jews who immigrated during the same period was around 363,000. [26] The following two observations help validate the foregoing statements about Jewish and Arab immigration to Palestine during the early 20th century and the benefits accruing to both races mainly through the unstinting work by the Jewish immigrants and their willingness to live in peace with their Arab neighbors.

> Those good Jews brought...prosperity over Palestine without damage to anyone or taking anything by force.[27]

> No one doubted that the Arabs had benefitted from Jewish immigration. Their numbers had almost doubled between 1917 and 1940. Wages had gone up, and the standard of living had risen more than anywhere else in the Middle East [28]

The United Nations, inspired by the continuing accomplishments of the Zionists, recommended the partitioning of the Mandate territory into a Jewish state beside an Arab state. The area earmarked for the Jewish state housed a decidedly Jewish majority, with Jews numbering about 650,000 and constituting one-third of the entire mandate population. More than 70 percent of the land identified for the Jewish state belonged to the British Mandate as opposed to being owned privately.[29] Approximately 277 rural Jewish communities stretched throughout the countryside.[30] Tel Aviv, a major Israeli city located on the country's Mediterranean coastline, grew from 550 people in 1911 to 230,000 in 1948.[31]

The British Mandate ended on May 14, 1948, and the State of Israel came into existence. The Jews, after a seemingly endless period of over 2,000 years of diasporic expulsion and maltreatment by anti-Semites the world over, finally satiated their yearning to reestablish themselves as an identifiable, self-governed people. Their return from exile and the undertaking's culmination into a national homeland became a reality.

The historic attainment of statehood notwithstanding, the road ahead for the fledgling state of Israel was not and has not been one bereft of trials and tribulations. Israel had to overcome the intricacies of state-building and installing a viable political infrastructure. The new state had to accommodate successive waves of immigrants and refugees, most of whom fled Arab countries. Israelis had to contend with the incessant menace of wars and terrorism, and navigating avenues to peaceful coexistence with covetous Arabs and Muslims who, although already occupying over 99 percent of Middle Eastern territories, sought to displace and/or annihilate the Jews, who lived on less than one percent of the region's land space. As a matter of fact, less than 24 hours after Israel became a state on May 14, 1948, an axis of five Arab/Muslim nations i.e., Egypt, Syria, Transjordan, Lebanon, and Iraq, invaded Israel. The war lasted 15 months, until the newly formed Israeli Defense Forces (IDF) repelled the invaders, but not before 6,000 Israelis, or approximately one percent of the country's population lost their lives. (See *Israel – Against All Odds (Volume II)* Chapter Two - *The Israeli/Palestinian Conflict*, for more on the foregoing subject). The Jews also struggled to maintain their ancient religious and ethical traditions amidst national and international incompatibility and hostility. Many of the challenges and hindrances continue to plague the nation of Israel today.

ANSWERING THE CRITICS OF ZIONISM

The Zionist movement, despite its evident success, has not been without its critics, some of them vehemently opposed to the undertaking. Among the various arguments and denunciations leveled against the movement are the following.

1. Zionism is an unlawful form of nationalism.

2. Zionism is racist because of the flight & expulsion of Palestinian refugees

3. Zionism opposes the "legitimate right" of Palestinians to return to Israel

4. Zionism's "Law of Return" is a racial law

5. Zionism serves to displace Palestinian Arabs.

6. Zionism empowers Israel to be an Apartheid regime.

The author addresses the allegations against the Zionist movement in the following discussions.

IS ZIONISM AN UNLAWFUL FORM OF NATIONALISM?

It is expedient to define the term "nationalism" before venturing to answer the captioned question.

Nationalism is a multifaceted social, political or religious configuration that characterizes the inimitability or uniqueness of a particular nation. The primary objectives of a nationalist undertaking relate to the securing and maintaining of jurisdiction through authority and self-governance and ensuring sovereignty over a territory of historical importance such as an original homeland, or a race or group. Nationalism contends that a nation, for instance, should govern itself, exclusive of outside interference or meddling. The doctrine is inescapably intertwined with the principle of self-governance or self-determination.

Nationalism also revolves around developing and sustaining a national identity predicated on communal characteristics such as culture, language, race, religion, political goals or a belief in common ancestry.[32] Nationalism is fiercely linked with the preservation of a nation's culture, and a sense of pride in a nation's accomplishments. Consequently, the ideology runs parallel with the notion of patriotism.

Scholars used the term "nationalism," from the late 18th century onward, to exemplify the intention of a nation to pursue political autonomy and self-determination. History records nationalist movements in 19th century Germany, Italy, Greece, Serbia, Poland, Latin America, and 20th century China and Africa. There are many varieties of the mindset, among which are the following: (a) Integral nationalism (b) Civic or Liberal nationalism (c) Ethnic nationalism (d) Religious nationalism (e) Left-Wing nationalism (f) Right-wing nationalism (g) Territorial nationalism, and (h) Racial nationalism.

Contrary to generally accepted protocol, which leans toward a ready dismissal of nationalism as maleficent or oppressive, the doctrine may be *positive* or *negative, good* or *bad,* or *inclusive* or *exclusionary.*

Given the above explanation of the nature and characteristics of nationalism, it seems appropriate to classify Zionism as a nationalist endeavor, but is the Zionist movement an unlawful or illegal form of the pursuit? Negative or exclusionary nationalism relates to a majority ethnic group's attempt to exclude and persecute minorities, often to the accrual of various benefits for the overassertive group. The presumption is that negative nationalism accords little or no significance to global or international standards of justice and fair play. Those who practice negative or exclusionary nationalism generally target the socially and economically fragile and encourage their constituents to vent their frustrations on minorities who supposedly threaten their livelihood in one way or another. Promoters of negative nationalism sometimes direct their animosity toward minorities who are to adhere to a religious persuasion that differs from the predominant belief system of the land.

Zionism upholds or indorses none of the foregoing political, social, or religious foibles.

Israel is a democracy that boasts an enviable record of furthering the noble principles relative to (a) Civil Liberties (b) Multiculturalism and (c) Equality before the Law. It is unfathomable that leaders of other nations level charges of exclusionary or negative nationalism against the Jewish state. Furthermore, the allegations of wrongdoing take on an outrageously ironic guise when many of the leaders who accuse Israel of negative nationalism exercise jurisdiction over governmental regimes that are blatantly nationalistic in deleterious ways, with a shameful history of discrimination and maltreatment of their minority populations. The author volunteers a few examples of such duplicity and treachery later in this subsection.

Israel – A Unique Democratic Nation

Israel and Civil Liberties

Religious Freedom – Israel is the only Middle Eastern country in which non-Jewish populations coexist and thrive with adherents of the primary faith (Judaism), instead of being persecuted and/or proscribed from living among those who subscribe to the central or ascendant worldview. As a matter of fact, although Israel is a Jewish state, it formally recognizes 15 religions, including Islam, the Baha'is, and Druze faiths, as well as Chaldaic and many other Christian denominations, among other belief systems. Israeli law mandates the protection of the holy sites of all religions. Each religious community enjoys unrestrained liberty to exercise its faith, observe its holy days and administer its internal functioning.

112

Freedom of Assembly & Freedom of Expression – The freedom to assemble, and to express oneself freely is the right of all Israeli citizens—Jewish or non-Jewish.

While hate speech and incitement to violence are infringements of the law, and indeed they should be in any civilized, constitutionalist society, expressing differences of opinion in any sphere of social, political and religious life in Israel is legal. Israeli-Arab members of the Knesset (the unicameral national legislature of Israel) have been known to criticize the Jewish State and from the floor of the Knesset no less.

The abundance of daily newspapers in Hebrew, Russian, Arabic, French and English help confirm the presence of free speech and communication in Israel. There are multiple hundreds of periodicals, numerous radio and TV stations, and ready access to the foreign press in the Jewish state. The Internet also avails all Israelis the freedom to express themselves.

Civil Rights – Israel's broad-minded, liberal legislation guarantees protection of the rights of all minorities.

Israel & Multiculturalism

Contrary to what those opposed to Israel's existence as a self-governing state would propagandize, and what others who are obsessed with misrepresenting the truth about the country's social, political and religious infrastructure would intimate, the Jewish nation is a pluralistic society. The following cultural characteristics of Israel might be a source of surprise to some and a conduit of dismay to others who labor under a swath of denial.

1. Eighty percent of Israelis are people of Jewish ancestry derived from various ethnicities and races.

2. Many of the Jews emigrated from the Middle East, Ethiopia, India, Russia, the USA. and Europe.

3. Refugees from Arab and Muslim Middle Eastern and North African countries and their descendants comprise over half of Israel's Jewish population.[33] Israel's non-Jewish population account for twenty percent of the nation's population and includes Arab Muslims, Arab Christians, non-Arab Christians, Druze, Bedouins, Circassians, Asians, and others.[34]

Israel & Legal Equality

Palestinians in the Territories, although they are not Israeli citizens, enjoy the facility to petition the nation's highest courts in legal matters. The Court administers its duties based on the merits of each case and as a matter of fact, often rules in favor of the Palestinians. A May 5, 2003, *New York Times* article lends credence to the aforementioned statement.

> *One of the most unusual aspects of Israeli law is the rapid access that petitioners, including Palestinians, can gain to Israel's highest court. In April 2002, during the fiercest fighting of the current conflict (the Israeli-Palestinian conflict) ... the high court was receiving and ruling on petitions almost daily.*[35]

Israel & the Right to Vote

The entitlement of every Israeli citizen to vote or not to vote is an inalienable right granted to all Israeli citizens. The nation's non-Jewish citizens, or its minority constituents, trace such a privilege to Israel's Declaration of Independence. Election Day in Israel is a national holiday and voter turnout generally scales eighty percent, which is higher than even the voter turnout in the USA. The Israeli electoral system accommodates various political parties that endorse a wide range of opinions i.e. Communist, religious, Arab, and secular standpoints. The multiparty system represents a departure from the traditional two or three-party arrangement that typifies most other democratic structures.

Israel Singled Out for Disparagement

Why does there exist an international perception of Israel as a nation that is negatively or selfishly nationalistic?

The concept of nationalism is generally at odds with the viewpoint of globalism or the conception of a common global community. The foregoing assessment notwithstanding, there is a demarcation between positive nationalism and negative nationalism as alluded to earlier. *The presumption is that negative nationalism evades global responsibilities while positive nationalism pursues domestic accountabilities.* The reverse psychological play upon the italicized words in the preceding sentence leaves room for the assumption that negative nationalism may also evade domestic responsibilities and positive nationalism may also pursue global obligations.

Furthermore, the theory of the development of a unified global community is nonsensically idealistic when one considers the overwhelmingly diverse social, political and religious agendas that hold sway in the multitudinous societies around the world. The very unpredictable situation as it relates to politics and religion in Europe and the Middle East, among other areas, makes it especially difficult to contemplate the emergence of any kind of global world order whereby there would be a common, undergirding framework for lasting international camaraderie and cooperation. In other words, globalism today is woefully absent while nationalism, at least to some extent, exists almost everywhere.

A society that demonstrates an unambiguous penchant for positive nationalism is more predisposed to be tolerant and accommodating toward foreign nations because its people are acquainted with the mores of good citizenship and social justice. A society that exhibits traits associated with negative nationalism, where for instance, dictators, autocrats, and despots assume power, lacks the wherewithal to conform to standards and etiquette that appeal to international inclusiveness.

The recent emergence of ISIS (*Islamic State of Iraq & Syria*), the international terrorist organization, the members of which mercilessly and unhesitatingly slaughter anyone who does not subscribe to their unfathomably dark and heinous agenda, has prompted the rulers of some nations to rethink their social and political strategies and adopt a nationalistic approach toward ensuring national security. ISIS' ability to spread its tentacles of hate and destruction across the globe makes people wary and apprehensive. Also, conflicts within certain Muslim fundamentalist countries in the Middle East whereby many thousands of people become displaced and seek refuge in a freer, democratic nations around the world, create a worrisome problem for the recipient nations that face the daunting prospect of allowing probable terrorists entry into their countries as refugees swarm their borders. Many fearful people within countries prepared to accommodate refugees from warn-torn nations may capitulate toward acknowledging nationalism, especially positive nationalism, as an answer to the problem at hand.

The foregoing having been said, negative nationalists tend to prey on people who experience the throes of social and economic instability. People who feel unobligated toward one another in a nation that displays negative nationalistic tendencies are wont to discriminate against minorities in their midst, and even rail against foreigners outside their borders in a misguided quest for a status of social or political, or even religious dominance. People whose livelihoods might be threatened relish the opportunity to target others whom they somehow may blame for their misfortune and on whom they can vent their frustrations.

In all of this, Israel is made out to be the villain, even though its nationalistic policies proceed from justice and fair play. Zionism, which is a form of positive nationalism, is a commendable undertaking and is a proven success, given the breadth and latitude of Israel's unique democratic processes.

If Zionism is racist merely because it is nationalist, then all nationalism is representative of racism. Consequently, all nations that claim to be structured on nationalist principles also should be marginalized and ostracized from the global community, as is Israel. Anti-Zionism essentially advocates that one or more of the following suppositions are true.

1. Jews are not a nation.

2. Jews only relate to Judaism as a historical nexus.

3. Evidence linking Jews to the Old Testament (Torah) history is questionable.

4. Jews originated from Eastern Europe, not the Middle East.

5. Jews do not constitute a homogeneous group.

6. Jews have partnered with imperialists, Nazis and other oppressors throughout history.

7. Zionism essentially amounts to tyrannizing the Palestinians.

The foregoing allegations are false and unsubstantiated and do not coincide with the truth about the Jewish State of Israel, which, in its Zionist undertaking, embodies the moralities of positive or inclusive nationalism.

The Jews' history is littered with episodes of discrimination, persecution, and subjugation in their homeland and in countries around the world. Debauched occupiers expelled Jews from the lands of their ancestors multiple times over the centuries and banished them to diverse nations in which they were never welcome. During World War II, Jew-hatred or anti-Semitism bourgeoned into the Holocaust—history's deadliest incidence of genocide—and the unmitigated slaughter of over six million people of Jewish ancestry in Europe. The Jews, more than any other group of people, have the right to return to their homeland i.e. Israel and reestablish or develop an infrastructure that is unique to their social, political and religious needs and character. Zionism or the reestablishment, development, and protection of the nation of Israel is nationalism, but it is positive nationalism. It is nationalism that is eminently justifiable!

Negative Nationalism in Many Countries Goes Unnoticed While Many People Decry Israel's Positive Nationalism

It is distressing that the majority of Middle Eastern countries, most of them Muslim theocracies, pro-actively and systematically evict Jews, Christians, and other religious minorities without allowing them to return to lands that were their homes for thousands of years. Effectively, these nations practice nationalism—negative or exclusionary nationalism—yet the world at large neglects to level discriminatory nationalist charges against these nations and instead demonizes Israel as illegally nationalist. The following extract from a *Jerusalem Post Christian Edition* article, published in partnership with the *International Christian Embassy Jerusalem* (ICEJ) in February 2011 reveals some alarming statistics about the disappearance of Christians in Middle Eastern countries. The title of the article is *The Tragic Decline of Middle East Christianity – Communities Dwindle under Pressure.*

Egypt – Out of an estimated population of over 80 million residents, Christians number eight percent or 6.4 million with the vast majority being Coptic Christians.

Iran – Out of an estimated population of around 70 million, Christians make up no more than 0.5 percent or around 350,000.

Iraq – Out of an estimated population of around 29 million residents, the Christian community numbers less than 500,000 or under two percent of the population.

Jordan – Out of an overall population of around six million, some two percent or 120,000 people are Christians.

Lebanon – Out of a general population of four million, the Christian population dropped from a near majority several decades ago to as low as 35 percent or approximately 1.5 million.

Palestinian Territories – Demographics vary widely on the general population: West Bank (1.4 to 2.4 million), Gaza (1.2 million to 1.5 million). Christians today number less than two percent; down from 10 percent some 40 years ago. No more than 3,000 Christians remain in Gaza.

Syria – Out of a general population of over 20 million, Christians make up around six percent or 1.2 million.

Turkey – The general population numbers around 78 million, while the Christian community is down to under 0.03 percent or less than 200,000. There were huge drops in the Greek Orthodox and Armenian Orthodox communities over the past century.

(Sources: US State Department, CIA World Factbook)

Recent upsurges of negative nationalism in Europe seem to solicit only token responses from global observers—unlike the frenetic rejoinders to so-called unlawful Israeli or Jewish nationalism.

In Austria, for instance, the rise in popularity of the nation's far-right Freedom Party and its performance in the 2016 general elections is essentially a resurgence of exclusionary nationalism. The Freedom Party's unabashed agenda, which calls for stronger border defenses and tougher controls on immigration and asylum seekers, is a departure from the traditional political and social missions of one of Europe's more stable democracies.

France's *National Front Party*, which lost in the country's the 2017 general elections, nevertheless embodies a growing number of voters who lean toward unbridled nationalism. Marie Le Pen, the National Front's leader, unapologetically embraces anti-globalization and anti-immigration policies. Le Pen is a formidable advocate of authoritarian politics and opposes immigration and fields an obsession with securing the country's borders. Negative nationalism has been on a rise in France since the 1980s, when the party's founder, Jean-Marie Le Pen, Marie Le Pen's father, won a seat in the European Parliament in 1984.

Additionally, terror attacks in Paris, Nice and elsewhere in Europe, combined with seemingly endless streams of refugees and immigrants, particularly from Syria and other Muslim nations, leave many French citizens apprehensive. They feel endangered physically and economically.[36] Sociologist Michèle Lamont, the Robert I. Goldman Professor of European Studies at Harvard University, offered the following statement in connection with the aforementioned outlook.

> *What the French have witnessed, especially since the attacks over the last two years, (has left many feeling) 'we're not a home anymore, and these people who are here in our country as guests are totally destroying our quality of life....(they) are coming in and stealing our resources.'*[37]

Switzerland too is a prominent player on the burgeoning European nationalist stage. The right-wing Swiss People's Party, also known as the Democratic Union of the Centre (SVP), is the largest political assembly in the nation. The October 18, 2015, federal elections showed a shift due to voter concerns about refugee immigration. The SVP won a record number of seats, taking a third of the 200 lower-seat house. The party received the highest proportion of votes of any Swiss political party since 1919, when the nation first adopted a proportional representation electoral system.[38] As the veteran Swiss nationalist, Christoph Blocher, advocates without reservation, the SVP's mission is to make Switzerland fiercely independent and equipped to defend traditional values and combat "asylum chaos" across Europe.

The Southeast Asian nation of Indonesia, the fourth most populous country in the world (population of around 200 million), and the largest economy in the region finds itself in the throes of economic, cultural and territorial issues from a nationalistic perspective. Indonesians express their dissatisfaction at what they deem foreign interference in the nation's affairs and demand greater international recognition of the country's status in the global arena. Politicians, intellectuals, and leaders of religious and social organizations, and ordinary citizens as well, regularly declare that foreign countries regularly demonize, exploit and mistreat Indonesia and do not accord the nation the respect it deserves as a major nation of the region, the latter that includes Malaysia and Australia.

Ethnic Chinese in Indonesia found themselves at the receiving end as negative nationalism reared its ugly head during a recent currency crisis, and Indonesians, fearful of an economic collapse, responded to the volatile situation by resorting to violence. A CNBC September 2015 article, confirming the reality of the crisis, reported that the Indonesian rupiah plunged to 14,280 units against the US dollar, the lowest since July 1998.[39]

Recent actions of the incumbent Prime Minister of India, Mahendra Modi, indicate a leaning toward the adoption of a national policy that reeks of religious exclusionism. The strategy, epitomizing Modi's *Bharatiya Janata Party's* (BJP) staunch stand for Hinduism, India's main religion that numbers 80 percent of the country's 1.3 billion people, is worrying, to say the least. Modi himself is a Hindu, and is a vocal supporter of the worldview, notwithstanding the expectation that the Prime Minister's office in such a large democracy should project an image of religious neutrality or pluralism.

A wave of disturbances by Hindu nationalists in recent years placed Modi in an unenviable, embarrassing position. Sikh, Christian and Muslim minorities are understandably discomfited by the belligerence of Hindu nationals and feel threatened physically, emotionally and economically.

They fear the establishment of Hinduism as a national religion with numerous frightful repercussions for non-Hindus across the country.

On June 2, 2016, police clashed with armed protesters from the Hindu Netaji sect occupying a park in the city of Mathura, a city in the North Indian state of Uttar Pradesh. Some 24 people lost their lives and authorities arrested over 300 protesters. The Hindu militants had occupied the park for two years, demanding that India's parliament disband, and the posts of president and prime minister be abolished.[40] The escalating instances of disagreement between Hindu nationals and Indian secularists can only serve to undermine Mahendra Modi's already deteriorating reform agenda, deepen the country's political polarization, and temper economic growth.

The author volunteers the following two paragraphs as a personal aside in connection with Narendra Modi's departure from religious freedom and inclusionism.

My wife Pamela and I were sponsors of a young Indian girl via the auspices of Compassion International, a Christian humanitarian child sponsorship organization dedicated to the long-term development of children living in poverty around the world. Early in 2017, we received notification from Compassion International that we could no longer support our sponsored child in India and our financial assistance would be redirected to help better the life of a young Haitian child. Upon inquiry, we learned that Compassion International and other Christian humanitarian organizations no longer could continue operations in the Asian country. Organizations were free to offer assistance to impoverished children in India, we learned, but could not preach the Christian Gospel. The ban pertained not only to Christian organizations, but to Muslim, Sikh, Jewish, and other non-Hindu groups.

Shortly afterward, we read about Indian Prime Minister Narendra Modi's concerted drive to promote Hinduism in India at the expense of other belief systems. Modi's approach represents not only a nationalist undertaking but a negative and exclusionary strategy of excommunicating and oppressing people who do not subscribe to the tenets of Hinduism. The outrage is today a fact of life in one of the world's largest democracies.

And people ridicule minuscule Israel for being nationalist…positively nationalist!

The foregoing are examples of nations around the world that are not only nationalist but negatively or prejudicially separatist. Yet the world at large pays scant attention to such troubling developments, and instead single out the nation of Israel, which is positively nationalist, as an exclusionary nation that abhors globalism and mistreats its ethnic minorities. The Jewish nation's Zionist program, they say, ignores international connectedness and discriminates against resident non-Jews.

In would seem in most instances, criticism or denouncement of Zionism as an illegitimate nationalist movement is nothing more than a façade for expressing anti-Semitic sentiments. As Abraham (Abe) Foxman (born May 1, 1940), former National Director of the *Anti-Defamation League* and currently the League's National Director Emeritus said, "...anti-Zionism constitutes anti-Semitism if Zionism is the only nationalism being opposed." Put alternatively, when criticism of Israel retrogresses into attempts to demonize the country and delegitimize its right to exist as a Jewish state, such condemnation becomes anti-Semitism. When people adjudge Zionism a conspiratorial scheme to subjugate and take over the world, it is arrant evidence of anti-Semitism at work.

THE PALESTINIAN REFUGEE CRISIS - IS IT ZIONIST RACISM?

If anyone were to be blamed for the Palestinian refugee crisis, it should be the Arab Palestinians themselves and the collaborating Arab nations that went to war with Israel after Palestine refused to accept and abide by UN Resolution 181, enacted in 1947 and that sought to partition Palestine into Jewish and Arab states.

Had the Palestinians accepted UN Resolution 181 instead of engaging in war in an avaricious attempt to seize the whole British Mandate, an independent Palestinian-Arab state would today exist alongside Israel. The refugee crisis remains the contentious and polarizing issue it is because of the continued rejection by Palestinians and Arabs of a two-state solution that would require Arabs and Jews to coexist and cooperate with one another. Very many Palestinians and Arabs view such an agreement as anathema to their socio-religious convictions. Another reason for the importunate Palestinian refugee crisis is the refusal by Arab nations, which comprise over ninety-nine percent of the Middle Eastern region, to assimilate Palestinian refugees into their midst. Instead, Arab leaders leave the refugees in their plight and misuse them as leverage in their incessant, shameless pursuit to destroy the Jewish state of Israel.

Some Arab leaders in Palestine, since the early 20th century, expressed their unalloyed dislike for the Jewish community. Many of these hatemongers identified with the rising Nazi movement and enflamed their followers with hatred and dislike for Jews. Arabs engaged in mob attacks

121

against Jews in 1920, 1921, 1929 and 1936-1939. A noted Nazi accomplice was Haj Amin El-Husseini, a Palestinian Arab leader and Grand Mufti of Jerusalem (1921-1937). Haj Amin El-Husseini met with Adolf Hitler, the German dictator in 1941 and petitioned the Nazi leader for assistance in exterminating the Jews of Palestine. Following is an excerpt from an official German record of the meeting between Adolf Hitler and El-Husseini at the Reich Chancellory in Berlin on November 28, 1941.

> *The Arab countries were firmly convinced that Germany would win the war and that the Arab cause would then prosper. The Arabs were Germany's natural friends because they had the same enemies as had Germany, namely the English, the Jews and the Communists. Therefore they were prepared to cooperate with Germany with all their hearts and stood ready to participate in the war, not only negatively by the commission of acts of sabotage and the instigation of revolutions, but also positively by the formation of an Arab legion.*[41]

El-Husseini helped recruit a Bosnian *Schutzstaffel* (SS) unit on behalf of Adolf Hitler. The Schutzstaffel was a major paramilitary organization under Hitler and the Nazi Party (NSDAP) in Nazi Germany, and later throughout German-occupied Europe during World War II.

Had there been no war (Israel's War of Independence) instigated and begun by the Palestinians and their Arab co-conspirators in 1948, there would have been no refugees. The Jews in the Palestine region had no other recourse but to defend themselves against turncoat Arabs and the armies of an evil axis of Arab nations, namely Egypt, Syria, Transjordan, Lebanon, and Iraq. The newly formed Israeli Defense Forces (IDF) somehow were able to defeat the invaders over a course of 15 months of mayhem and bloodshed, during which 6,000 Israelis lost their lives. Israel's War of Independence lasted from 1948 to 1949.

The Israelis were entirely justified to refuse to allow Palestinians who fought against them to return to Israel after the war. These people were, by definition, traitorous collaborators with an enemy obsessed with destroying the Jewish nation. They refused to live in a Jewish state and/or capitalize on the opportunity to create one for themselves and coexist peacefully alongside people of Jewish ancestry.

IS ZIONIST OPPOSITION TO THE SO-CALLED "LEGITIMATE RIGHT" OF PALESTINIAN REFUGEES TO RETURN TO ISRAEL A RACIST OR DISCRIMINATORY POLICY?

It is commonly misrepresented protocol for supporters of the so-called "Palestinian cause" to accuse Israel of violating the Fourth Geneva Convention in relation to an ostensible "right" of Palestinian refugees of the aftermath of the 1948-1949 war to return to Israel. Also, pro-Palestinian activists and members of the international community allude to UN Resolution 194, adopted by the UN General Assembly on December 11, 1948, toward the end of the Arab-Israeli War, as granting the "right" to Palestinian refugees to return to their homes.

A United Nations Human Rights panel headed by a French judge, Christine Chanet, alleged that Israel violates the Fourth Geneva Convention by building Jewish communities in Judea and Samaria. Chanet declared that *"To transfer its own population into an occupied territory is prohibited because it is an obstacle to the exercise of the right to self-determination."* The judge's pronouncement was hardly surprising, especially to those accustomed to the United Nations' track record of prejudice and intolerance in its dealings with the Jewish State of Israel. (See *Israel – Against All Odds (Volume II)* Chapter One - *The United Nations and Israel – A History of Discrimination*)

A passable analysis of the previously mentioned issues bring to the fore, some revelations that dispute the generally held view that Israelis wrongfully deny Palestinian refugees the right to return to Palestine or Israel.

Article 49 (Jewish Settlements in Judea and Samaria (the West Bank), and Geneva Convention, IV, Relative to the Protection of Civilian Persons in Time of War) came into existence after World War II. Multiple millions of people were deported, displaced and massacred during the war, with outright genocide perpetrated against Jews and Gypsies. The architects of Article 49 of the Geneva Convention felt commissioned to help prevent a replication of the horrendous cruelty and evil that accompanied Nazism.

Article 49, paragraph 6 states, *"The Occupying Power shall not deport or transfer parts of its own civilian population into the territory it occupies."* A careful reading of the foregoing stipulation along with an evaluation of the context in which its originators drafted the document brings two pivotal observations to the fore. Firstly, the legislation refers to forced transfers of the population that result in endangering an overpowered nation's existence, not a voluntary settlement in open areas, even if the region in question is indeed an occupied one. Secondly, Judea, Samaria, and East Jerusalem as well, are not occupied territories. Such a perspective derives from a legal standpoint as discussed below, even though a strong alternative that disputes the contention Israel occupies the region proceeds from the fact that (a) the Palestine region has been the homeland of Jews for over three thousand years, long before Arab and Muslim invaders overran the territory (b) history records brutal episodes of Arab and Muslim subjugation and occupation in Middle Eastern countries over the centuries, and (c) Middle Eastern Arabs and Muslims were parties to a premeditated exodus into the Palestine area during the years after the 1948-1949 Israeli War of Independence in order to swarm the land and afterward claim an ancestral linkage.

The foregoing observations notwithstanding, the case for a solid legal argument against the allegation that Israel occupies Judea, Samaria and Eastern Jerusalem stems from the following observations.

(a) Article 2 of the Geneva Convention clearly states that the Fourth Geneva Convention only applies to two or more high contracting parties, which makes Judea and Samaria ineligible since the international community never recognized Jordan's annexation of these territories.

(b) Egypt never annexed Gaza.

(c) There has never been a Palestinian Arab state throughout history.

(d) According to the San Remo Resolution* of April 25, 1920, and the Palestine Mandate of July 24, 1922, Judea and Samaria, East Jerusalem, and Gaza were all earmarked to be part of a Jewish state.

(e) The aforementioned agreements continue to be relevant today since Article 80 of the United Nations Charter maintains that all mandates of the League of Nations remain valid.

* Adopted on April 25, 1920, during the San Remo conference, the *San Remo Resolution* was an agreement among post-World War I allied powers (Britain, France, Italy, Japan). The *Mandate for Palestine* emerged from this resolution; it incorporated the *1917 Balfour Declaration* and the *Covenant of the League of Nations* Article 22. Britain was to establish a "national home for the Jewish people" in Palestine. Britain's subsequent violation of the Palestine Mandate (in 1922 and 1923) did not alter the legality of such an agreement.

No nation is under any obligation to admit enemy belligerents within its borders. Palestinian refugees are not Israeli citizens. They are essentially enemies of the Jewish state who do not wish to become citizens, but who instead clamor for the destruction of Israel and its Jewish inhabitants. It is commonsensical to presume the admission of millions of Palestinian refugees into Israel would eventually lead to an Arab majority, the members of whom would be reluctant to live in peace alongside their Jewish neighbors.

Paradoxically, the same people who advocate a "right of return" to Israel for undeserving refugees seek to abolish the Israeli "Law of Return" for Jews to return to their homeland. Were the Israeli "Law of Return" abolished, Israel would not be the national home of the Jews, and the Jewish people would be unable to exercise their right of self-determination. Under such circumstances, an international law grounded in justice and fair play i.e., the Jews' "Law of Return" would be abandoned at the expense of a so-called right i.e., the Palestinians' "Right of Return," the latter that transgresses every semblance of reason and legitimacy.

Arab governments, during and after the Israeli War of Independence, promised refugees they would return to their homes in Palestine. The demagogues unabashedly promoted their intention to dismantle the Jewish state demographically and inundate it with Palestinian Arabs, as expressed in the following two pronouncements.

If Arabs return to Israel – Israel will cease to exist.

Gamal Abdel Nasser, President of Egypt, 1961[42]

> *The demand for the return of the Palestinian refugees...is tantamount to the destruction of Israel.*

As'ad Abd-Al Rahman, Palestinian Authority Minister of Refugee Affairs, 1999[43]

The 2018 Gaza Strip Protests

The ready proclivity by the Palestinians and their supporters to plunge headlong into reckless and vicious acts of aggression against the Israelis was painfully obvious during the 2018 Palestinian protests along the Gaza Strip, near the Israeli border.

Palestinian organizers referred to the protests as the "Great March of Return" and dovetailed the uprisings with the usual controversial demands that hallmarked decades of confusion and unsubstantiated allegations by a people obsessed with harming and killing Israelis and Jews instead of working toward reconciliation and peaceful coexistence. The protesters demanded that Palestinian refugees and their descendants be allowed to return to what is now Israel and protested the blockade of the Gaza Strip. They also denounced the 2018 relocation of the United States Embassy in Israel from Tel Aviv to Jerusalem.

Tens of thousands of Palestinians participated in the demonstrations at different times. Protests that were initially peaceful became raucous as protesters stormed the border, threw stones and Molotov cocktails at the Israeli troops, launched kites bearing incendiary devices, and caused damage to Israeli property. At least 110 Palestinians died between March 30 and May 15, 2018.

The world at large was quick to condemn Israel for its retaliation and "unnecessary" violence, while it neglected to chastise the Palestinians for transforming a supposedly peaceful demonstration into one of unbridled violence and for venting their hatred on the Israelis who were only defending themselves. It was a reaction that has become commonplace over the years whereby misguided and misinformed people condone mayhem and murder by some i.e. Palestinians and Palestinian terrorists and condemn defensive strategies by those who attempt to protect themselves i.e. Israelis and Jews.

Israeli Prime Minister Benjamin Netanyahu defended the deadly response to the Gaza protests by the Israeli military and endeavored to put the Palestinian offensive and Israeli retaliation into proper perspective. In an interview with "CBS Evening News" anchor Jeff Glor, Mr. Netanyahu bared his feelings about the protests and the Palestinians' sinister agenda of malice and misinformation. Excerpts from the May 15, 2018 article read as follows:

> Netanyahu said, "Hamas is pushing people with a view of a massive infiltration into Israel, openly declaring their goal is to destroy Israel. They're paying these people. So it's…it's not the peaceful demonstrations that you think about."

> "They're pushing civilians, women, children into the line of fire with the view of getting casualties…We try to minimize casualties. They're trying to incur casualties in order to put pressure on Israel, which is horrible."

> Netanyahu said he doesn't see any circumstance where he would be open to talks with Hamas in the current climate…As long as they seek our destruction, what am I going to talk about?" he said.

The Israeli newspaper *Haaretz*, the longest running periodical currently still in print in Israel, carried an article about the 2018 Gaza protests titled "Hamas Called Gaza a "Peaceful Protest" and the World Fell for It" on May 21, 2018. The report articulated the observations of Israeli Defense Forces (IDF) Brigadier General Ronen Manelis as they related to the protests.

> Hamas has repeatedly lied about its true intentions and the protests in (the) Gaza Strip and the world "fell for it."

> According to the IDF spokesman, despite weeks of lying to the world over the "violence on the border between Gaza and Israel," Hamas also made "rare acknowledgments of truth" which the general claimed, "are especially revealing."

> For example, "Hamas itself has confirmed that 80% of those killed in the violent riots last Monday were members of a terrorist group, not innocent civilians. Several more of the fatalities were claimed by Palestinian Islamic Jihad.

> Manelis also quoted one of Hamas' co-founders, MahmoudAl-Zahar, as telling Al Jazeera, "When we talk about 'peaceful resistance,' we are deceiving the public." ... Manelis claimed some in the media helped Hamas by publishing its lies rather than the facts.

> The IDF spokesman blamed Hamas for the violence (and deaths) and said that the Gaza group "can lie – to the world, to Palestinians and to their own commanders and operatives – but I am proud that the IDF will never lie or use Israeli civilians or soldiers as pawns."

THE ISRAELI "LAW OF RETURN" - IS IT RACIST?

History attests to the fact that Jews, unlike any other group of people, have suffered expulsion, ostracism, persecution, and annihilation, in their homeland and abroad. Scattered in lands across the globe for thousands of years, they have been derided, stigmatized, mistreated and cheated of the niceties of basic or common existence. Centuries of religious, political, social, economic and other forms of anti-Semitism or Jew hatred reached a head with the Holocaust that took place in the mid-twentieth century during the Second World War.

Even before the onset of the Holocaust, easily the deadliest genocide in history, diasporic Jews were contemplating a return to the Land of Israel. The acknowledged father of modern political Zionism, Theodor Herzl

127

(1860-1904), set in motion in the late nineteenth century, the mission that would come to be known as the Zionist cause.

The 1950 Law of Return, as stipulated in Israel's Declaration of Independence, states that *"the State of Israel will be open to the immigration of Jews and the ingathering of exiles from all countries of their dispersion."* The law codified the undertaking to gather Jews from around the world by granting them the right to settle in Israel and gain automatic citizenship.

One of the major goals of the Israeli Law of Return is to ensure a Jewish majority in Israel. Today, over 20 percent of Israeli citizens are Arab, and this number could continue to rise. The Law of Return offsets the high Arab birth rate by enabling the naturalization of thousands of Jewish immigrants to Israel each year.[44] Furthermore, the law postulates that any Jew may relocate to Israel and become a citizen without having to submit to a naturalization process. Non-Jewish aspirants who wish to become Israeli citizens must undergo a naturalization process.

Another primary objective of the Jewish Law of Return is to provide a safe-haven and national home for Jews dispersed across the world. Tragically, the mission met with an unexpected and unprecedented obstacle in the form of the Holocaust, during and after which Jews who fled Nazi persecution met with closed doors in just about every country of the world. Very many Jews suffered the terrible fate of being trapped in hostile host countries and dying therein. Should the Law of Return be abolished, as anti-Zionists insist it should, the fundamental aim of the establishment of Israel as a national home for the Jews would be negated?

Notwithstanding the aforementioned observation, Israel does not summarily blacklist non-Jewish immigrants. The Jewish state, however, employs circumspective procedures when dealing with Arab applicants for Israeli citizenship, as the Jews remain at loggerheads with Palestinians, who are deadly confrontationists bent on killing Jewish men, women, and children, and who refuse to live in peace with people of Jewish ancestry.

DID ZIONISTS DISPLACE PALESTINIAN ARABS?

Palestinian Arabs, falling prey to anti-Zionist propaganda in the early nineteen-twenties, around the beginning of the British Mandate and throughout the Mandate period that ended in 1947, were cajoled into thinking that Zionists planned to confiscate their homes and other belongings and banish them to foreign lands.

There were about 660,000 Arabs in Palestine at the beginning of the British mandate in 1922. The number grew to about 1.3 million at the end of the Mandate in 1947. Some 735,000 Arabs resided in areas that would later become Israel after the 1948-1949 War of Independence. Immediately after the United Nations partitioned Palestine in 1947, the Palestinians, abhorring living in peace with the Jews, initiated attacks against them. Jewish underground groups understandably retaliated and much bloodshed ensued. Many civilians, Jewish and Palestinian, lost their lives. Many Arabs, although their standard of living in Palestine exceeded the quality of life of fellow Arabs in neighboring countries, chose to flee Palestine as a result of incessant fighting, hoping to return to Palestine later, after, as Arab leaders led them to believe, the Jews would be vanquished.

The Jews, however, were victorious over the Palestinians, and subsequently enacted legislation prohibiting the return of refugees. The law preventing Arabs from reentering Palestine was justifiable given the fact that Palestinian refugees committed themselves to undermining the Jewish or Israeli government and exterminating people of Jewish ancestry. The flight and expulsion of Palestinian refugees, while due to a certain extent to the actions of Jewish revolutionaries, and in some instances, misrepresentation by factions of the Israeli army, were not, as anti-Zionists charge, in keeping with any aspect of Zionist doctrine. The refugee crisis was the aftermath of a war created by the reckless, ill-advised leadership of Arab and Muslim rulers in the region.

Historians estimate that between 472,000 and 750,000 (scholars are divided as to the exact count) Palestinian Arabs fled the region that later became Israel for a number of reasons. Among the motives behind the Palestinians' flight from Israel were the following two weighty issues.

1. Arab leaders encouraged Palestinians to leave Israel in order to stay out of the path of advancing Arab armies. The leaders promised a sure and swift victory for the Arabs and a quick return for refugees to a conquered Israel.

2. Many Palestinians exited Israel in terror as fabricated tales of Israeli atrocities led to widespread panic.[45]

The undermentioned statements by prominent Arabs and a Palestinian newspaper editor bring to the fore, the fact that hateful, covetous Arab leaders were the malefactors behind the exodus of Palestinians from Israel during the mid-20th century and not Israelis or Jews who Arabs and Muslims blame for the displacement of Palestinian Arabs. The remarks echo the feelings of deceived Palestinians and other Arabs after the 1948-1949 Israeli War of Independence. The first statement refers to a plan for Arab and Muslim women and children to leave Israel and to return after an envisaged victory over the Israelis.

> We will smash the country. The Arabs should conduct their wives and children to safe areas until the fighting has died down. – Iraqi Prime Minister Nuri Said, 1948[46]

> Since 1948 we have been demanding the return of the refugees to their homes. But we ourselves are the ones who encouraged them to leave. Only a few months separated our call to them to leave and our appeal to the United Nations to resolve on their return. – Haled al Azim, Syrian Prime Minister, 1948-1949 [47]

> The Arab armies entered Palestine to protect the Palestinians...but instead, they abandoned them, forced them to emigrate and to leave. – Palestinian President Mahmoud Abbas, 1976.[48]

> The fabricated atrocity stories about Deir Yassin "were our biggest mistake... Palestinians fled in terror." – Hazem Nusseibeh, editor of the Palestine Broadcasting Service's Arabic news in 1948.[49]

IS THE JEWISH STATE OF ISRAEL SIMILAR TO AN "APARTHEID REGIME?"

Critics of Zionism accuse the Israeli government of replicating an environment similar to the one that existed in South Africa during the "Apartheid" years. Apartheid was a system of institutionalized racial segregation and discrimination in South Africa between 1948 and 1991.[50]

Native Africans endured much suffering under South African Apartheid rule. After the enactment of apartheid laws in 1948, institutionalized racial discrimination became the order of the day. Race laws impacted every aspect of social life, including a prohibition of marriage between non-whites and whites, and the sanctioning of "white-only" jobs. Blacks did not have an equal voice and faced discriminatory employment practices, including having to contend with sub-par remuneration. "Grand apartheid" involved comprehensive racial segregation and measures such as the removal of black people from white areas and the creation of black homelands. "Lesser" or "petty apartheid" was the practice of segregation in the routine of daily life i.e., in lavatories, restaurants, railway cars, buses, swimming pools, and other public facilities.

In 1950, the Population Registration Act required that all South Africans be racially classified into one of three categories: white, black (African), and colored (of mixed decent). The colored category included major subgroups of Indians and Asians. Classification into these categories was based on appearance, descent, and social acceptance.

The treatment of Arab minorities in Israel differs vastly from the contemptible and unfair dealing meted out to non-white Africans during the apartheid era. Israeli Arab citizens vote and participate in government along with Jewish citizens. Arab Israeli citizens, contrary to misinformation peddled by those who accuse the Jewish State of being an Apartheid regime, may exercise the right to purchase and own land. Israeli Arabs enjoy legal protection against discrimination in governmental agencies and at work. Arabs and Jews are free to intermarry.

In 1948, after the termination of the British Mandate, 160,000 Arabs who resided within Israel's borders accepted the invitation to become Israeli citizens. Effectively, these people chose peace over war and discord and exercised their democratic right to help select governmental representatives of their choice. As a matter of fact, the new citizens proceeded to elect three Israeli-Arabs to the first Knesset, or the Israeli parliament. [51] Subsequent to the resolution of the War of Independence postwar problems, Arab-Israeli citizens experienced a degree of freedom, a level of education, healthcare, and prosperity that exceeded similar privileges experienced by average citizens residing in every other Arab country. Israeli-Arabs today number over 1.25 million and continue to have access to a relatively high standard of living. The following statement by Dr. Talal Al-Shareef, a columnist of the Palestinian newspaper *Al-Quds* (May 27, 1999) attests to the aforementioned observations.

> *Israel has proved that for fifty years its real power is in its democracy, guarding the rights of its citizens, applying laws (equally) to the rich and poor, the big and small...and in the participation of the nation in the development of institutions according to ability and efficiency and not according to closeness to (the ruler).[52]*

JUDAISM, CHRISTIANITY, AND ISLAM ALL ENDORSE A ZIONIST MOVEMENT

It is not implausible, especially for students of comparative religion and adherents of certain religious worldviews i.e. Judaism, Christianity, and Islam, to presume that Almighty God himself endorsed a Zionist movement that would take place in modern times. According to the Holy Books of each of the belief systems, the Land of Israel (Eretz Israel or Palestine) is a region of the land God promised to the Jews.[53] The doctrinal and/or theological dissimilarities among the scriptural texts, i.e. the Hebrew Bible, the Greek Bible, and the Quran, are irrelevant for the purpose of the issue at hand. Suffice it to say that adherents of the three major religions number about 3.8 billion or 55 percent of the world's population of 7.1 billion people.[54] Consequently, more than half the world's inhabitants may appeal to historical incidence, from a religious standpoint, in connection with ownership of the Land of Israel, even though Muslims of today generally choose to digress from Quranic pronouncement in relation to the matter. See passages from the Quran below that tell about God gifting the Land of Israel to the Jews.

The following extract from the Bible (the Old Testament) speaks clearly about God bestowing a wide expanse of land to the patriarch Abraham and his descendants, indeed much more territory than what people today consider Israel.

> On that day God made a covenant with Abram (Abraham) and said, 'To your descendants I give this land, from the river of Egypt to the great River, the Euphrates – the land of the Kenites, Kenizzites, Kadmonites, Hittites, Perizzites, Rephaites, Amorites, Canaanites, Girgashites, and Jebusites.'[55]

Pointed scholarship reveals that the tribes or groups of people lived in what is today Egypt, Sudan, Lebanon, Jordan, Syria, Iraq, part of Asian Turkey, and all of Israel, including Gaza and the West Bank. The lands are "occupied" (the pun is intentional) today by people who are not Jews. Ironically, Jews, to whom the Old Testament says Almighty God gifted the lands, have never had control of the territories that belong to them.

The Quran contains the following statement about God giving the Land of Israel to the Jews.

> Pharaoh sought to scare them (the Israelites) out of the land (of Israel): but we (Allah) drowned him (Pharaoh) together with all who were with him. Then We (Allah) said to the Israelites: 'Dwell in this land (the Land of Israel). When the promise of the hereafter (End of Days) comes to be fulfilled, We (Allah) shall assemble you (the Israelites) altogether (in the Land of Israel).[56]

In addition to the forgoing scriptural passages that speak about God gifting the Land of Israel and other Middle Eastern territories to the Jews, the Hebrew and Greek Bibles (Judaism and Christianity) and the Quran (Islam) proclaim the regathering of Jews in Israel (Zionism), and their re-establishment as a nation, in the following excerpts from the holy books.

The Bible, in the Old Testament Book of Ezekiel 36:24-28, ESV (Judaism and Christianity) states:

> I will take you from the nations and gather you from all the countries and bring you into your own land. I will sprinkle clean water on you, and you shall be clean from all your uncleannesses, and from all your idols I will cleanse you. And I will give you a new heart, and a new spirit I will put within you. And I will remove the heart of stone from your flesh and give you a heart of flesh. And I will put my Spirit within you, and cause you to walk in my statutes and be careful to obey my rules. You shall dwell in the land that I gave to your fathers, and you shall be my people, and I will be your God.

The Quran, in Sura 17:104 (Islam), reads:

> And thereafter We (Allah) said to the children of Israel: 'Dwell securely in the Promised Land. And when the last warning will come to pass, we will gather you together in a mingled crowd.'

In the final analysis, the Zionist movement, bolstered by the various arguments in favor of its mission in the preceding discussions, and its seeming parallelism with scriptural assertions in the holy books of Jews, Christians and Muslims—three of the world's most prominent religious groups—has been, and continues to be a justified and successful endeavor at liberating, reestablishing and protecting a people who have suffered and have been marginalized around the world for many centuries.

Chapter Five

THE HOLOCAUST

What is the Jew? ...What kind of unique creature is this whom all the rulers of all the nations of the world have disgraced and crushed and expelled and destroyed; persecuted, burned and drowned, and who, despite their anger and their fury, continues to live and flourish.

...A people such as this can never disappear. The Jew is eternal. He is the embodiment of eternity.

Leo Tolstoy (1828-1910) - Russian novelist and moral philosopher

An Overview

The *Holocaust* (from the Greek *holos*, "whole" and *kaustos*, "burnt"), also known as the *Shoah* (from the Hebrew, *HaShoah*, "the catastrophe"), ranks as history's deadliest genocide. The slaughter, engineered by Adolf Hitler of Nazi Germany and leaders of collaborating nations during 1941 to 1945, resulted in the deaths of about six million European Jews, around two-thirds of the Jewish population of Europe.[1] Close to one and one half million of the victims were children. Alternative counts of Holocaust casualties include an additional five million non-Jewish people exterminated by Nazi mass murderers, yielding an astonishing total of eleven million victims.

Holocaust atrocities occurred throughout Nazi Germany, German-occupied territories and territories controlled by allies of the fascist nation. Countries occupied by the Nazis during the Second World War included Czechoslovakia, Austria, the Netherlands, Belgium, Luxembourg, France, Denmark, Yugoslavia, Greece, Norway, and Western Poland. These lands were home to many millions of Jews, as was Nazi Germany itself.

The Holocaust was a component of the Nazi regime's wider diabolical scheme to oppress and annihilate various ethnic and political groups in Europe. The Nazi *Schutzstaffel* (SS, Protective Squadron) and its armed wing, the Waffen-SS, led the charge in coordinating and implementing the genocide, under instruction from the uppermost echelon of Germany's leadership. Every facet of the Nazi bureaucracy directly or indirectly played a role in planning and effecting the slaughter of millions of Jews and non-Jews in Europe during the Second World War. Victims of Nazi carnages included religionists, the mentally and physically disabled, political opponents, prisoners of war, homosexuals, and black people. The Nazis and their collaborators utilized over 42,000 specially designated facilities in Germany and German-occupied territories to herd and hold prisoners for slave labor, mass murder, and other human rights abuses.[2] Historians estimate that over 200,000 people participated in Holocaust perpetrations during 1941 to 1945.[3]

The Nazis persecuted and butchered the Jews and non-Jews in phases. The ultimate stage of the Holocaust called the "Final Solution to the Jewish Question" (*die Endlosung der Judenfrage*), was an elaborate scheme to exterminate the Jews in Europe. The German government enacted laws to ostracize Jews from civil society, prominent legislation of which were the Nuremberg Laws of 1935. The Nazis developed a network of concentration camps, beginning in 1933, and formed ghettos following the outbreak of World War II in 1939. In 1941, as the war progressed, and as Germany overrode new territory in Eastern Europe, specialized paramilitary units called *Einsatzgruppen* slaughtered around two million Jews and non-Jews, often in mass shootings.[4] Afterward, it became common practice for the Nazis to transport prisoners by freight trains to extermination camps and mercilessly end their lives. Those who somehow survived the ordeal of the journey to the camps were summarily killed in gas chambers. Such horrendous practices persisted until the end of World War II in 1945.

Jewish resistance to the Nazi juggernaut that persecuted and annihilated millions of Jews and non-Jews was relatively stymied and ineffective. Such a fact notwithstanding, there was sporadic opposition as people driven to desperation sought to defend themselves and their families. The 1943 Warsaw Ghetto uprising in Poland represented a notable departure from the acquiescent mindset to which the beleaguered and helpless Polish people became accustomed. Thousands of inadequately armed Jewish combatants fought off Waffen-SS soldiers and held them at bay for four weeks.

The Waffen-SS was the armed wing of the Nazi Party's SS organization. Its formations included men from Nazi Germany, along with volunteers and conscripts from both occupied and unoccupied lands.[5]

Overall, it is estimated that about 20,000 to 30,000 Jewish partisans battled the Nazis and their allies in Eastern Europe. Jews in France mounted the French Resistance, which mainly took the form of a guerrilla campaign against the Nazis and the Vichy French authorities. All told, there were over a hundred armed Jewish insurgencies.

THE EMERGENCE OF NAZI GERMANY

Germany's resounding defeat in World War I occasioned the Versailles Treaty (*French: Traite de Versailles*), a major peace treaty enacted at the end of the conflict. The legislation terminated the state of war between Germany and the Allied Powers, which, in the main, consisted of Russia, Serbia, France, the United Kingdom, Italy, Belgium and the United States of America. The Versailles Treaty served to humiliate the German Empire to no small extent. Germany lost much of its prewar territory, saw its armed forces shrink, and had to pay reparations to the allied powers. The Versailles pact further demeaned the Germans by insisting they accept responsibility for the war itself.

A new parliamentary government named the Weimar Republic assumed leadership in Germany after the demise of the nation's World War I regime. The new leadership, however, failed to address adequately, the burdensome effects of runaway inflation, high unemployment, and a shaky economy. The worldwide depression triggered by the 1929 New York stock exchange crash further accentuated the foregoing indicators of economic chaos. In addition, the state of affairs in the republic whereby class and political differences grew among the members of a disillusioned populace, added to the woes of the new government.

January 30, 1933, was an ill-fated day. It was the day President Paul von Hindenburg named Adolf Hitler, the leader of the National Socialist German Workers (Nazi) Party, chancellor of Germany. Hitler's party had performed well enough in the general elections of 1932 for him to secure the appointment as the country's political leader. The Nazi Party capitalized on the tense, and probably incendiary socio-political climate to entice the country's electorate to support its revolutionary agenda, which revolved around victimizing the incumbent and weak Weimar government, and targeting the nation's Jews, whom the Nazis unwarrantedly and brazenly blamed for Germany's misfortunes. The Nazis also sought to antagonize the communists who, up to the time of the 1932 elections, comprised a strong political force in the country.

The Nazi Propaganda Machine

One of the Nazis' primary tools in swaying public sentiment against the Jews in Germany and other European nations was its propaganda mechanism. The Nazis cunningly utilized the newspaper *Der Sturmer* (The Stormer/Attacker/Striker) to promulgate animosity and disdain for people of Jewish ancestry. Der Sturmer was a weekly German tabloid-format newspaper published by Julius Streicher, the leader of a regional branch of the Nazi Party, from 1923 to the end of World War II. It was a significant part of Nazi propaganda and was putridly anti-Semitic.[6]

The front page of every issue of the newspaper carried the nauseating slogan, "The Jews are our misfortune!" The publication regularly mocked Jews and depicted them as repulsive and animalistic. Nazi propaganda portrayed Jews as bacteria that fed off the host nation (Germany), poisoned its culture, seized its economy, and enslaved its workers.[7] Dehumanized images of Jews already in use by anti-Semites became part of the new government's propaganda repertory. Among such depictions of Jews were parasites, leeches, devils, rats, bacilli, locusts, vermin, spiders, blood-suckers, lice, and poisonous worms.[8] The Der Sturmer newspaper became widely popular and by 1938 boasted a readership of about a half million subscribers.

Adolf Hitler, during his election campaign, relented somewhat on his attacks on Jews, and instead emphasized the importance of national unity and formidable leadership. Hitler adopted the appearance of a peacemaker during the electoral process. However, he swiftly reverted to being an anti-Semitic demagogue after securing the office of the leader of Germany.

Hitler and the Nazis sought after full control of the Reichstag, the German parliament after he became chancellor. The Nazis, aided and abetted by the governmental means at their disposal, proceeded to antagonize and harass the members of the other political parties in an effort to crush all opposition. Party leaders were put in jail and political meetings outlawed. A fire destroyed the Reichstag building on February 27, 1933, while the election campaign was underway. Many people felt the Nazis were responsible for the conflagration, but Hitler somehow succeeded in having blame cast on the communists. Consequently, the German ruler garnered more votes for his party.

German democracy effectively ended with the so-called conviction of the Communists for the Reichstag fire. Hitler immediately legislated sweeping social and political changes ostensibly aimed at controlling the Communists, but that were oppressive measures tailored to asphyxiate all opposition to the Nazi regime. The Nazis forbade people to assemble and took away their rights to privacy. They also essentially outlawed freedom of the press and the freedom of expression. Hitler and the Nazi Party subsequently garnered nearly 44 percent of the vote at the March 5, 1933, general elections and bolstered by an additional eight percent of the Conservative vote, secured a majority position in the government.

The Rise of Nazism

The March 23, 1933, Enabling Act empowered Adolf Hitler to pursue his dictatorial agenda proactively. The Nazi propaganda machine attained full throttle and silenced all critics of Hitler's march toward dictatorship, while sophisticated police and military force emerged unhindered.

The *Sturmabteilung* (SA, Stormtroopers), functioned as the original parliamentary wing of the Nazi Party. The organization helped the Nazis in no small way to undermine the German democratic establishment and played a significant role in Hitler's rise to power in the 1920s and 1930s. The Stormtroopers undertook numerous pursuits of intimidation and destabilization of the opponents of the Nazi Party. They provided protection for Nazi rallies and assemblies, disrupted the gatherings of competitor organizations, fought against the paramilitary units of opposing parties, especially the Red Front Fighters League (*Rotfrontkampferbund*) of the Communist Party of Germany (KPD), and persecuted Slavic and Romani citizens, unionists and Jews. Ernst Roehm, an early Nazi Party member and close friend of Adolf Hitler, was a co-founder of the SA.

Leaders of the *Reichswehr* (the German Armed Forces), along with Hermann Göering, Joseph Goebbels, and senior officers of the Gestapo and the SD, who viewed the vast number of SA members as an existential threat, persuaded Hitler to believe that Ernst Roehm's SA posed a serious conspiratorial threat that required a harsh and swift resolution. [9] The SD fabricated information about an assassination plot on Hitler's life and lied about an SA scheme to assume power. [10] Additionally, reports reached the SD and Gestapo that the vulgarity of the SA's behavior was damaging the party and was even making anti-Semitic conduct seem less palatable. [11]

The *Sturmabteilung* (SA) effectively ceased to exist after Hitler ordered the "blood purge" of 1934. The event became known as the Night of the Long Knives (die Nacht der langen Messer) or, in Germany, the Rohm Putsch, whereby the Reichswehr murdered up to 200 people.[12] The "blood purge" took place in Nazi Germany from June 30 to July 2, 1934. The brutal crushing of the SA and its leadership sent a clear message to everyone that opposition to Hitler's regime could be fatal. [13] It struck fear across the Nazi leadership as to the tangible concern of the reach and influence of Heinrich Himmler's (see below) intelligence collection and policing powers.[14]

The *Schutzstaffel* (SS), a major paramilitary organization that served as Hitler's personal bodyguard (see below), superseded the *Sturmabteilung* (SA), although the latter was not formally dissolved until the Third Reich's eventual submission to the Allied Powers in 1945.

The Schutzstaffel (SS) was an organization that began as a small guard unit known as the *Saal-Schutz* (Hall Protection), which comprised of NSDAP volunteers who provided security for party meetings in Munich.[15] Heinrich Himmler, a leading officer of the Nazi Party and later Commander of the Replacement Army and General Plenipotentiary for administration of the entire Third Reich, joined the *Schutzstaffel* in 1925 and subsequently transformed the unit into Nazi Germany's foremost agency of surveillance and terror within Germany and German-occupied Europe during the Second World War.

The *Schutzstaffel* (SS) consisted of two principal factions, i.e. the *Allgemeine* SS (General SS) and the *Waffen* SS (Armed SS). The *Allgemeine* SS enforced the racial policies of Nazi Germany and carried out general policing activities, while the *Waffen* SS encompassed special combat units within Nazi Germany's military. The *Schutzstaffel* SS was responsible, more than any other Nazi group, for the genocidal annihilation of an estimated 5.5 to 6 million Jews in the Holocaust.[16] It's members was responsible for many war crimes and crimes against humanity during World War II.

The *Gestapo* (Geheime Staatspolizei) or the Secret State Police, was the official secret police of Nazi Germany and German-occupied Europe. Hermann Goering, the German politician, military leader and a leading member of the Nazi Party, created the *Gestapo* in 1933. Most people considered Goering the second most powerful man in Germany after he helped Adolf Hitler ascend to Germany's highest political office in the same year. Goering passed the mantle of leadership to the SS national leader Heinrich Himmler in 1934.

The *Sicherheitsdienst (full title Sicherheitsdienst des Reichsfuhrers SS, or SD)*, was the intelligence agency of the SS and the Nazi Party in Nazi Germany. The unit emerged in 1931 as a secret branch of the Nazi Party. The organization was the first Nazi Party group established and was essentially a sister unit to the Gestapo, which the SS infiltrated heavily after 1934. Reinhard Heydrich, the Sicherheitsdienst's first director, purposed to subject every individual within the Third Reich's jurisdiction to continuous supervision.[17] His objectives included the control and destruction of political opponents and the intimidation of the general population.

Heydrich was second in importance to Heinrich Himmler in the Nazi SS organization. He was nicknamed "The Blond Beast" by the Nazis and

"Hangman Heydrich" by other people. Heydrich had insatiable greed for power. He was a cold, calculating manipulator without human compassion, and was one of the leading planners of Adolf Hitler's "Final Solution"—the Nazi plan to exterminate the entire Jewish population of Europe.

Toward the end of 1934, Adolf Hitler had assumed absolute control of Germany, and his campaign of unprecedented depravity and cold-bloodedness against the Jews especially had reached unbelievable heights. The formidable German military and police infrastructure enabled the Nazis to hound and persecute Jews and other opponents at will and without reservation.

The Nazis accused the Jews of corrupting a pure German culture with their "foreign" and "mongrel" attitude and influence. The German propaganda machine portrayed Jews as wicked and cowardly, while they represented Germans as honest, hardworking and brave. The Nazis also accused the Jews of weakening the country's economy through their prominence in various fields of endeavor such as finance, commerce, literature, theater, and the arts. A government-sponsored misinformation scheme gave rise to racial anti-Semitism, which was markedly dissimilar to the religious anti-Semitism fostered by the traditional Christian Church for many centuries prior.

The differentiation between the standpoints notwithstanding, history records evidence of an indirect collaboration between Nazi oriented racial and political anti-Semitism and traditional Christian anti-Semitism. Contemptible, misguided religionists and German supremacists conflated their abhorrent viewpoints during World War II years to target and persecute Jews. For instance, four hundred years after its initial publication, the Nazi Party displayed the famed German theologian Martin Luther's publication *On the Jews and their Lies* during Nuremberg rallies, and the city of Nuremberg presented a first edition of Luther's work to Julius Streicher, the editor of the Nazi newspaper Der Sturmer. The periodical (Der Sturmer) described *On the Jews and Their Lies* as the most radically anti-Semitic tract ever published.[18]

THE BANISHMENT OF JEWS FROM SOCIETY

The Nazis perceived themselves as superior to other races and ethnicities. Leni Yahil, nee Leni Westphal, the accomplished German-born Israeli historian states:

The word "Aryan," derived from the study of linguistics, which started in the eighteenth century and at some point determined that the Indo-Germanic (also known as Aryan) languages were superior in their structures, variety, and vocabulary to the Semitic languages that had evolved in the Near East. This judgment led to a certain conjecture about the character of the peoples who spoke these languages; the conclusion was that the "Aryan" peoples were likewise superior to the "Semitic ones."[19]

The Nazis deviously enmeshed their racial theories about "Aryan" supremacy with the revolutionary theories of the British naturalist Charles Darwin, namely, Darwin's "survival of the fittest" hypothesis, to justify their maltreatment of the Jews. Germans, they assumed, were the strongest and the fittest and destined to subjugate and govern others, while Jews, being weak and racially deficient, faced certain extinction. Judah Rumney, the Polish philosopher, as early as 1939, alluded to Darwin's influence on Hitler, and the Italian dictator Benito Mussolini as well. Rumney stated:

Both Mussolini and Hitler avow their adherence to this philosophy of war. Hitler in "Mein Kampf" argues that the world must be ruled according to the natural law of the survival of the fittest: In constant war, mankind has become great – in eternal peace it must perish.[20]

The perennial controversy surrounding the scientific validity of evolutionary theory, and the author's staunch position as a grassroots, Biblical Christian and pro-creationist notwithstanding, it is easy to see demagogues like Hitler and Mussolini, and other social Darwinists as well, mistakenly applying Darwin's biological theories to social phenomena. Hitler's misrepresentation of Darwin's ideas, especially his interpretation of evolutionary theory's premise of "natural selection" and its relation to the struggle for existence among different species of living things, facilitated to a considerable extent, the Nazis' horrendous "final solution" plot. Hitler's construal of the "survival of the fittest" premise encompassed, in his warped, hate-fueled mind, the annihilation of all opponents, "inferiors," and those who did not support his twisted agenda.

As persecution of the Jews increased exponentially, the Nazis enacted legislation to restrict Jewish participation and involvement in public, social, and even private spheres of activity. Jews had to relinquish professional jobs, give up their businesses and property, and vacate the public school system. The Nazis burned books written by Jews and terrorized the latter in every echelon of society. In due course, the quality of the lives of Jews degenerated to the bottommost plateau of fear, deprivation, and suffering.

The *Nuremberg Laws* announced on September 15, 1935, at an annual Nazi party rally, were among the most oppressive and restrictive mandates aimed at excluding Jews from German society. Unanimously enacted by the Reichstag, [21] the Laws embodied two distinct sets of legislations i.e., the *Reich Citizenship Law* and the *Law for the Protection of German Blood and German Honor.* The legislation concretized many of the racial theories that underpinned Nazi ideology. The Nazis deprived German Jews of their rights to citizenship, and Jews instead became "subjects" of Hitler's Reich.

The *Law for the Protection of German Blood and German Honor* prohibited marriages and extramarital intercourse between Jews and Germans and forbade the employment of German females under 45 in Jewish households. The *Reich Citizenship Law* declared that only those of German or related blood were eligible to be Reich citizens; the remainder were state subjects, without citizenship rights.[22] This law was effectively a means of stripping Jews, Roma, and other "undesirables" of their legal rights and their citizenship.[23] Over the ensuing years, the Nazis legislated 13 ancillary laws that further marginalized the Jewish community in Germany.[24] Jewish families, for instance, were ineligible to submit claims for subsidies for large families, and Jews could not transact business with Aryans.[25]

Many thousands of Jews fled Germany and settled in countries such as Belgium, Czechoslovakia, England, France, and Holland. European Jews found it more difficult to relocate to other lands. Authorities subjected Jews worldwide to harsh immigration procedures and delimited quotas, and forced them to wait for inordinately long periods of time before allowing them to immigrate to countries where they could avoid persecution.

The *Evian Conference* was held in Evian, France in July 1938 after Germany annexed Austria in March of that year. US President Franklin D. Roosevelt called for an international conference to promote the emigration of Austrian and German Jewish refugees and create an international organization to address the growing refugee problem. The meeting yielded no resolution to the dilemma at hand. Hitler consequently concluded most countries were reluctant to offer assistance to the Jews who sought to escape from Germany and its occupied territories. He became emboldened to pursue his anti-Jewish agendas without reservation.

Kristallnacht (The Night of Broken Glass)

On November 7, 1938, in Paris, a seventeen-year-old German/Polish Jewish refugee named Herschel Grynszpan shot and killed the third secretary of the German embassy, Ernst vom Rath. The Nazis, in response to Ernst vom Rath's shooting, or as many historians posit, in expediting a pre-planned pogrom of the Jews, bared to the world at large, a precursor of one of history's vilest and darkest atrocities that would take place some years later—the Holocaust.

On November 9, 1938, the Nazis unleashed a night of organized terror, called *Kristallnacht*, or the *Night of the Broken Glass*, during which they burned and destroyed Jewish businesses, homes, and synagogues, and mercilessly beat Jewish men, women and children, killing some of them. Local police, acting upon prior directives, did not intervene as the Nazi Stormtroopers carried out their despicable acts. A major objective of the night's events was to arrest as many Jews as possible with a view toward deporting them to concentration camps.

The United States Holocaust Memorial Museum records the following statement about *Kristallnacht* and the manifestation of the callous and insidious nature that was the Nazi mindset.

> *German propaganda minister Joseph Goebbels and other Nazis carefully organized the pogroms. In two days, over 250 synagogues were burned, over 7,000 Jewish businesses were trashed and looted, dozens of Jewish people were killed, and Jewish cemeteries, hospitals, schools, and homes were looted while police and the fire brigades stood by. The pogroms became known as Kristallnacht, the "Night of Broken Glass, for the shattered glass from the store windows that littered the streets.*
>
> *The morning after the pogroms, 30,000 German Jewish men were arrested for the "crime" of being Jewish and sent to concentration camps, where hundreds of them perished. Some Jewish women were also arrested and sent to local jails. Businesses owned by Jews were not allowed to reopen unless they were managed by non-Jews. Curfews were placed on Jews, limiting the hours of the day they could leave their homes.[26]*

The United States Holocaust Memorial Museum notes the following key dates and events relative to the "Night of Broken Glass" or

Kristallnacht. The deep, unbridled hatred for the Jews by the Nazis, and the latter's readiness to give vent to their vile predispositions were startling.

Germany Expels 17,000 Polish Jews—On October 28, 1938, Germany expelled close to 17,000 Polish Jews and forced them across the border into Poland. Polish authorities refused entrance to the Jews. The majority of the deportees ended up in a no-mans-land between the two countries, near a place called Zbaszyn. The parents of Hershel Grynszpan, a 17-year-old Polish Jew living in Paris, France, were among the deportees.

Young Polish Jew Shoots German Diplomat—On November 7, 1938, Herschel Grynszpan shot Ernst vom Rath, a diplomat attached to the German embassy in Paris. Grynszpan apparently acted out of despair over the fate of his parents, who the Nazis banished, along with other Polish Jewish deportees, to a no-mans-land between Germany and Poland. The Nazis used the shooting to fan anti-Semitic fervor, claiming that Grynszpan did not act alone, but was part of a wider Jewish conspiracy against Germany. Vom Rath died two days later.

German Leaders Encourage Radical Response—German propaganda minister Joseph Goebbels delivered a passionate anti-Semitic speech to the Nazi party faithful on November 9, 1938, in Munich. The party members were commemorating the abortive Nazi Putsch of 1923 (Adolf Hitler's first attempt to seize power). After the speech, Nazi officials ordered the Stormtroopers (SA) and other party formations to attack Jews and to destroy their homes, businesses, and houses of worship. The violence against Jews lasted into the morning hours of November 10 and became known as Kristallnacht—the "Night of Broken Glass." The Nazis killed several dozen Jews, arrested tens of thousands more and sent them to concentration camps.

The Nazi state imposed a fine of one billion *Reichsmarks* (an equivalent of $400 million US in 1938) on the Jewish community in Germany. Authorities ordered Jews to clean up and make repairs after the pogrom and barred them from collecting insurance for the damages. Instead, the state confiscated payments owed by insurers to Jewish property holders. In the aftermath of the pogrom, the Nazis systematically excluded Jews from all areas of public life in Germany.[27]

Reinhard Heydrich, second in command of the SS after Heinrich Himmler, worked in consort with Joseph Goebbels to orchestrate the dreadful events of *Kristallnacht*. A 2009 *History.com* article cites the following statistics reported by Heydrich to Hermann Goering, a prominent Nazi Party leader.

> In Heydrich's report to Hermann Goering after Kristallnacht, the (following) damage was assessed: "...815 shops destroyed, 171 dwelling houses set on fire or destroyed...119 synagogues were set on fire, and another 76 completely destroyed...20,000 Jews were arrested, 36 deaths were reported and those seriously injured were also numbered at 36...
>
> ...The extent of the destruction was actually greater than reported. Later estimates were that as many as 7,500 Jewish shops were looted, and there were several incidents of rape...[28]

The warped mentality of those who subscribed to Nazi ideology came to the fore through the expulsion of the Nazi rapists from the Nazi Party and their subsequent indictment—a relatively harsh sentence given the fact that the Nazis who murdered Jews during Kristallnacht avoided interrogation and/or trial because they were merely following orders. The racial laws that governed Nazi attitude and behavior forbade sexual intercourse between Jews and Gentiles. Transgression of such a law, as perverse as the decree was, amounted to a crime greater than murder! The Nazi rapists were not put on trial for the offense of rape, which was criminality that warranted prosecution, but because they had sex, albeit forcibly, with women of an "inferior" or "lesser" race.

THE "JEWISH QUESTION" & THE "FINAL SOLUTION"

The *Jewish Question* is a term that refers to the discussion of a wide range of issues pertaining to the status and treatment of Jews in European society and elsewhere. The debate revolved around the civil, legal, national and political status of Jews as a minority, particularly within Europe in the eighteenth and nineteenth centuries. Drawing from the liberal principles championed during the *Age of Enlightenment* (1715-1789), and the radical social and political ideas that hallmarked the *French Revolution* (1789-1799), intellectuals within the socio-political arenas of Western and Central Europe sought to devise strategies to address the implications germane to the Jewish presence in the region. Issues at hand included Jewish quotas and segregation, Jewish assimilation, Jewish emancipation, and Jewish enlightenment.

Prominent American author and Holocaust historian Lucy S. Dawidowicz, in her book *The War Against the Jews*, opines that the term

"Jewish Question," as interpreted in Western Europe, was a neutral expression for the negative attitude toward the apparent and persistent singularity of the Jews as a people against the background of rising political nationalism and new nation-states. Dawidowicz writes that "the histories of Jewish emancipation and European anti-semitism are replete with proffered 'solutions to the Jewish question.'" [29] The phrase "the Jewish Question" was bandied around since the 1880s with anti-Semitic connotations. Also, proponents and adversaries of the establishment of an autonomous Jewish homeland or a sovereign state expediently utilized the pros and cons of the "Jewish Question" over many decades to support their propositions for possible resolutions to the contentious issue.

Adolf Hitler, the Nazi dictator and Chancellor of Germany during World War II, thought he knew of a *Final Solution* to the Jewish Question!

On January 20, 1942, senior government officials of Nazi Germany and SS leaders participated in a conference in the Berlin suburb of Wannsee. The purpose of the meeting, convened at the behest of the director of the Reich Main Security Office SS—*Obergruppenfuhrer* Reinhard Heydrich, was to secure the cooperation of the administrative leaders of various government departments in the implementation of a final solution to the Jewish question. The "solution" called for the deportation of all Jews who resided in German-occupied Europe to Poland, where they would be systematically exterminated. During the meeting, Heydrich outlined plans for the Nazis to gather European Jews from east to west and transport them to extermination or death camps in the occupied (General Government) region of Poland.

The persecution of European Jews increased exponentially after the German invasion of Poland in September 1939. The indiscriminate killing of men, women, and children, however, began in June 1941 after the start of *Operation Barbarossa* against the Soviets, whereby the Nazis, prodded by ideological fixation, sought to conquer the Western Soviet Union in order to repopulate the land with Germans.

On July 31, 1941, Hermann Goring, one the Nazi Party's highest-ranking leaders, authorized Reinhard Heydrich via written diktat to prepare and submit a plan for a "total solution to the Jewish question" in territories under German control and to coordinate the participation of the various government branches. At the January 20, 1942, Wannsee conference, Heydrich revealed that after the completion of the mass deportation of European Jews, the SS would assume full charge of the exterminations.

Although the Nazis murdered members of national and ethnic groups besides Jews, such as Soviet prisoners of war, Polish intellectuals, gypsies, and Romanis, they marked only the Jews for systematic slaughter. Jews were to receive "Special Treatment" (*Sonderbehandling*), whereby the Nazis would use poisonous gas to kill men, women, and children methodically. Records retrieved from the Auschwitz-Birkenau death camp note the cause of death of Jews who died through gassing as "SB," the first two letters of the two German words for "Special Treatment." The Auschwitz-Birkenau Memorial and Museum estimates that German authorities sent 1.3 million people, 1.1 million of them Jewish, to the camp during its existence.[30]

The *Final Solution* culminated in the *Holocaust* (1942-1945), whereby ninety percent of Polish Jews, and two-thirds of the Jewish population of Europe, met their deaths.[31]

HITLER'S GHETTOS, CONCENTRATION CAMPS, AND EXTERMINATION CAMPS

The Nazis, after they invaded Poland in 1939, set up *ghettos* across occupied Europe in order to segregate and confine Jews, and Gypsies in some instances, into small areas of certain towns and cities. Such a strategy enabled the Nazis to monitor the activities of the Jews closely and contributed toward the latter's exploitation. A major objective of establishing ghettos was to prevent Jews from living amongst Germans. Nazi ideology taught that Germans belonged to a superior Aryan race while Jews originated from inferior stock. Jews, should they live amongst Germans, would contaminate and degrade their Aryan superiors. The Nazis also felt that the Jews, faced with the appalling living conditions in the ghettos, would fall sick and perish.

Ghettos were extremely crowded and unsanitary. The chronic lack of food, water, fuel shortages, and severe winter weather resulted in repeated outbreaks of disease and sickness, and a high mortality rate. Housing units were unheated during winter, and food rationed whereby Ghetto residents received much lower allocations than Poles and Germans, with Germans receiving the highest allocations by far. Jews in the ghettos had to wear identifying badges or armbands with a yellow Star of David. Jews living in the ghettos performed forced labor for the German Reich.

Holocaust historians make mention of several types of ghettos, including *open ghettos*, *closed ghettos*, *work ghettos*, *transit ghettos*, and *destruction ghettos*.[32] Ghettos in Nazi-occupied Europe, especially in Poland, often had barbed-wire fences, or carried gates. The Nazis established the first ghetto in Lodz, Poland, on February 8, 1940, into which the Nazis forced almost one-third of the city's total population or about 155,000 Jews.

The *Warsaw Ghetto* was the most populated ghetto in Poland. It was home to over 400,000 Jews, who occupied an area of only 1.3 square miles or 3.4 kilometers. It housed an average of 7.2 individuals per room, who subsisted on rationed food.[33] The Nazis deported Jews from the Warsaw Ghetto to Nazi camps and mass-killing centers. In the summer of 1942, at least 254,000 Ghetto residents traveled to the Treblinka extermination camp during *Großaktion Warschau* under the guise of "resettling in the East" over the course of the summer.[34] Historians estimate the death toll among the Jewish inhabitants of the Warsaw Ghetto to be at least 300,000 killed by bullet or gas,[35] and about 92,000 who died from rampant hunger and hunger-related diseases, the Ghetto uprising, and during the final destruction of the Ghetto.[36, 37]

The Warsaw ghetto was the scene where, in 1942, the largest ghetto uprising took place. Other major ghettos were located in Poland at Krakow, Bialystok, Lvov, Lublin, Vilna, Czestochowa, Kovno in Lithuania, and Minsk in Belarus.

The ghettos served another purpose—one with cruel and iniquitous intent, in addition to the aforementioned objectives. They represented round-up centers that facilitated the assemblage of large numbers of ill-fated Jews who the Nazis later would send to extermination or death camps. Viewed from the foregoing perspective, scholars determine that many of the later ghettos existed only for brief periods of time as the Nazis systematically destroyed the ghettos after deporting their Jewish occupants to forced-labor and extermination camps with the implementation of Hitler's "Final Solution" in 1942. A further heartrending reality of life in the ghettos was the compulsory function of Nazi-appointed Jewish councils and Jewish monitoring police to facilitate the deportation of Jews to extermination or death camps.

Nazi Germany maintained *concentration camps* (*Konzentrationslager,* KZ or KL) throughout the territories it occupied and controlled prior to and during the Second World War. The Dachau concentration camp in Germany, set up in 1933 after Adolf Hitler became Chancellor and his Nazi party acquired control over the country's police force, was the first of its kind.

At the outset, the Nazis used the camps to detain and torture political opponents and union organizers, and contained around 45,000 prisoners.[38] Heinrich Himmler's SS took full control of the police and the concentration camps throughout Germany in 1934–35 and expanded the role of the camps to hold so-called "racially undesirable elements," such as Jews, criminals, homosexuals, and Romanis.[39] The number of people in the camps, which had fallen by then to 7,500, grew again to 21,000 by the start of World War II and peaked at 715,000 in January 1945.[40]

In the aftermath of World War II, when the Allied forces entered concentration camps at Dachau, Bergen-Belsen, Mauthausen, Gross-Rosen, Jasenovac, Plaszow, Buchenwald, Sachsenhausen, Auschwitz, and other camps in Germany and Europe, the world was stunned by the images that evinced the stark brutality and evil of Adolf Hitler's Nazis. People maimed and emaciated, but still alive, lay alongside those who were dead. Many were virtual skeletons *(Muselmanner)*. The scenes were heartrending and confirmed the merciless practice by the Nazis to imprison people who were not of the so-called superior "Aryan" race, and mistreat, torture and kill them.

The Allied forces liberated the camps between 1944 and 1945. The lead editors of the *Encyclopedia of Camps and Ghettos* (1933-1945) of the United States Holocaust Memorial Museum, Geoffrey Megargee and Martin Dean, cataloged some 42,500 Nazi ghettos and camps throughout Europe, spanning German-controlled areas from France to Russia and Germany itself, which were in operation from 1933 to 1945. They reckon that 15 to 20 million people died and/or were prisoners at the sites.[41]

A *concentration camp* differed from an extermination camp. Extermination camps served the specific purpose of murdering Jews and other targeted groups of people en masse (see below). The foregoing observation notwithstanding, numerous thousands of people lost their lives in concentration camps. The Nazis subjected inmates of concentration camps to rigorous forced labor, cruel mistreatment, starvation, sickness, and random executions. While more than three million Jews lost their lives in extermination or death camps, several hundred thousand perished in concentration camps in Germany and Nazi-occupied European countries. The Nazis classified concentration camps according to purpose and function i.e. forced labor camps, work and reformatory camps, prisoner of war (POW) camps, transit camps, police camps, women camps, and ghetto camps.

Initially, the inmates of concentration camps comprised of political adversaries of the Nazi regime. Later, other people such as Jews, gypsies, and criminals became inmates as the Nazis intensified their efforts to promote and uphold their racial ideology of Aryan exclusivity and supremacy. The fact that law-abiding people i.e., Jews, gypsies and other special interest groups had to live amongst criminal elements in concentration camps was of little importance to the Nazis, who relegated anyone who did not support their insidious agenda of hate and persecution to a status of a criminal against Nazism anyway. Hitler and his followers considered Jews inherently undesirable and proscribed them from joining the ranks of the Aryan "super race," even if, as seldom as it happened, they indicated some sort of allegiance or willingness to embrace Nazism.

The Reichstag Fire Decree of February 28, 1933, empowered the Nazis' to detain people and hold them in "protective custody" (*Schutzhaft*). The legislation served as a launching pad for an organized and centrally administered concentration camp system, which fell under the jurisdiction of the notorious leader of the SS and the German police, Heinrich Himmler.

Life in a concentration camp was painstakingly protracted and arduous. Inmates usually occupied overcrowded barracks and slept in undersized "bunk beds." *Forced labor camps* were especially unbearable, whereby inmates performed difficult physical tasks for 12 hours a day. They wore rags, were underfed, and continuously faced the risk of corporal punishment. Residents who were old, sick, or otherwise incapable of enduring the cruel, laborious pace of a forced labor camp died horribly as the Nazis gassed, injected or gunned them down. Some of the pitiable, defenseless souls became the subjects of horrible pseudo-scientific experiments and often died in the process. The term *"Muselmanner,"* mentioned earlier, referred to a concentration camp inmate who was so undernourished that he or she, although alive, resembled a living skeleton. A Muselmanner's existence was painful and lingering, and death often was a welcome release.

Forced labor was a key stratagem of the Nazis' overall plan in dealing with the "Jewish problem," and also a means through which the concentration camps remained economically viable, especially after the outbreak of World War II when the Nazi war effort required heavy fiscal funding. As the war progressed and Adolf Hitler and other Nazi leaders devised a "Final Solution to the Jewish Question," the Germans exterminated Jews in increasing numbers. The role of Jewish concentration camp inmates as forced laborers ironically diminished as more and more of them perished in gas chambers or from execution. Additionally, in a scheme to help ensure the escalated killing of Jews, the Nazis introduced a sinister and inhuman directive in 1941 that stipulated Jewish laborers should be "worked to death."

Historians mention the existence during World War II of a total of 22 main concentration camps (*Stamlager*) and approximately 1,200 affiliate camps. In addition, thousands of smaller camps were strewn across

German-controlled Europe. While an entirely accurate count is beyond computation, scholars estimate that at least 500,000, and maybe as many as 750,000 people died as a result of slave labor, starvation and sickness in Nazi concentration camps during 1933 to 1945. The National WWII Museum (New Orleans) volunteers the following statistics about inmate mortality in Nazi concentration camps during the Second World War. The list is not an exhaustive one, and details relate only to major camps.

Dachau (Germany) Labor Camp – 200,000 inmates; 32,000 deaths; first German concentration camp, established in 1933

Buchenwald (Germany) Labor Camp – 250,000 inmates; 56,000 deaths; the largest concentration camp in Germany

Mauthausen (Austria) Labor Camp – 195,000 inmates; 95,000 deaths; included more than 50 sub-camps

Bergen-Belsen (Germany) Collection Point - 70,000 deaths

Flossenberg (Germany) Labor Camp – 100,000 inmates; 30,000 deaths

Dora-Mittelbau (Germany) Labor Camp - 60,000 inmates; 20,000 deaths; provided slave labor for German V-2 rocket production

Gross-Rosen (Germany – Poland today) Labor Camp and *Nacht und Nebel* Camp – 125,000 inmates; 40,000 deaths; included up to 60 sub-camps

Ravensbrueck (Germany) Labor Camp for women – 150,000 inmates; 90,000 deaths

Westerbork (Netherlands) Transit Camp – 102,000 Dutch Jews deported to extermination camps

Sachsenhausen (Germany) Labor Camp – 200,000 inmates; 100,000 deaths

Plaszow (Poland) Labor Camp – 150,000 inmates; 9,000 deaths; it was from this camp that German industrialist Oscar Schindler saved 1,200 Jews

Drancy (France) Transit Camp – 70,000 French Jews deported to extermination camps

Theresienstadt (Germany – Czech Republic today) Transit Camp and Ghetto – 140,000 inmates; 35,000 deaths

Stuthof (Poland) Labor Camp – 110,000 inmates; 65,000 deaths; first concentration camp built by Germans outside Germany

Neuengamme (Germany) Labor Camp – 106,000 inmates; 43,000 deaths

Natzweiler- Struthof (France) Labor Camp and *Nacht und Nebel* Camp – 40,000 inmates; 25,000 deaths; the only German-built concentration camp in France (Vichy France controlled the others)

Jasenovac (Yugoslavia – Croatia today) Concentration and Extermination Camp – 100,000 inmates; 100,000 deaths

(Source: The National WWII Museum, New Orleans, By the Numbers: The Holocaust, www.nationalww2museum.org/learn/education/for...by...numbers/holoc aust.html)

During the years 1939-1945, the Nazis utilized *extermination camps* or *death camps* in the genocidal killing of three million Jews; half of the six million Jews annihilated in the Holocaust. The victims of the Holocaust died primarily by gassing and also in mass executions and through extreme work under starvation conditions.[42, 43]

The idea of mass extermination with the use of stationary facilities built exclusively for that purpose was a result of earlier Nazi experimentation with the chemically manufactured poison gas during the secretive Action T4 euthanasia program against hospital patients with mental and physical disabilities.[44] The Nazis adapted, expanded, and applied the technology during the war to unsuspecting victims of many ethnic and national groups. The Jews, however, were the primary targets, accounting for over 90 percent of the extermination camp death toll.[45]

The Germans established the first extermination camp in Chelmno, Poland. Soon after, they constructed three more death camps in Blezec, Treblinka, and Sobibor. There were six extermination camps in total, all in occupied Poland. The remaining camps were located at Auschwitz-Birkenau and Majdanek. The principal objective behind the construction of the six death camps in Poland was to murder people, especially Jews, *en masse*. There were at least two death camps outside Poland i.e. Jungfernhof in Latvia and Maly Trostinets in Byelorussia. The Nazis built the Polish extermination camps within a relatively short time. The camps at Chelmno, Belzec, Treblinka, Sobibor, Auschwitz-Birjenau, and Majdanek all became operational from December 1941 to December 1942. The camps stood near railway lines in inconspicuous, rural areas in the General Government region of occupied Poland. Such settings were conducive to transporting

152

large numbers of prisoners and reduced the possibility of inquiries by German and international observers.

The extermination camps were much akin to industrial plants and were efficiently organized. The camp at Auschwitz-Birkenau housed advanced gassing facilities and reflected a high level of technology. Two crematoria could be accessed via elevators from the gas chambers underground, where the Nazis killed the Jews and then transported their bodies to the crematoria for incineration.

The most common method of murdering Jews in the extermination camps was by the use of gas chambers. German soldiers herded prisoners into the gas chambers, after which camp officials closed the chamber doors. They then released exhaust gas (in Blezec, Sobibor, and Treblinka) or poison gas in the form Zyclon B or A (in Auschwitz- Birkenau and Majdanek) in the chambers. The use of gassing trucks was another method of killing Jews. At the Chelmno death camp, for instance, the Nazis forced Jews into trucks and then redirected the exhaust fumes into the crowded cabins and suffocated the trapped, helpless occupants.

The extermination camp at Belzec functioned from May 1942 to August 1943. During the time of its operation, 600,000 Jews lost their lives in the camp's gas chambers. The death camp at Sobibor also began its operations in May 1942 and ceased functioning in October 1943. Approximately 250,000 Jews perished in Sobibor's gas chambers. The Treblinka extermination camp functioned from July 1942 to November 1943. As many as 900,000 Jews died at this death camp. The camp at Auschwitz-Birkenau also functioned as a work camp or forced labor facility. Auschwitz-Birkenau was the Nazis' largest killing center and historians estimate that between 1 and 2 million Jews lost their lives there. Nine out of ten of the death camp victims were Jews.

The death camp at Majdanek claimed the lives of between 60,000 and 80,000 Jews. Like the camp at Auschwitz-Birkenau, the camp at Majdanek also functioned as a work camp. The facility began gassing people in October 1942 and ended its operations in the autumn of 1943.

Yet another means of exterminating Jews and other dissident groups of people was by mass shooting. Operation Harvest Festival (*Aktion Erntefest*), which took place at the Majdanek death camp and its sub-camps, was a prime example of heartless Nazi cruelty. Aktion Erntefest took place on November 3 and 4, 1943.[46] The SS, in an undertaking to exterminate the remaining Polish Jews in the Lubin reservation and the Lubin Ghetto within the general Government territory, killed over 43,000 Jews. Virtually the entire Jewish workforce disappeared. [47] *Aktion Erntefest* was the single largest German massacre of Jews during World War II.

Upon arrival at the extermination camps, German SS soldiers and other security personnel confiscated the inmates' clothes and other belongings. Generally, the prisoners were encouraged to think they were relocating to places where living conditions were better and where they could find jobs. Consequently, most of them traveled with whatever items of value they owned. SS soldiers and other extermination camp staff, and even Jewish inmates under direction were known to search the dead bodies of inmates for valuables, including their teeth for gold.

During the last six months of Hitler's rule, as the German armies retreated, the Nazis held "death marches" whereby they forced the remaining concentration camp prisoners to march to locations in occupied territory. Starving and sick Jews had to walk for hundreds of miles. Most of them died or were gunned down along the way.

The death marches often lasted for weeks at a time. Up to 250,000 people died due to the appalling conditions they faced either through marching on foot or being herded into freight cars.[48] Elie Wiesel, Holocaust survivor and winner of the 1986 Nobel Peace Prize, describes in his 1958 book *Night* how he and his father, Shlomo, were forced on a death march from Buna to Buchenwald.[49]

The number of Nazi extermination camp victims was staggering. National WWII Museum (New Orleans) lists the six camps, all in Poland, and estimates of the number of casualties at each location during World War II.

Auschwitz-Birkenau (Poland) – Over 1,000,000 deaths

Belzec (Poland) – 435,000 deaths

Chelmno (Poland) – 150,000 deaths

Majdanek (Poland) – 78,000 deaths

Sobibor (Poland) – 200,000 deaths

Treblinka (Poland) – 870,000 deaths

JEWISH OPPOSITION AND RESISTANCE

The Nazis' relentless onslaught against the Jews severely curtailed the efforts of the latter to oppose and resist their tormentors. The military might of the Germans pitted against men, women, and children who were totally defenseless, and the overbearing social and political pressure exerted by ideologically obsessed "Aryan" supremacists, left the Jews at a pitiable disadvantage on various fronts.

The foregoing observation notwithstanding, the Jews were not entirely without recourse, albeit more often than not in stymied, inconsequential comportment. Merely staying alive under the inhuman living conditions that prevailed in ghettos, concentration camps and labor camps constituted a form of defiance against the Nazis. Trying to observe the rules of basic hygiene amidst widespread unsanitary conditions was also a kind of opposition to Nazi expectation that the Jews would succumb to punishment meted out to them, as was the Jews' steadfast resolve to practice their religious traditions. Still, other means of resistance took the form of attempts by Jews to escape from ghettos and concentration camps. Many who succeeded in fleeing the ghettos and camps resorted to living in forests and mountains. Those who moved out of forested areas had to contend with the residents of adopted locales and partisan groups that were often hostile.

The limited opportunity for physical and/or forceful opposition and resistance did not preclude the Jews from staging occasional armed revolts. Jews engaged in armed challenges in the ghettos of Vilna, Bialystok, Bedzin-Sosnowiec, Cracow, and Warsaw. The uprising in Warsaw, Poland, from August 1, 1944, to October 2, 1944, was the largest single military undertaking by any European resistance unit against the Nazis during World War II.[50]

The *Warsaw Uprising* (Polish: *Powstanie Warszawskie*; German: *Warschauer Aufstand*) was a major offensive by the Polish resistance Home Army (Polish: *Armia Krajowa*) to liberate Warsaw, the capital, and largest city in Poland, from German occupation. A plan was in place for the uprising to overlap with the approach of the Soviet Union's Red Army into the eastern suburbs of the city and the simultaneous retreat of the German forces.[51] The Soviet Army's advance fell short, however, and the Germans were able to regroup and defeat the Polish resistance, destroying the city of Warsaw in the process. The Poles fought for sixty-three days, essentially unassisted by outside allies, especially the Red Army, before falling to the Nazis.

The Warsaw uprising began on August 1, 1944, and was a component of a more extensive plan, *Operation Tempest*. Operation Tempest, sometimes referred in English as *Operation Storm*, was a series of anti-Nazi uprisings conducted during World War II by the Polish Home Army (Armia Krajowa, AK), the dominant force in the Polish resistance.

The principal objective of the Operation Tempest offensive was to seize control of cities and areas occupied by the Germans while they were preparing their defenses against the advancing Soviet Red Army. Polish underground civil authorities planned to assume power before the arrival of the Soviets. The Poles anticipated driving out the German occupiers of their city and participating in the greater battle with Germany and the Axis powers. A secondary objective was to liberate Warsaw and empower the Polish Underground State before the Soviets could descend upon the city and enable the Soviet-backed Polish Committee of National Liberation to take control. Also, the Poles feared the threat of the Germans rounding up their able-bodied men for service in their labor camps. The call for action on August 1, 1944, was in response to directives from Moscow via radio for the uprising to begin.

The Soviet Union's Red Army unexpected inaction and disregard for the Poles' request for help was a major factor in the Poles' crushing defeat. In the initial stages of the uprising, the Poles secured control over most of central Warsaw, but the Soviets ignored their efforts to establish radio contact and refused to advance beyond the city limits. Fierce fighting between the Poles and Germans took place all the while. By September 14, Polish forces under the Soviet high command gained control of the east bank of the Vistula river opposite the locations manned by the resistance fighters, but only 1,200 men managed to reach the west bank and there was no reinforcement by the Red Army. Additionally, although Soviet air support could have been possible after only about five minutes of flying time from a nearby air base, such assistance never materialized. The Soviets' refusal to go to the aid of the Polish resistance fighters fanned allegations that Joseph Stalin, the leader of the Soviet Union, tactically withheld his troops from aiding the Poles and consequently facilitated their downfall.

Scholars suggest that among the reasons Joseph Stalin halted the Soviets from advancing into Warsaw and helping in the Polish uprising, was to hasten the Poles' overthrow and weaken their resistance to eventual Soviet occupation and control of the region. The Hungarian-British author and journalist Arthur Koestler referred to the Soviet attitude during the Warsaw uprising as "one of the major infamies of this war which will rank for the future historian on the same ethical level with Lidice."[52] The *Lidice massacre* was complete destruction of the village of Lidice in the Protectorate of Bohemia and Moravia (now in the Czech Republic) in June 1942 upon orders of Adolf Hitler and *Reichsfuhrer SS* Heinrich Himmler in reprisal for the assassination of Reich Protector Reinhard Heydrich in the late spring of 1942.

The Germans retreated after allied forces, albeit too late to prevent the destruction of Warsaw and considerable loss of life, joined in the uprising. Following are activity dates by some of the allies that participated in the uprising and opposed the Nazis who, by the end of the 63-day battle, left the city of Warsaw in ruins.

Polish Underground State: August 1. 1944 – October 2, 1944

Royal Air Force, including Polish Squadrons: August 4, 1944 – September 21, 1944

US Army Air Force: Only on September 18, 1944

Polish First Army: From September 14, 1944

Soviet Air Force: From September 13, 1944

The casualties of the Warsaw Uprising, as alluded to earlier, were staggering. The following excerpt from an August 2013 article by The New World Encyclopedia details the tragic consequences of the battle.

> ...Losses on the Polish side amounted to 18,000 soldiers killed, 25,000 wounded, and over 250,000 civilians killed, mostly in mass executions conducted by advancing German troops. Casualties on the German side amounted to over 17,000 soldiers killed and 9,000 wounded. During the urban combat – and after the end of hostilities, when German forces acting on Hitler's orders burned the city systematically, block after block—an estimated 85 percent of the city was destroyed.[53]

There were instances of Jewish revolts in the death camps of Sobibor, Treblinka, and Auschwitz. These uprisings were mostly unsuccessful, given the vastly superior military capability of the German forces. Such retaliation, however, was spiritually and psychologically immeasurable, as it instilled hope that one day the Nazis would be defeated.

HOLOCAUST DENIAL AND DISTORTION

Notwithstanding history's solid documentation of the Holocaust, an event of inconceivable hatred, persecution and slaughter, unparalleled up to this day, there are those who, for various ill-judged reasons, deny the mid-twentieth century Nazi genocide of six million European Jews and five million non-Jewish people ever took place. Holocaust denial is the act of denying the genocide of Jews in the Holocaust during World War II.[54]

157

Holocaust deniers ply their craft of disinformation and shamelessness notwithstanding the fact that the tens of thousands of prisoners who survived the Auschwitz-Birkenau death camp were witnesses to the atrocities perpetrated there; even though camp inmates left behind thousands of depositions, accounts, and memoirs, and despite the fact allied forces and researchers retrieved multitudinous quantities of documents, photographs and material objects from the camp. Holocaust deniers essentially attempt to reject the incontrovertible truth that the Nazi extermination/labor camp at Auschwitz-Birkenau was the scene of genocide.

Holocaust deniers claim the Nazis never planned to exterminate the Jews i.e., the "Final Solution to the Jewish Question" was a fabrication, and poison gas chambers in extermination or death camps such as those in Auschwitz-Birkenau, Majdanek, Belzec, Treblinka, Chelmno, and Sobibor never existed. Also, they say Nazi authorities did not use extermination camps and gas chambers to mass murder Jews.[55]

More recent Holocaust denials revolve around the suggestions that the figure of six million Jewish deaths is an exaggeration, and that the actual number of Jews killed was about five hundred to six hundred thousand.[56] Some imprudent deniers even posit that the German-born Jewish child diarist and writer Anne Frank, who documented her life as Jew hiding from the Nazis from 1942 to 1944 during the German occupation of Netherlands, did not maintain a diary, and that "The Diary of a Young Girl" (originally *Het Achterhuis* – The Secret Annex), is a forgery.

While deniers customarily single out the Auschwitz-Birkenau death camp for attention, their proclivity to deny the fact of the Holocaust, the existence of gas chambers, and the truth of the mass annihilation of Jews and others nevertheless broadens to include all the Nazi concentration and extermination camps during the Holocaust years of 1933 to 1945 in Germany and Europe. In other words, denying that the Nazis murdered Jews en masse at Auschwitz-Birkenau is tantamount to suggesting the Germans did not carry out mass killings at any other concentration camp or extermination camp during World War II.

Why do people deny the Holocaust?

Holocaust denial really began with the Nazis themselves, mainly for political reasons, as they sought to evade international opinion and prevent Allied and neutral nations from finding out about the extermination of Jews and other people in German-occupied countries. The Nazis went to great lengths to conceal the truth about mass exterminations from the residents of occupied countries, and even from people in ghettos and prisoners in concentration camps, the latter who often mistakenly felt transportation trips from camps served to relocate them to locations where there were better living and working conditions, but where instead they found death. The siting of concentration and labor camps in remote rural areas also served the intent of keeping people in the dark about the Nazis' clandestine, sinister activities.

Modern-day Holocaust deniers, who are mostly individual dissenters, lend credence to a number of impulsions. Some are simply controversialists who are unmindful of the consequences and repercussions of their actions. Other deniers seek to profit financially from the venture by writing books, implementing Internet websites, and traveling around the world and lecturing to neo-Nazis and other hate groups. Many deniers nurture an obsession with facilitating a dismantling of the State of Israel, which they feel was founded upon sentiment derived from a misrepresentation of the truth about the Holocaust by Jews who courted sympathy from the international community. Still, other Holocaust deniers capitulate to a nauseating desire to revitalize Nazism and redeem the perceived dignity of the "Aryan race" or to present fascism and other radical political movements as acceptable ideologies. The various stimuli notwithstanding, all Holocaust deniers are anti-Semitic to at least a certain extent and are party to a conspiratorial mindset and a willingness to portray Jews as repulsive, greedy and untrustworthy, and as unconscionable deceivers who blame the Nazis unfairly for the crime of genocide.

Holocaust Denial Exists in Many Parts of the World

Holocaust denial exists worldwide, including in Europe, the United States of America and Canada. The movement currently experiences exponential growth in the Middle East, where Muslim autocracies utilize the mindset in their unceasing war against Israel, and in the former Soviet Union, where anti-Semitism runs rampant.

The following excerpt from a *Los Angeles Times* December 16, 2006 article by Ayaan Hirsi Ali, an American Somali immigrant who served in the parliament of the Netherlands until early 2006, brings to the fore the intense hatred for Jews, and the bias harbored by the predominantly Muslim populace of Somalia and other African Muslim nations and in the Middle East as well, in connection with the Holocaust.

...My head was reeling from what happened to 6 million Jews in Germany, Holland, France and Eastern Europe...I learned that innocent men, women and children were separated from each other. Stars pinned to their shoulders, transported by train to camps, they were gassed for no other reason than for being Jews...I saw pictures of masses of skeletons, even of kids. I heard horrifying accounts of some of the people who had survived the terror of Auschwitz and Sobibor.

I told my half-sister all this and showed her the pictures in my history book. What she said was as awful as the information in my book. With great conviction, my half-sister cried, 'It's a lie! Jews have a way of blinding people. They were not killed, gassed or massacred. But I pray to Allah that one day all the Jews in the world will be destroyed.'

She was not saying anything new. As a child growing up in Saudi Arabia, I remember my teachers, my mom and our neighbors telling us practically on a daily basis that Jews are evil, the sworn enemies of Muslims, and that their only goal was to destroy Islam. We were never informed about the Holocaust.[57]

In December 2006, when Ayaan Hirsi Ali wrote the forgoing Los Angeles Times article, the incumbent Iranian President Mahmoud Ahmadinejad, at a special conference he called to investigate the Holocaust, publicly denied that the Holocaust ever took place. In the article, Ali expressed shock and dismay at the "silent acquiescence" of Ahmadinejad's denial by mainstream Muslims around the world. Ali lamented the inaction by Muslim leaders in Riyadh, Cairo, Lahore, Khratoum and Jakarta in condemning the Iranian president. He also asked why the 57 members of the Organization of the Islamic Conference were silent on the issue.

The Holocaust denial mindset typified by Middle Eastern Arab and/or Muslim sentiment engenders a form of anti-Semitism that reverberates in the ongoing Israeli/Palestinian conflict. Indeed, there seems to exist an entrenched nexus between Palestinian animosity for the Israelis and Middle Eastern Muslim abhorrence of people of Jewish ancestry. *Israel – Against All Odds (Volume II)* Chapter Two, *The Israeli-Palestinian Conflict* contains a detailed discussion about the Israeli/Palestinian dispute.

The following individuals number among the more notorious Holocaust deniers around the world. There are many others, whose names are not shown here for lack of space.

1. *David Irving* (United Kingdom) – An untrained historian who has no qualms about professing his pro-Nazi sympathies, Irving failed in his libel action against Professor Deborah Lipstadt. In 2000, Penguin books exposed Irving to the world as a racist, anti-Semitic, and far-right polemicist whose work sought to exonerate Adolf Hitler for the crimes of the Nazi regime.

2. *Nick Griffin* (United Kingdom) – The leader of the far-right British National Party whom the courts found guilty of inciting racial hatred.

3. *Robert Faurisson* (France) – Considered by many to be one of the foremost Holocaust deniers, Faurisson spoke on behalf of fellow denier Nick Griffin. French authorities proscribed Faurisson from teaching in the nation's universities for denying the Holocaust.

4. *Albert Szabo* and *Istvan Gorkos* (Hungary) – These men are under judicial investigation in Hungary for denying the Holocaust.

5. *Dariusz Ratajczak* (Poland) – Opole University lecturer fired from his job and put on trial for Holocaust denial. The court dismissed the charges against Ratajczak on the grounds of "negligible social harmfulness."

6. *Fred Leuchter* (USA) – Leuchter produced the 1988 "Leuchter Report" that purported to offer scientific evidence that there were no gas chambers in Auschwitz. Notwithstanding the presentation by Leuchter of a façade of graphs, analyses, and calculations, opponents thoroughly discredited Leuchter's report and proved he fabricated the data.

7. *Mark Weber* (USA) – The director of the Institute for Historical Review (IHR) since 1995. The IHR is perhaps the foremost Holocaust denial organization in the Western world. Weber is a former member of the Nazi National Alliance.

8. *Ernst Zundel* (Germany) – Zundel is one of the world's leading Holocaust deniers. Canadian officials deported Zundel to Germany to stand trial for Holocaust denial. Convicted and imprisoned in Germany, Zundel gained his freedom in 2010.

9. *Gemar Rudolf* (Germany) – Rudolf is a chemist whose publication of the controversial "Rudolf Report" led to his prosecution in 1995. Rudolf subsequently fled to the USA, where he sought asylum. United States authorities denied Rudolf asylum in 2006. The

German government jailed Rudolf upon his deportation from the USA to the country.

10. *Lady Michele Renouf* (France) – Former model turned Holocaust denier Michele Renouf is a close acquaintance of David Irving. She runs her own Telling Films broadcast as a channel for her anti-Semitic tirades. She speaks regularly on the Iranian-owned *Press TV* and sits on the International "Holocaust" Research Committee (IHRC), an Iranian based Holocaust denial undertaking.

11. *Gerd Honsik* (Austria) – Honsik is a leading Holocaust denier and far-right activist, who has been in jail many times. Honsik is the author of "Hitler Innocent" in which he attempts to exonerate Hitler and the Nazis for their murderous deeds.

12. *Dr. Herbert Schaller* (Austria) – Schaller is a prominent Holocaust denier and lawyer who specializes in defending Nazis and "revisionists." Schaller's clients include Ernst Zundel, David Irving, Pedro Vareia and Otto Ernst Remer, the veteran Nazi leader who ruthlessly killed many of the 1944 bomb plot conspirators who tried to kill Adolf Hitler.

Legislation Outlawing Holocaust Denial

In the aftermath of World War II, several European nations enacted legislature geared toward preventing surviving Nazis and neo-Nazis from denying the truth about the horrible crimes committed by Hitler's Nazi regime. Holocaust denial is one such infraction. As a matter of fact, some countries earmark Holocaust denial as an especially objectionable transgression and consider the offense and its promotion a form of racial incitement against Jews.

The undermentioned countries currently prohibit the practice of Holocaust denial. Perpetrators of the crime are subject to prosecution and incarceration—Austria, Belgium, Czech Republic, France, Germany, Lithuania, the Netherlands, Poland, Romania, Slovakia, Spain, Switzerland, and Israel. The United Kingdom and Canada do not specifically proscribe Holocaust denial, but effect general laws to prosecute those who incite hatred. The United States of America's constitution guarantees the right of free speech, irrespective of social, moral or political content. Notwithstanding the nauseating reality of the predilection by some to deny the truth of the Holocaust, the author is inclined to support the American perspective of freedom of expression. Such a right is an indispensable predisposition in any open and civilized society. Choice, not compulsion or coercion, marks a genuine response. This is not to say a frank response may not be unreasoned and/or farcical.

A well-known, definitive legal court case surrounding Holocaust denial was Irving vs Lipstadt (2000) whereby Holocaust denier David Irving (see above) sued Emory University Holocaust scholar Deborah Lipstadt for libel. Lipstadt had made reference to Irving's historical misrepresentation about the Holocaust in her book, *Denying the Holocaust: The Growing Assault on Truth and Memory* (Free Press, 1993). Irving also sued Lipstadt's British publisher, Penguin Books. The trial took place in London, England and lasted ten weeks. The judge decided the case in favor of the defendants, Lipstadt and Penguin Books.

David Irving, in essence, lost the case because of his shameless manipulation of historical facts and his manifestly anti-Semitic disposition. As the case progressed, it was evident that the issues at hand were Irving's inclination to mislead the court, and his deficient research, instead of the truth or its absence thereof as it related to the Holocaust. The presiding judge ruled that David Irving was an anti-Semite, a racist and a falsifier of the historical record.

In what many construed an unlikely source of support for Holocaust victims and Jews around the world in general, the Cuban dictator Fidel Castro, in September 2010, derided the former Iranian President and autocrat Mahmoud Ahmadinejad for denying the Holocaust ever took place. In a CBS News article dated September 7, 2010, Castro advised Ahmadinejad to learn to "understand the 'unique' history of anti-Semitism." The article quoted the South American leader as saying:

> I don't think anyone has been slandered more than the Jews. I would say much more than the Muslims. They have been slandered much more than the Muslims because they are blamed and slandered for everything. No one blames the Muslims for anything.
>
> ...The Jews have lived an existence that is much harder than ours. There is nothing that compares to the Holocaust.[58]

Holocaust Denial Is Unfounded and Unsubstantiated

The fact that many allied nations—countries directly involved in the fight against Nazi Germany during World War II (see above)—instituted Holocaust denial legislation with a view toward prosecuting deniers of the

Nazi regime's atrocities against Jews and non-Jews, is in itself solid indication that the Holocaust did take place.

The term "denial" relates to the ill-advised strategy and methodology of Holocaust deniers to distinguish them from legitimate historians who challenge orthodox interpretations of history through the use of established historical inquiry. Holocaust deniers generally prefer to describe their work as a revisionist undertaking and take offense to any intimation that what they do amounts to a denial of the truth. The foregoing claim notwithstanding, the methodologies of Holocaust deniers are often based on a predetermined conclusion that ignores overwhelming historical evidence to the contrary.[59]

Holocaust denial revolves around the allegation that the Holocaust is an exaggeration or a hoax arising out of a deliberate Jewish conspiracy to further the interest of Jews at the expense of the interests of other peoples. Holocaust denial is representative of anti-Semitic conspiracy, and as alluded to earlier, is illegal in several countries.[60]

Historians point to the fact that after World War II the Jewish population in Eastern Europe had dwindled by about six million, including one and one-half million children. Additionally, the Nazis left a substantial measure of documentation behind, including films and photographs. There even exists footage of aerial surveillance of Nazi extermination camps by allied forces. In 2006, German authorities agreed to make public, the so-called "Holocaust Archives" stored in the north-central German town of Bad Arolsen. The archives presumably contain clues to the fates of 17.5 million people. The 25 kilometers of aged papers include typed lists of Jews, homosexuals and other persecuted groups, files on children born in the Nazi Lebensborn program to breed a master race, and registers of arrivals and departures from concentration camps.

A March 6, 2017 *ThoughtCo* (a reputable Internet-based educational organization) article bared the following excerpts of information on Nazi files about the Holocaust. The title of the article was *Nazi Files on 17.5 million Revealed after 60 Years - 50 Million Pages of Nazi Records Made Public in 2006.*

> *After 60 years of being hidden away from the public, Nazi records about the 17.5 million people—Jews, Gypsies, homosexuals, mental patients, handicapped, political prisoners and other undesirables—they persecuted during the regime's 12 years in power will be open to the public.*

The ITS (International Tracing Service) Holocaust Archive in Bad Arolsen, Germany contains the fullest records of Nazi persecutions in existence. The archives contain 50 million pages, housed in thousands of filing cabinets in six buildings. Overall, there are 16 miles of shelves holding information about the victims of the Nazis.

The documents—scraps of paper, transport lists, registration books, labor documents, medical records, and finally death registers—record the arrest, transportation, and extermination of the victims. In some case, even the amount and size of the lice found on the prisoners' heads were recorded.

This archive contains the famous Schindler's List, with the names of 1,000 prisoners saved by factory owner Oskar Schindler who told the Nazis he needed the prisoners to work in his factory.

Records of Anne Frank's journey from Amsterdam to Bergen-Belsen, where she died at the age of 15, can also be found among the millions of documents in this archive.

The Mauthausen concentration camp's "Totenbuch," or Death Book, records in meticulous handwriting how, on April 20, 1942, a prisoner was shot in the back of the head every two minutes for 90 hours.

The Mauthausen camp commandant ordered these executions as a birthday present for Hitler.

Toward the end of the war, when the Germans were struggling, the record keeping was not able to keep up with the extermination, and unknown numbers of prisoners were marched directly from trains to gas chambers in places like Auschwitz without being registered.[61]

The *International Committee of the Red Cross* (ICRC), after managing the Bad Arolsen archives since 1955, handed them over to an international commission of eleven countries in January of 2013. Experts anticipate that such a strategy could maximize the potential for the proficient academic study of the archives.

Many Holocaust survivors documented their experiences in memoirs and other reports. The USC Shoah (Holocaust) Foundation – *The Institute for Visual History and Education*, formerly *Survivors of the Shoah Visual*

History Foundation, a nonprofit organization dedicated to producing audio-visual interviews with survivors of and witnesses to the Holocaust and other genocides, conducted nearly 52,000 video testimonies between 1994 and 1999 in 32 languages in 56 countries in relation to the Holocaust.[62]

The majority of the video testimonies revolved around the experiences of Jewish survivors, rescuers and aid providers, Sinti and Roma survivors, liberators, political prisoners, Jehovah Witness survivors, war crimes trial participants, eugenic policies survivors, non-Jewish forced laborers, and homosexual survivors.[63]

A salient consideration often overlooked today by those who seek to question the veracity of Holocaust activities is the fact that the Nazis and other Germans themselves never attempted to deny participating in the crimes of which they were accused. In court cases on five continents, such as the Nuremberg, Auschwitz, Frankfurt Auschwitz, Dachau, Belsen, and Neuengamme trials, authorities established a clearly demarcated judicial record of the Holocaust for posterity.

One may ask why the Nazis tried to conceal or destroy evidence of their misdeeds by incinerating and/or burying the countless bodies of murdered Jews to evade the ramifications of international inquiries but left behind the multitudinous millions of documents, pictures, and films stored in the "Holocaust Archives?" Did the Germans neglect to trash the documents and other pieces of information because they did not contain incriminating information about millions of Jews? Consequently, are the claims about the Nazis burning and destroying the remains of Jews and other victims unfounded and untrue? Answers to questions such as the foregoing may not be forthcoming until historians and analysts complete the laborious, intricate task of analyzing the "Holocaust Archives" to an extent that allows the formulation of informed decisions.

Alternatively, one may presume that the Nazis, realizing defeat at the hands of the Allied forces toward the end of the War was imminent, were so preoccupied with disposing of millions of dead bodies so they might escape the rigors of international prosecution and possible condemnation to death, simply ran out of time to direct their attention to the trove of documents and other records of the fates of over seventeen million European people. They had no opportunity to destroy the archived information! Some experts feel the "Holocaust Archives," which evidences the Nazis' penchant for detailed recordkeeping, might have been more extensive if the Nazis had not suspended the exercise after they directed their efforts toward herding Jews and other victims into gas chambers.

The histrionics of Holocaust deniers notwithstanding, the popular consensus of opinion is that research and analysis of the "Holocaust Archives" will confirm the Holocaust did take place during World War II, and that Adolf Hitler and the Nazi regime perpetrated atrocities against Jews and other targeted groups that beforetime were unheard of by way of numerical significance, brutality and inhumanness.

Poland's Holocaust Denial Law

The Polish government enacted a law in February of 2018 that many consider a form of Holocaust denial and even an expression of anti-Semitism. Polish President Andrzej Duda signed the legislation ahead of an assessment of the proposal being undertaken by the country's Constitutional Tribunal. The new law drew much indignation from Israel, the United States and France, and Jewish organizations around the world.

The law makes it illegal to accuse the Polish nation of complicity in crimes committed by Nazi Germany, including the atrocities perpetrated during the Holocaust. Additionally, it becomes a crime to use terms such as "Polish death camps' in reference to the camps that stood in Auschwitz and other locations in Nazi-occupied Poland. Such an infraction incurs a three-year prison sentence.

Jewish groups in Poland expressed deep concern about the safety and fair treatment of people of Jewish ancestry and report that the controversial law is already leading to a growing wave of intolerance, xenophobia, and anti-Semitism.

A statement from Poland's Jewish organizations calling on the government to address the issue with a view toward retracting or overturning the legislation reads as follows.

> We believe this law to be poorly constructed and detrimental to open discussion of history. If Poland's government believes that even sporadic mentions of 'Polish Death Camps' must be criminalized, certainly the rising intolerance and anti-Semitic hatred in our country should be subject to similarly serious measures. Our government possesses the legal instruments to combat hatred but lacks political will. We call upon our politicians to change course.[64]

It is ironic that Holocaust denial is a crime in many countries, especially in Europe, whereas the law enacted recently in Poland makes it illegal to claim or imply that certain aspects of the atrocity, whereby some Poles aided and abetted the unprecedented slaughter of multiple millions of Jews and others, took place. It is a dichotomous perspective that boggles the mind.

In reality, the recent Polish law is simply another example of Holocaust denial and/or a demonstration of anti-Semitic sentiment.

THE END OF THE WAR & THE CULMINATION OF ONE OF HISTORY'S DARKEST ERAS

Allied forces, as they descended on the German army toward the end of World War II, gradually liberated the inmates who remained in Nazi concentration and extermination camps. The Soviet forces freed the prisoners at the Majdanek death and labor camp near Lublin, Poland, in July 1944. The Soviets liberated the inmates of the Auschwitz-Birkenau extermination and labor camp in January 1945, and the British set the Bergen-Belsen (near Hanover, Germany) collection point camp residents free in April 1945. The Americans liberated inmates of the Dachau labor camp in April 1945.

After the war ended, between 50,000 to 100,000 Jewish survivors were scattered across three zones in what was previously German-occupied Europe but then became regions under American, British, and Soviet jurisdiction. The number increased to about 200,000 within a year. The American zone held more than ninety percent of the Jewish *displaced persons* (DP's). The Jewish DP's chose to remain in the newly designated zones and would not return to their former homes i.e. their places of abode under Nazi rule. The memories of their experiences were too painful, and they were fearful of anti-Semitic neighbors who remained behind. The Jewish DP's, therefore, languished in DP camps while authorities made arrangements to relocate them to Palestine, and later Israel, the United States, South America, and other countries. According to Holocaust scholar David S. Wyman, the last DP camp closed in 1957.[65]

The Second World War effectively culminated on September 2, 1945, having begun some six years earlier on September 1, 1939. The Allied Forces overcame the Nazis, and Adolf Hitler ignominiously took his own life. One of the darkest eras in history was over. The aftermath, or the conflagration's lingering, deleterious effects, however, would beleaguer multitudinous millions in Europe and around the world for decades to come.

The undermentioned statistics as they relate to the casualties of World War II are estimates, as would be most such tallies. Retrieved from the website of The Holocaust Memorial Center, 6602 West Maple Road, West Bloomfield, MI 48322, USA, they read like the materialization of a nightmare, which is what the Holocaust really was.

Number of Jews Murdered During the Holocaust (1939 - 1945)

Country	Jewish Victims
Africa	526
Albania	200
Austria	65,000
Belgium	24,387
Czechoslovakia	277,000
Denmark	77
Estonia	4,000
France	83,000
Germany	160,000
Greece	71,301
Hungary	305,000
Italy	8,000
Latvia	85,000
Lithuania	135,000
Luxembourg	700
Netherlands	106,000
Norway	728
Poland	3,001,000
Romania	364,632
Soviet Union	1,500,000
Yugoslavia	67,122
Total Deaths	6,258,673

The tragedy and heartbreak of the Holocaust, and ironically, the human capacity for survival and hope, comes to the fore in the following reflections by (a) Rabbi Yisrael Meir Lau, a Holocaust survivor who was only eight years old in 1945 when allied forces liberated Buchenwald, the Nazi concentration camp in which he was a prisoner since he was seven, and (b) Annelies Marie Frank (Anne Frank), the German-born Jewish child diarist who documented her life hiding from the Nazis from 1942 to 1944 during the German occupation of the Netherlands.

I remember the looks of horror on the faces of the American soldiers when they came in and stared around them.

I was afraid when I saw them.

I crept behind a pile of dead bodies and hid there, watching them warily. Rabbi Herschel Schachter was the Jewish chaplain of the division. I saw him get out of a jeep and stand there, staring at the corpses.

He has often told this story, "...how he thought he saw a pair of living eyes looking out from among the dead."

It made his hair stand on end, but slowly and cautiously he made his way around the pile, and then, he clearly remembers coming face-to-face with me, an eight-year-old boy, wide-eyed with terror.

In heavily-accented American Yiddish, he asked me, 'How old are you, mein kind?' There were tears in his eyes.

'What difference does it make?' I answered, warily. 'I'm older than you, anyway.'

He smiled through his tears and said, 'Why do you think you're older than me?'

And I answered, '...Because you cry and laugh like a child. I haven't laughed in a long time, and I don't even cry anymore. So which one of us is older?' – (Rabbi Yisrael Meir Lau)

Who has inflicted this upon us? Who has made us Jews different from all other people? Who has allowed us to suffer so terribly up till now? It is God that has made us as we are, but it will be God, too, who will raise us up again. If we bear all this suffering and if there are still Jews left, when it is over, then Jews, instead of being doomed, will be held up as an example.

Who knows, it might even be our religion from which the world and all peoples learn good, and for that reason and that reason alone do we have to suffer now. We can never become just Netherlanders, or just English, or representatives of any country for that matter; we will always remain Jews, but we want to, too. – (Annelies Marie Frank – Anne Frank)

The conclusion of *Israel – Against All Odds (Volume I)* and a Preview of the Contents of *Volume (II)*

Jews have been indisputably the most persecuted people in the annals of history.

At the source of Jew-hatred in its myriad forms is anti-Semitism, a sinister and vile mindset that has existed since Old Testament times or for thousands of years. Anti-Semites pervade social, religious, economic and political confines, even mainstream Christianity, and their dislike for people of Jewish ancestry often translate into mindless persecution and slaughter, such as the atrocities perpetrated by the Nazis and their collaborators during the Second World War in the mid-twentieth century whereby over six million Jews met their deaths in the *Holocaust*.

Despite the seemingly insurmountable hardships and challenges Jews have faced throughout the centuries, they persist and even progress in today's societies. They leave their enemies awe-struck at their resilience and their will to survive. It seems as though Israel and Jews, in general, enjoy the auspices of a kind of divine providence.

ISRAEL and Jews around the world continue to progress and stand tall today—against all odds!

In *Israel – Against All Odds (Volume I)*, which covered the history of Anti-Semitism or Jew hatred from its beginnings to the time of the Holocaust during World War II that took place in the mid-twentieth century, the following issues were addressed:

(a) The global hatred of anti-Semitism and its many forms

(b) A brief history of the anti-Semitic mindset

(c) The sin of Christian anti-Semitism

(d) Zionism – The reestablishment, development and protection of the Nation of Israel

(e) The Holocaust

Following is a preview of the contents of *Israel – Against All Odds (Volume II)*

Israel - Against All Odds (Volume II)

Introduction

- Why Iran Cannot Be Trusted

- A Summary of Iranian Sanctions (1979-2017)

- Iranian Sanctions Relief & Sanctions Reinstatement after the JCPOA Enactment

- Appeasing the Murderous Dragon (Iran)

Chapter Five: **The Shocking Truth about the Iranian-American Hostage Exchange**

- The Iranian – American Hostage Exchange

- Ransom Payment for Hostages?

- Lies, Misrepresentation & Inveiglement

- The Nuclear Deal – Iran's Legal Path to the Bomb

- Barack Obama's Legacy Project

Chapter Six: **"Shalom" Will Come**

- The Jewish Ideal of Peaceful Co-existence with Others

- Israel – Besieged from All Fronts

- Israel – Still Standing

- Destiny of the Jews – Judaic Eschatology

- Destiny of the Jews – Christian Eschatology

- Shalom Will Come

Notes

Chapter One

1. https://www.adl.org/news/press-releases/adl-global-100-poll?_ga=1.122160264.2000096670.1457648735%22%20%5C1%20%22.Vw0Wh_krJhE

2. ADL – Anti-Semitism in the USA, April 6, 2017 - In First, New ADL Poll Finds Majority of Americans Concerned About Violence against Jews and Other Minorities, Want Administration to Act.

3. https://www.adl.org/news/press-releases/in-first-new-adl-poll-finds-majority-of-americans-concerned-about-violence

4. Israel 101, 2018– www.standwithus.com; www.cufi.org Page 32 Israel – Small Country. Big Ideas enjoyed by the world.

5. Friedrich Wilhelm Adolph Marr (November 16, 1819-July 17, 1904) was a German agitator and publicist, who popularized the term "antisemitism" (1881). Definition at the Online Etymology Dictionary.

6. Israel 101, 2018 – www.standwithus.com; www.cufi.org Israel's Size Compared to Arab World. Page 2.

7. Harap, Louis (1987). Creative awakening: the Jewish presence in twentieth-century American literature, 1900-1940s. Greenwood Publishing Group. p. 24. ISBN 978-0-313-25386-7

8. United States Holocaust Memorial Museum. "Antisemitism in History: Racial Antisemitism, 18751945." HolocaustEncyclopedia.https://www.ushmm.org/wlc/en/article.php?ModuleId=10007171. Accessed on 3/3/2017.

9. (Segel, BW and Levy, RS. *A Lie and a Libel: The History of the Protocols of the Elders of Zion.* University of Nebraska Press (1995), p. 30. ISBN 0803242433)

10. (Allah in the West: Islamic Movements in America and Europe By Gilles Kepel, Stanford University Press, 1997 pp. 68-69.)

11. (Wim Klooster (University of Southern Maine): Review of Jews, Slaves, and the Slave Trade: Setting the Record Straight. By Eli Faber. Reappraisals in Jewish Social and Intellectual History. William and Mary Quarterly Review of Books. Volume LVII, Number 1. by Omohundro Institute of Early American History and Culture. 2000)

12. Harap, Louis (1987). Creative awakening: the Jewish presence in twentieth-century American literature. Greenwood Publishing Group. p. 76. ISBN 978-0-313-25386-7.

13. Kandel, Eric R. (2007). In search of memory: the emergence of a new science of mind. W. W. Norton & Company. p. 30. ISBN 978-0-393-32937-7.

14. Friedrich Nietzsche, 1886, (0MA 1 475). Nietzsche der philosoph un Politiker, 8, 63, et passim. Ed. Alfred Baeumler, Reclam 1931

15. http://israelforever.org/news/modern_anti-semitism/ Modern Anti-Semitism: Bernard-Henri Levy at the U.N. Copyright 2017

16. http://israelforever.org/news/modern_anti-semitism/ Modern Anti-Semitism: Bernard-Henri Levy at the U.N. Copyright 2017

17. Michael Burleigh, Project Syndicate – Confronting a New Era of Anti-Semitism, https://www.project-syndicate.org/commentary/anti-semitism-europe-us-by-michael-burleigh-2017-04

18. Michael Burleigh, Project Syndicate – Confronting a New Era of Anti-Semitism, https://www.project-syndicate.org/commentary/anti-semitism-europe-us-by-michael-burleigh-2017-04

19. http://www.timesofisrael.com/liveblog_entry/simon-wiesenthal-center-urges-us-task-force-on-anti-semitism/

20. www.jerusalemonline.com/news/world-news/the-jewish-world/analysis-why-is-anti-semitism-on-the-rise-within-america-26926

21. www.jerusalemonline.com/news/world-news/the-jewish-world/analysis-why-is-anti-semitism-on-the-rise-within-america-26926

22. www.jerusalemonline.com/news/world-news/the-jewish-world/analysis-why-is-anti-semitism-on-the-rise-within-america-26926

23. www.jerusalemonline.com/news/world-news/the-jewish-world/analysis-why-is-anti-semitism-on-the-rise-within-america-26926

24. https://www.algemeiner.com/2017/03/01/why-were-the-7000-antisemitic-incidents-under-obama-largely-ignored/

25. https://www.algemeiner.com/2017/03/01/why-were-the-7000-antisemitic-incidents-under-obama-largely-ignored/

Chapter Two

1. J. Miller (ed.) Teshuvot Ge'onei Mizraho'u-Ma'arav (1888) 31a, no. 133)

2. Israel scrambles Palestinian 'right of return' with Jewish refugee talk "Palestinian and Israeli critics have two main arguments: that these Jews were not refugees but eager participants in a new Zionist state, and that Israel cannot and should not attempt to settle its account with the Palestinians by deducting the lost assets of its own citizens, thereby preventing individuals on both sides from seeking compensation."

3. "The Unbearable Silence about the Jewish Refugees." Gatestone Institute. Michael Curtis. December 14, 2012 https://www.gatestoneinstitute.org/3498/jewis

4. "Warm British welcome for Jews fleeing Nazis a 'myth.' " Phys.org / University of Manchester. February 27, 2013

5. http://www.jewishvirtuallibrary.org/jsource/vjw/Egypt.html #5

6. http://www.jewishvirtuallibrary.org/jsource/vjw/Egypt.html

7. http://www.jewishvirtuallibrary.org/jsource/vjw/Egypt.html

8. "Jews of Libya." Jewish Virtual Library.

9. "Jews of Libya." Jewish Virtual Library.

10.
(http://jewishencyclopedia.com/view.jsp?artid=567&letter=
)

11. Source: Jacob Marcus, The Jew in the Medieval World: A
Sourcebook, 315-1791, (New York: JPS, 1938), 3-7

12. ABC/Reuters (29 January 2008). "Black Death 'discriminated'
between victims (ABC News in Science)." Australian
Broadcasting Corporation.

13. "Health. De-coding the Black Death." BBC. 3 October 2001.
Retrieved 21 March 2017

14. Austin Alchon, Suzanne (2003). A pest in the land: new world
epidemics in a global perspective. University of New Mexico
Press. p. 21. ISBN 0-8263-2871-7.

15. Gottheil, Richard; Strack, Hermann L.; Jacobs, Joseph (1901–
1906). "Blood Accusation." Jewish Encyclopedia. New York:
Funk & Wagnalls.

16. Dundes, Alan, ed. (1991). The Blood Libel Legend: A
Casebook in Anti-Semitic Folklore. University of Wisconsin
Press. ISBN 978-0-299-13114-2.

17. http://www.jewishvirtuallibrary.org/host-desecration-of

18. United States Holocaust Museum, Jewish Badge – Origins,
Holocaust   Encyclopedia,
https://www.ushmm.org/wlc/en/article.php?ModuleId=100
08212

19. "Bogdan Chmelnitzki leads Cossack uprising against Polish
rule; 100,000 Jews are killed and hundreds of Jewish
communities are destroyed." Judaism Timeline 1618–1770,
CBS News. Accessed April 20, 2017

20. "The peasants of Ukraine rose up in 1648 under a petty
aristocrat Bogdan Chmielnicki. ... It is estimated that 100,000
Jews were massacred and 300 of their communities
destroyed." Oscar Reiss. The Jews in Colonial America,
McFarland & Company, 2004, ISBN 0-7864-1730-7, pp. 98–
99.

21. Davitt, Michael (1903). Within the Pale. London: Hurst and
Blackett. pp. 98–100.

22. Rosenthal, Herman; Rosenthal, Max (1901–1906). "Kishinef (Kishinev)." In Singer, Isidore; et al. Jewish Encyclopedia. New York: Funk & Wagnalls Company.

23. Antisemitism: A Historical Encyclopedia of Prejudice and Persection, Volume 2, L–Z, ed. Richard S. Levy (Santa Barbara, CA: ABC-CLIO, 2005), s.v. "Odessa Pogroms."

24. Yonah Alexander, Kenneth Myers (2015). Terrorism in Europe. Rutledge Library Editions, RLE: Terrorism & Insurgency. Rutledge. pp. 40–41. ISBN 1317449320

25. John Doyle Klier, Shlomo Lambroza (2004). Pogroms: Anti-Jewish Violence in Modern Russian History. Cambridge University Press. p. 381. ISBN 0521528518.

26. Encyclopedia Judaica vol. 13 pp. 699-700. Grigoriev was a Red Army officer at the time. Timkov, O. Otaman Grigoryev: Truth and Myth.

27. "The Murder of a Race." The Nation. 114. 8 March 1922.

28. The Encyclopedia & Dictionary of Zionism & Israel, copyright 2005 – The Killing Trap – Genocide in the 20th Century by Manus I. Midlarsky, pg. 46, Cambridge University Press.

29. Elias Heifetz, "The Slaughter of the Jews in the Ukraine in 1919," Forgotten Books, 2016, P 180.

30. N. Gergel "The pogroms in the Ukraine in 1918-1920" [YIVO Annual of Jewish Social Science. Vol. 6. New York, 1951 p. 245] the number of killed is 50-60 thousand.

31. Elias Tcherikower [Di Ukrainer pogromen in yor 1919. New York, 1965 p 333] the number of killed is 50-60 thousand.

32. 2013 Anti-Defamation League https://www.adl.org/sites/default/files/documents/assets/pdf/education-outreach/Brief-History-on-Anti-Semitism-A.pdf

33. 2013 Anti-Defamation League https://www.adl.org/sites/default/files/documents/assets/pdf/education-outreach/Brief-History-on-Anti-Semitism-A.pdf

34. Thomas Williams Ph.D., Roman Jews Give Pope Francis Standing Ovation for Holocaust Remembrance: http://www.breitbart.com/big-

government/2016/01/17/roman-jews-give-pope-francis-standing-ovation-for-holocaust-remembrance/

35. Lewis, Bernard (1984). The Jews of Islam. Princeton: Princeton University Press. ISBN 0-691-00807-8 pp.10, 20

36. Lewis, Bernard (1987). The Jews of Islam. Princeton: Princeton University Press. ISBN 0-691-00807-8 pp. 9, 27

37. Assaleh, Abu-Mohammed (1828). Historia dos soberanos mohametanos: das primeiras quatro dysnastias e de parte da quinta, que reinarao na Mauritania. Jozé de Santo Antonio Moura (trans.). Lisbon: Academia Real das Sciencias de Lisboa. p. 117. Retrieved 2017-04-27.

38. Roudh el-Kartas: Histoire des souverains du Maghreb, p. 459, at Google Books.

39. Granada by Richard Gottheil, Meyer Kayserling, Jewish Encyclopedia. 1906 ed.

40. Yehudah Ratzaby, Galut Mawza', Sefunot (Volume Five), Ben-Zvi Institute: Jerusalem 1961, p. 339 (Hebrew)

41. Yosef Qafiḥ (ed.), "Qorot Yisra'el be-Teman by Rabbi Ḥayim Ḥibshush," Sefunot, Volume 2, Ben-Zvi Institute: Jerusalem 1958, pp. 246-286 (Hebrew); Yosef Qafiḥ, Ketavim (Collected Papers), Vol. 2, Jerusalem 1989, p. 714 (Hebrew

42. Frankel, Jonathan: The Damascus Affair: 'Ritual Murder,' Politics, and the Jews in 1840 (Cambridge University Press, 1997) ISBN 0-521-48396-4 p.1

43. Report of the Commission on the disturbances of August 1929, Command paper 3530 (Shaw Commission report), p. 65.

44. Ross, Stewart (2004). Causes and Consequences of the Arab-Israeli Conflict. Evans Brothers. p. 22. ISBN 0237525852.

45. "אירועים ביטחוניים בתולדות משמר העמק [Security events in the history of Mishmar HaEmek]." Mishmar HaEmek website (in Hebrew). Retrieved 28 April 2017.

46. Kaplan, Robert. D. "In Defense of Empire." The Atlantic Apr. 2014: 13-15. Print.

47. Martin Gilbert. The atlas of Jewish history, William Morrow and Company, 1993. pg. 114. ISBN 0-688-12264-7.

48. Pappe, Ilan (2002) 'The Rise and Fall of a Palestinian Dynasty. The Husaynis 1700-1948. AL Saqi edition 2010. ISBN 978-0-86356-460-4. pp.309,321

49. Cohen, Aharon (1970) Israel and the Arab World. W.H. Allen. ISBN 0-491-00003-0. p.312

50. Vatikiotis, P.J. (1992). The History of Modern Egypt (Fourth ed.). Baltimore: Johns Hopkins University. p. 443. ISBN 0-8018-4214-X.

51. John F. Burns, "In the Islamic Middle East, Scant Place for Jews" Week in Review, New York Times, July 25, 1999.

52. Friedman, Saul S. (1989). Without Future: The Plight of Syrian Jewry. Praeger Publishers. ISBN 978-0-275-93313-5

53. Le Figaro, March 9, 1974, "Quatre femmes juives assassins a Damas," (Paris: International Conference for Deliverance of Jews in the Middle East, 1974), p. 33.

54. "Aliens Act of 1937," Cape Town Holocaust Centre, retrieved May 8, 2017

55. Rise of the South African Reich, Brian Bunting http://web.archive.org/web/20070715031456/http://www.anc.org.za/books/reich4.html

56. Linder, Douglas O. (2010). "The Nelson Mandela(Rivonia) Trial: An Account." University of Missouri-Kansas City

57. Turpin-Petrosino, Carolyn (2013). The Beast Reawakens: Fascism's Resurgence from Hitler's Spymasters to Today's Neo-Nazi Groups and Right-Wing Extremists. Taylor and Francis. There are hate groups in South Africa. Perhaps among the most organized is the Afrikaner Resistance Movement or AWB (Afrikaner Weerstandsbeweging). Included in its ideological platform are neo-Nazism and White supremacy.

58. "Separation, even after apartheid; Many whites fear for life after Mandela," (21 June 2013) National Post, Ontario

59. "Icasa hears decade-old racist row | News | National | Mail & Guardian" Mg.co.za. Retrieved 2017-05-17.

60. 'We look our past in the eye; similarly, our future' Dan Newling in South Africa reports on the debate over university discovery of Nazi's 'race index' tools

61. Government minister's slurs anger South African Jews Global News service of the Jewish people.

62. Hajaig 'must apologise or go' News24. The ANC and anti-semitism. Politicsweb. South Africa Jews slam deputy FM's anti-Semitic comments. The Jewish World

63. Allison, Simon (2013-10-16). "Africa Check: No evidence to support ANC leader's claim that 98% of property owners in Cape Town are 'white' and 'Jewish.'" Daily Maverick. Retrieved 2017-05-17.

Chapter Three

1.   Greenspoon, Leonard; Hamm, Dennis; Le Beau, Bryan F. (1 November 2000). The Historical Jesus   Through Catholic and Jewish Eyes. A&C Black. p. 78. ISBN 978-1-56338-322-9

2.   Singer, Thomas; Kimbles, Samuel L. (31 July 2004). The Cultural Complex: Contemporary Jungian Perspectives on Psyche and Society. Routledge. p. 33. ISBN 1-135-44486-2.

3.   Nostra Aetate: a milestone - Pier Francesco Fumagalli.

4.   THOMAS OF MONMOUTH, Life and Miracles of St. William of Norwich, ed. JESSOP and JAMES (Cambridge, 1896); VACANDARD, Question du meutre rituel in Etudes de critique et d'histoire religieuse, III (Paris, 1912); STRACK, Blut in Glauben and Aberglauben (Munich, 1900); Acta SS., III March; THURSTON, Antisemitism and the Charge of Ritual Murder in The Month, XC (London, 1898), 561; LEA, Santo Nino de la Guardia in English Historical Review, IV (London, 1889), 229.

5.   William Nicholls, Christian Antisemitism: A History of Hate (Aronson, 1995)

6.   Parfitt, Tudor (1985) 'The Year of the Pride of Israel: Montefiore and the blood libel of 1840.' In: Lipman, S. and Lipman, V.D., (eds.), The Century of Moses Montefiore. Oxford: Oxford University Press, pp. 131-148.

7.   Malamud, Bernard, ed. (1966). The Fixer. POCKET BOOKS, a Simon & Schuster division of GULF & WESTERN CORPORATION. ISBN 0-671-82568-2.

8. Feldberg, Michael (ed.) (2002). "The Massena Blood Libel." Blessings of Freedom: Chapters in American Jewish History. New York: American Jewish Historical Society. ISBN 0-88125-756-7.

9. Landman, Isaac (ed.) (1929). Christian and Jew: A Symposium for Better Understanding. New York: Horace Liveright. pp. 371–372. OCLC 415207. Retrieved December 5, 2008.

10. William Nicholls, Christian Antisemitism: A History of Hate (Aronson, 1995

11. Martyr, J., & Slusser, M., 2003 – Dialogue with Trypho - Selections from the Fathers of the Church, Rev. Ed. –United States of America: Catholic University of America Press.

12. Simona Rich, May 14, 2017, 160 AD Letter Explains How Jesus Fulfilled the Law and the Mystery of Passover https://www.simonarich.com/melito/

13. Roberts, A., & Donaldson, J., 2001- Ante-Nicene Christian Library: Translations of the Writings of the Fathers down to A.D. 325. Volume 23: The Writings of Origen, Volume 2: Origen contra Celsum, Books II-VII. United States of America: Adamant Media Corporation.

14. Chrysostom, J., 1999 – Discourses Against Judaizing Christians, The Fathers of the Church, 68. United States of America: Catholic University of America Press.

15. Thomas L. McDonald, August 28, 2013. St. Augustine & the Jews. Wonderful Things. https://thomaslmcdonald.wordpress.com/2013/08/28/st-augustine-and-the-jews/

16. Fathers of the English Dominican Province, trans. Summa Theologica. 2, rev. ed. 22 vols. London: Burns, Oates & Washbourne, 1912-36; reprinted in 5 vols., Westminster, MD. Christian Classics, 1981.

17. Romans 11:25-26 (New International Version

18. Part III of Aquinas' Summa Theologica

19. Charry ET. Supersessionism. in Green JB, Lapsley J, Miles R, Verhey A (editors). Dictionary of Scripture and Ethics. Baker Academic, 2011. ISBN 9780801034060

20. Johnson LT. Christians and Jews: Starting Over - Why the Real Dialogue Has Just Begun. Commonweal magazine. January 31, 2003.

21. Carroll, James. Constantine's Sword: The Church and the Jews. Boston: Houghton Mifflin, 2001. Print. p. 58

22. Carroll, James. Constantine's Sword: The Church and the Jews. Boston: Houghton Mifflin, 2001. Print. p. 50

23. Martin Luther, That Jesus Christ Was Born a Jew (1523) – Excerpts

24. Luther, Martin. On the Jews and Their Lies, cited in Michael, Robert. "Luther, Luther Scholars, and the Jews," Encounter 46 – 1985- No. 4:343-344

25. Hendrix, Scott H. "The Controversial Luther," Word & World 3/4 (1983), Luther Seminary, St. Paul, MN, p. 393: "And, finally, after the Holocaust and the use of his anti-Jewish statements by National Socialists, Luther's anti-Semitic outbursts are now unmentionable, though they were already repulsive in the sixteenth century. As a result, Luther has become as controversial in the twentieth century as he was in the sixteenth." Also see Hillerbrand, Hans. "The legacy of Martin Luther," in Hillerbrand, Hans & McKim, Donald K. (eds.) The Cambridge Companion to Luther. Cambridge University Press, 2003.

26. Ellis, Marc H. Hitler and the Holocaust, Christian Anti-Semitism, Baylor University Center for American and Jewish Studies, Spring 2004, slide 14.

27. Excerpt from "Ad Quaelstiones et Objecta Juaei Cuiusdam Responsio," by John Calvin; The Jew in Christian Theology, Gerhard Falk, McFarland and Company, Inc., Jefferson, NC and London, 1931.

28. Do Not Trust a Fox in the Meadow, and Do Not Trust a Jew by his Word, Elvira Bauer – Sturmer Press, 1936

29. Adolf Hitler - In a speech before the Reichstag (Berlin, Germany), 1936

30. See also Luke 18:31-34, New International Version (NIV); Matthew 16:21-23, NIV.

31. Acts 4:27 (New International Version

32. Finegan, Jack (1992). The Archaeology of the New Testament. Princeton: Princeton University Press. p. 26.

33. Schalit, A. (1969). "Konig Herodes: der Mann und sein Werk." Studia Judaica 4. Berlin: de Gruyter: 648ff.

34.   France, Richard T. (1979). "Herod and the Children of Bethlehem." Novum Testamentum (21): 98–120.

35.   N.S. Gill, Pontius Pilate, Thought Co, June 18, 2017. https://www.thoughtco.com/pontius-pilate-biography-120414

36.   The International Standard Bible Encyclopedia by Geoffrey W. Bromiley 1988 ISBN 0-8028-3785-9 p. 426

37.   Vernon K. Robbins in Literary studies in Luke-Acts by Richard P. Thompson (editor) 1998 ISBN 0-86554-563-4 pp. 200–201

Chapter Four

1. A.D. Herzl, Theodor (1988) [1896]. "Biography, by Alex Bein." Der Judenstaat [The Jewish state]. transl. Sylvie d'Avigdor (republication ed.). New York: Courier Dover. p. 40. ISBN 978-0-486-25849-

2. Guy Canivet, first President of the Supreme Court, Justice from the Dreyfus Affair, p. 15

3. Theodore Herzl, concluding words of The Jewish State, 1896. The Jewish State, by Theodore Herzl, (Courier Corporation, 27 Apr 2012), page 157

4. Tesler, Mark. Jewish History and the Emergence of Modern Political Zionism. Bloomington, IN: Indiana University Printing Press, 1994.

5. A.R. Taylor, "Vision and intent in Zionist Thought," in The Transformation of Palestine, ed. by I. Abu-Lughod, 1971, ISBN 0-8101-0345-1, p. 10

6. Herzl, Theodor (1896). "Palästina oder Argentinien?" Der Judenstaat (in German). sammlungen.ub.uni-frankfurt.de. p. 29 (31).

7. Gur, Nachman; Haredim, Behadrey. "'Kometz Aleph – Au': How many Hebrew speakers are there in the world?"

8. Harris, J. (1998) The Israeli Declaration of Independence Archived June 7, 2011, at the Wayback Machine. The Journal of the Society for Textual Reasoning, Vol. 7

9. Dore Gold, "Jerusalem in International Diplomacy: Demography," Jerusalem Center for Public Affairs, October 27, 2006

10. New York Times, April 28, 1903, pg. 6

11. British Consul in Jerusalem, Willam T. Young, to Colonel Patrick Campbell, May 25, 1839. Quoted in David Landes' "Palestine before the Zionists" Commentary, May 1976, pg. 22

12. "Israel Focus-Migration." Focus-migration.de.

13. "400 olim arrive in Israel ahead of Independence Day - Israel Jewish Scene, " Ynetnews.com.

14. DellaPergola, Sergio (2014). Dashefsky, Arnold; Sheskin, Ira, eds. "World Jewish Population, 2014". Current Jewish Population Reports. The American Jewish Year Book (Dordrecht: Springer).

15. Mishkenot Sha'ananim, jewishvirtuallibrary.org

16. Arieh L. Avneri, The Claim of Dispossession, 4th ed., 2005 pg. 12; Benny Morris, The Birth of the Palestinian Refugee Problem, 1947-1949, 1989, pgs. 17-18, Demography of Palestine, & Israel, the West bank and Gaza, Jewish Virtual Library.

17. Interim Report on the Civil Administration of Palestine to the League of Nations, June 1921.

18. Sir John Hope Simpson, "Palestine: Report on Immigration, Land Settlement and Development," 1930, pg. 5

19. Peel Commission Report, Chapter IX, July 1937.

20. Early Zionist account of settling, 1885). Benny Morris, Righteous Victims, 2001, pg. 133

21. Interim Report on the Civil Administration of Palestine to the League of Nations, June 1921

22. "Demography of Palestine and Israel, the West Bank and Gaza," Jewish Virtual Library.

23. Interim Report on the Civil Administration of Palestine to the League of Nations, June 1921

24. The Churchill White Paper, in Walter Laqueur and Barry Rubin (eds.), The Israel-Arab Reader: A Documentary History of the Middle East Conflict, 4th ed., 1987, pg. 45

25. Jewish National Fund, "JNF Centennial Celebration," JNF website at www.jnf.org

26. Howard Sachar - A History of Israel, 2000, pgs. 156, 167. Yehoshua Porath, Palestinian Arab National Movement, Vol. 2, 1977 pgs. 17-18, 39.

27. Syrian Alawi notable's letter to French Prime Minister, June 1936. Quoted in Daniel Pipes,' Greater Syria, 1990, pg. 179.

28. Walter Laqueur - A History of Zionism, 1989. Pg. 510

29. Moshe Aumann, Land Ownership in Palestine, 1880-1948, in Michael Curtis et al. The Palestinians, 1975, pg. 29.

30. Naftali Greenwood, Redeemers of the Land, October 18, 1999 as www.mfa.gov.il

31. The Economist, Tel Aviv. The Economist: Cities Guide.

32. Triandafyllidou, Anna (1998). "National identity and the other." Ethnic and Racial Studies. 21 (4): 593–612. doi:10.1080/014198798329784.

33. Loolwa Khazoom, Jews of the Middle East, MyJewishLearning.com; Howard Sachar, A History of Israel, 2000, pgs. 515-517.

34. MFA, "Minority Communities," MFA website

35. Greg Myre, Trial of Palestinian Leader Focuses Attention on Israeli Courts, New York Times, May 5, 2003.

36. Michele Lamont, the Robert I. Goldman Professor of European Studies; Professor of Sociology and African and African American Studies at Harvard University

37. Christina Pazzanese, Harvard Staff Writer, Harvard Gazette, February 27, 2017

38. Gerber, Marlène; Mueller, Sean (October 23, 2015). "4 Cool Graphs that Explain Sunday's Swiss Elections." The Washington Post

39. http://www.cnbc.com/2015/09/07/indonesian-rupiah-plunges-to-lowest-since-asian-financial-crisis.html

40. https://worldview.stratfor.com/article/what-hindu-nationalism-means-indias-future

41. Documents on German Foreign Policy 1918-1945, Series D, Vo XIII, London, 1964

42. Quoted in the Swiss Zibicher Woche, September 1, 1961.

43. Quoted in the Jordanian Al-Dustur, August 16, 1999

44. The Law of Return - An Immigration Policy to Ensure a Jewish Majority in the State of Israel. Copyright © 2002-2017 My Jewish Learning

45. Sachar, op. cit. pg. 333 "Israel & the Arabs, The 50 Year Conflict" BBC Documentary. Cited by CAMERA, "Pattern of Bias," July 1999.

46. Quoted in Nimr el-Hawari, Sir An-Nakbah, 1952

47. The Memoirs of Haled al Azim" 1973, Part 1, pgs. 386-387

48. Mahmoud Abbas, Falastin al-Thaura, March 1976, cited in "Palestine's Pawns," Wall Street Journal. June 5, 2003

49. Hazem Nusseibeh, interview in "Israel and the Arabs: The 50 Year Conflict" BBC Documentary, Cited in CAMERA, "Pattern of Bias," July 1999.

50. Myre, Greg (18 June 1991). "South Africa ends racial classifications." Southeast Missourian. Cape Girardeau.

51. Members of the first Knesset at http://www.knesset.gov.il/

52. MEMRI, "Palestinians Comment on Israeli Democracy," Special Dispatch Series No.34, June 4, 1999

53. Lifting the Veil: The True Faces of Muhammad & Islam. The Quran affirms the Biblical narrative that assigned the Promised Land to the Twelve tribes of Israel on BOTH sides of the river Jordan.

54. Adherents.com, 2014.

55. Genesis 15:18-21, NASB

56. Qur'an, "Night Journey," Chapter 17:100 -104)

Chapter Five

1. Martin Gilbert (The Holocaust: The Jewish Tragedy, 1985, p. 18; Bauer 2002, pp. 10–11; Snyder 2010, p. 412; Landau 2016,

p. 3; and Introduction to the Holocaust," United States Holocaust Memorial Museum. Retrieved 4 October 2017.

2. Encyclopedia of Camps and Ghettos, 1933–1945, United States Holocaust Memorial Museum.

3. Dan Stone 2010, p. 109, citing Bajohr & Pohl 2008, p. 10

4. Bergen, Doris (2016). War & Genocide: A Concise History of the Holocaust (Third ed.). Lanham, MD: Rowman & Littlefield. ISBN 978-1-4422-4228-9. p. 200.

5. George H. Stein (1984). "Operation Barbarossa". The Waffen SS: Hitler's Elite Guard at War, 1939-1945. Cornell University Press. ISBN 0801492750. pp. xxiv, xxv, 150, 153. 2

6. Claudia Koonz, The Nazi Conscience, p 228 ISBN 0-674-01172-4

7. United States Holocaust Memorial Museum, n.d.

8. United States Holocaust Memorial Museum, n.d.

9. Blandford, Edmund L. (2001). SS Intelligence: The Nazi Secret Service. Edison, NJ: Castle Books. ISBN 978-0-78581-398-9. pps. 67-78

10. Delarue, Jacques (2008). The Gestapo: A History of Horror. New York: Skyhorse. ISBN 978-1-60239-246-5.19 p.113

11. Kulva, Otto Dov (1984). "Die Nürnberger Rassengesetze und die deutsche Bevölkerung im Lichte geheimer NS-Lage und Stimmungsberichte." pps. 582-600

12. Kershaw, Ian (2008). Hitler: A Biography. New York, NY: W. W. Norton & Company. ISBN 978-0-393-06757-6. Pps.309-313

13. Kershaw, Ian (2000) [1999]. Hitler: 1889–1936: Hubris. New York: W. W. Norton & Company. ISBN 978-0393320350. Pps. 521-522.

14. Reitlinger, Gerald (1989). The SS: Alibi of a Nation, 1922–1945. New York: Da Capo Press. ISBN 978-0-306-80351-2. pps. 65-66

15. Michael, Robert; Doerr, Karin (2002). Nazi-Deutsch/Nazi-German: An English Lexicon of the Language of the Third Reich. Westport, CT: Greenwood Press. ISBN 978-031332106 p. 356

16. Evans, Richard J. (2008). The Third Reich at War. New York: Penguin Group. ISBN 978-0-14-311671-4. p. 318

17. Buchheim, Hans (1968). "The SS – Instrument of Domination." In Krausnik, Helmut; Buchheim, Hans; Broszat, Martin; Jacobsen, Hans-Adolf, eds. Anatomy of the SS State. New York: Walker and Company. ISBN 978-0-00211-026-6. pp. 166–167

18. (Ellis, Marc H. *Hitler and the Holocaust, Christian Anti-Semitism*, Baylor University Center for American and Jewish Studies, Spring, 2004, slide 14.)

19. Leni Yahil, The Holocaust: The Fate of European Jewry, New York: Oxford University, 1990, p. 36

20. Judah Rumney, Biology & War, Journal of Social Philosophy, Volume 4, Number 4, 1939, 329

21. Evans, Richard J. (2005). The Third Reich in Power. New York: Penguin. ISBN 978-0-14-303790-3 p. 544.

22. Kershaw, Ian (2008). Hitler: A Biography. New York: W. W. Norton & Company. ISBN 978-0-393-06757-6. p.345.

23. Wolfe, Stephanie (2014). The Politics of Reparations and Apologies. New York: Springer. ISBN 978-1-4614-9184-2 p.94

24. Shirer, William L. (1960). The Rise and Fall of the Third Reich. New York: Simon & Schuster. ISBN 978-0-671-62420-0. p. 233.

25. Burleigh, Michael; Wippermann, Wolfgang (1991). The Racial State: Germany 1933–1945. Cambridge; New York: Cambridge University Press. ISBN 978-0-521-39802-2 p.84

26. United States Holocaust Memorial Museum, The Night of the Broken Glass, The Holocaust: A Learning Site for Students, https://www.ushmm.org/outreach/en/article.php?ModuleId=10007697, January 2, 2017

27. United States Holocaust Memorial Museum, The Night of the Broken Glass, The Holocaust: A Learning Site for Students, https://www.ushmm.org/outreach/en/article.php?ModuleId=10007697, January 2, 2017

28. The Night of Broken Glass, History.com Staff, History.com, 2009, http://www.history.com/this-day-in-history/the-night-of-broken-glass, January 7, 2017, A+E Networks

29. Lucy Dawidowicz, The War Against the Jews, 1933-1945 – New York, 1975, pp. xxi-xxiii.

30. "Number of deportees by ethnicity". Auschwitz-Birkenau Memorial and Museum

31. Holocaust (David S. Wyman; Charles H. Rosneberg (1996) The World Reacts to the Holocaust. JHU Press. P.99) and Encyclopedia. "'Final Solution': Overview." United States Holocaust Memorial Museum. Archived from the original on March 2, 2013. Retrieved January 23, 2017

32. Types of Ghettos. United States Holocaust Memorial Museum, Washington, D.C. https://www.ushmm.org/wlc/es/article.php?ModuleId=10007 445.

33. Bains, Alisha (2016). World War II. A Political and Diplomatic History of the Modern World Series. Encyclopædia Britannica. pp. 190–200. ISBN 1680483528

34. Gutman, Israel (1998). Resistance: The Warsaw Ghetto Uprising. Houghton Mifflin Harcourt. pp. 118–119, 200. ISBN 0395901308.

35. Shapiro, Robert Moses (1999). Holocaust Chronicles. Published by KTAV Publishing. ISBN 0-88125-630-7 – via Google Books, 302 pages 300,000 Jews murdered by bullet or gas. p.35

36. Holocaust Encyclopedia (June 10, 2013) [2008]. "Warsaw Ghetto Uprising." US Holocaust Memorial Museum. Archived May 2, 2012 at the Wayback Machine.

37. Statistical data compiled on the basis of "Glossary of 2,077 Jewish towns in Poland" by Virtual Shtetl Museum of the History of the Polish Jews (in English), as well as "Getta Żydowskie" by Gedeon (in Polish) and "Ghetto List" by Michael Peters at ARC.

38. Evans, Richard J. (2005). The Third Reich in Power. New York: Penguin Group. ISBN 978-0-14-303790-3. p. 81

39. Evans, Richard J. (2005). The Third Reich in Power. New York: Penguin Group. ISBN 978-0-14-303790-3. pps. 87-90.

40. Evans, Richard J. (2008). The Third Reich at War. New York: Penguin Group. ISBN 978-0-14-311671-4. p.367

41. Lichtblau, Eric (March 1, 2013). "The Holocaust Just Got More Shocking." The New York Times. Retrieved 27 June 2014. When the research began in 2000, Dr. Megargee said he expected to find perhaps 7,000 Nazi camps and ghettos, based on postwar estimates. But the numbers kept climbing — first to 11,500, then 20,000, then 30,000, and now 42,500. For the map of more that 1,000 locations, see: Map of Ghettos for Jews in Eastern Europe. The New York Times. Source: USHMM.

42. Yad Vashem (2015). "The Implementation of the Final Solution: The Death Camps." The Holocaust. Yad Vashem The Holocaust Martyrs' and Heroes' Remembrance Authority.

43. Robert Gellately; Nathan Stoltzfus (2001). Social Outsiders in Nazi Germany. Princeton University Press. p. 216. ISBN 978-0-691-08684-2.

44. Holocaust Encyclopedia (20 June 2014). "Gassing Operations." United States Holocaust Memorial Museum, Washington, DC.

45. Russell, Shahan (12 October 2015). "The Ten Worst Nazi Concentration Camps." WarHistoryOnline.com.

46. Browning, Christopher R. (1998) [1992]. "Arrival in Poland" (PDF). Ordinary Men: Reserve Police Battalion 101 and the Final Solution in Poland. Penguin Books. p.138

47. Gruner, Wolf (2006). Jewish Forced Labor Under the Nazis: Economic Needs and Racial Aims, 1938-1944. Cambridge University Press. p. 271. ISBN 0521838754. On November 3 and 4, 1943, the SS launched one of the largest murder operations ever against Jewish forced laborers, the notorious "Aktion Erntefest" (Operation Harvest Festival) – 42,000 to 43,000 Jews were killed. p.271

48. The Holocaust Explained, The Wiener Library for the study of the Holocaust & Genocide, 2016. Originally Desogned & Developed by the London Jewish Cultural Centre

49. Wiesel, Elie (1960) [1958]. Night. New York: Hill & Wang.

50. Duraczyński, Eugeniusz; Terej, Jerzy Janusz (1974). Europa podziemna: 1939-1945 [Europe underground: 1939-1945] (in Polish). Warszawa: Wiedza Powszechna. OCLC 463203458.

51. Stanley Blejwas, A Heroic Uprising in Poland, 2004

52. Koestler, letter in Tribune magazine 15 September 1944, reprinted in Orwell, Collected Works, I Have Tried to Tell the Truth, p.374

53. Warsaw Uprising. (2013, August 11). New World Encyclopedia, Retrieved 17:58, January 29, 2017 from http://www.newworldencyclopedia.org/p/index.php?title=W arsaw_Uprising&oldid=972363

54. "Holocaust Denial and Distortion", United States Holocaust Memorial Museum website. Accessed September 28, 2017. "Holocaust denial is an attempt to negate the established facts of the Nazi genocide of European Jewry. Holocaust denial and distortion are forms of antisemitism. They are generally motivated by hatred of Jews and build on the claim that the Holocaust was invented or exaggerated by Jews as part of a plot to advance Jewish interests."

55. The kinds of assertions made in Holocaust-denial material include the following:

- Several hundred thousand rather than approximately six million Jews died during the war.

- Scientific evidence proves that gas chambers could not have been used to kill large numbers of people.

- The Nazi command had a policy of deporting Jews, not exterminating them. Some deliberate killings of Jews did occur, but were carried out by the peoples of Eastern Europe rather than the Nazis.

- Jews died in camps of various kinds, but did so as the result of hunger and disease (most died to the unavailability of food due to allied bombings). The Holocaust is a myth created by the Allies for propaganda purposes, and subsequently nurtured by the Jews for their own ends.

- Errors and inconsistencies in survivors' testimonies point to their essential unreliability.

- Alleged documentary evidence of the Holocaust, from photographs of concentration camp victims to Anne Frank's diary, is fabricated.

- The confessions of former Nazis to war crimes were extracted through torture. The nature of Holocaust denial: What is Holocaust denial? Archived July 18, 2011, at the Wayback Machine., JPR report No. 3, 2000.

56. "How many Jews were murdered in the Holocaust? How do we know? Do we have their names?" The Holocaust Resource Center Faqs, Yad Vashem website. See also appropriate section of the Holocaust article for the death toll, and concentration camp inmates died from sickness and/or starvation and not due to a Nazi policy of Jewish eradication.

57. Ayaan Hirsi Ali, Los Angeles Times, December 16, 2006. (http://www.latimes.com/news/la-oe-ali16dec16-story.html)

58. Alex Sundby, Castro Blasts Ahmadinejad for Holocaust Denial. CBS News, September 7, 2010. https://www.cbsnews.com/news/castro-blasts-ahmadinejad-for-holocaust-denial/

59. Predetermined conclusion:

"'Revisionism' is obliged to deviate from the standard methodology of historical pursuit because it seeks to mold facts to fit a preconceived result, it denies events that have been objectively and empirically proved to have occurred, and because it works backward from the conclusion to the facts, thus necessitating the distortion and manipulation of those facts where they differ from the preordained conclusion (which they almost always do). In short, 'revisionism' denies something that demonstrably happened, through methodological dishonesty." McFee, Gordon. "Why 'Revisionism' Isn't," The Holocaust History Project, May 15, 1999.

Alan L. Berger, "Holocaust Denial: Tempest in a Teapot, or Storm on the Horizon?" in Zev Garber and Richard Libowitz (eds), Peace, in Deed: Essays in Honor of Harry James Cargas, Atlanta: Scholars Press, 1998, p. 154.

60. Conspiracy theory:

"While appearing on the surface as a rather arcane pseudo-scholarly challenge to the well-established record of Nazi genocide during the Second World War, Holocaust denial serves as a powerful conspiracy theory uniting otherwise disparate fringe groups...." Introduction: Denial as Anti-Semitism, "Holocaust Denial: An Online Guide to Exposing and Combating Anti-Semitic Propaganda", Anti-Defamation League, 2001.

"Before discussing how Holocaust denial constitutes a conspiracy theory, and how the theory is distinctly American, it is important to understand what is meant by the term 'Holocaust denial.'" Mathis, Andrew E. Holocaust Denial, a Definition, The Holocaust History Project, July 2, 2004.

"Since its inception ... the Institute for Historical Review (IHR), a California-based Holocaust denial organization founded by Willis Carto of Liberty Lobby, has promoted the antisemitic conspiracy theory that Jews fabricated tales of their own genocide to manipulate the sympathies of the non-Jewish world." Antisemitism and Racism Country Reports: United States Archived June 28, 2011, at the Wayback Machine., Stephen Roth Institute, 2000

61. Lisa Katz, March 6, 2017, ThoughtCo https://www.thoughtco.com/nazi-files-revealed-after-60-years-2076562

62. "About Us". USC Shoah Foundation

63. "About Us". USC Shoah Foundation

64. James Masters and Antonia Mortensen, CNN. February 20, 2018 Poland's Jewish Groups Say Jews feel Unsafe since New Holocaust Law.

65. David S. Wyman, "The United States," in David S. Wyman, ed., The World Reacts to the Holocaust, Baltimore, MD: John Hopkins University Press, 1996, pp. 70710

BOOK SUMMARY

Jews are indisputably the most persecuted people in the annals of history.

At the source of Jew hatred in its myriad forms is anti-Semitism, a sinister and vile mindset that has existed since Old Testament times, that is, thousands of years. Anti-Semites pervade social, religious, economic and political confines, even mainstream Christianity, and their dislike for people of Jewish ancestry often translate into mindless persecution and slaughter, such as the atrocities perpetrated by the Nazis and their collaborators during the Second World War in the mid twentieth century whereby over six million Jews met their deaths in the Holocaust.

Anti-Semitism, instead of diminishing after the horrors of World War II, showed no sign of abatement, and it seems as though the entire world, with a few exceptions like the Jewish nation of Israel itself and the United States of America, is at loggerheads with Jews. Even international peacekeeping and monitoring organizations like the United Nations (and its numerous spinoff groups) are known to discriminate, sometimes barefacedly, against Jews and Israel. Middle Eastern Arabs and Muslims harbor intense loathing for Israel and Jews, and notwithstanding their occupancy of over ninety-nine percent of Middle Eastern territories, seek to covet the less than one percent of land in which Israelis reside—by any means necessary.

Despite the seeming insurmountable hardships and challenges Jews have faced throughout the centuries, they persist, and even progress in today's societies. They leave their enemies awe-struck at their resilience and their will to survive. It seems as though Israel and Jews in general enjoy a kind of divine providence.

ISRAEL and Jews around the world continue to stand tall today—against all odds!

ABOUT THE AUTHOR

Christopher Hugh Kawal Persaud was born in British Guiana (now Guyana) and immigrated to the USA in 1982.

Christopher was a financial services and income tax professional for most of his vocational years and served in various capacities in his native Guyana and in the USA. He retired in 2018. He is a writer, poet, and Christian apologist and to date has written nine full-length books to date, including a book of poetry.

Four of the author's books have won a total of nine international awards. The four award-winning books are (a) Evolution – Beyond the Realm of Real Science (2008, revised 2013) (b) The Da Vinci Code Revisited – A Conclusive Refutation of the Widespread, Sinister Lie (2010, revised 2013) (c) Contending for the Faith – 22 Methodical Arguments for Biblical Truth (2013) and (d) Blessings, Miracles & Supernatural Experiences – A Biblical Perspective; A Christian's Story (2015).

Persaud has also published many essays and articles on the worldwide Internet. He is married to Pamela and together they are the parents of three sons – Duane, Jason, and Justin.

The author's website can be accessed at:

www.christopherhkpersaud.com